Communications in Computer and Information Science 3144

Rationale

The CCIS series is devoted to the publication of proceedings of computer science conferences. Its aim is to efficiently disseminate original research results in informatics in printed and electronic form. While the focus is on publication of peer-reviewed full papers presenting mature work, inclusion of reviewed short papers reporting on work in progress is welcome, too. Besides globally relevant meetings with internationally representative program committees guaranteeing a strict peer-reviewing and paper selection process, conferences run by societies or of high regional or national relevance are also considered for publication.

Topics

The topical scope of CCIS spans the entire spectrum of informatics ranging from foundational topics in the theory of computing to information and communications science and technology and a broad variety of interdisciplinary application fields.

Information for Volume Editors and Authors

Publication in CCIS is free of charge. No royalties are paid, however, we offer registered conference participants temporary free access to the online version of the conference proceedings on SpringerLink (http://link.springer.com) by means of an http referrer from the conference website and/or a number of complimentary printed copies, as specified in the official acceptance email of the event.

CCIS proceedings can be published in time for distribution at conferences or as post-proceedings, and delivered in the form of printed books and/or electronically as USBs and/or e-content licenses for accessing proceedings at SpringerLink. Furthermore, CCIS proceedings are included in the CCIS electronic book series hosted in the SpringerLink digital library at http://link.springer.com/bookseries/7899. Conferences publishing in CCIS are allowed to use our online conference service (Meteor) for managing the whole proceedings lifecycle (from submission and reviewing to preparing for publication) free of charge.

Publication process

The language of publication is exclusively English. Authors publishing in CCIS have to sign the Springer CCIS copyright transfer form, however, they are free to use their material published in CCIS for substantially changed, more elaborate subsequent publications elsewhere. For the preparation of the camera-ready papers/files, authors have to strictly adhere to the Springer CCIS Authors' Instructions and are strongly encouraged to use the CCIS LaTeX style files or templates.

Abstracting/Indexing

CCIS is abstracted/indexed in DBLP, Google Scholar, EI-Compendex, Mathematical Reviews, SCImago, Scopus. CCIS volumes are also submitted for the inclusion in ISI Proceedings.

How to start

To start the evaluation of your proposal for inclusion in the CCIS series, please send an e-mail to ccis@springer.com

Massimo Mecella · Arend Rensink ·
Leszek Maciaszek
Editors

Software Technologies

20th International Conference, ICSOFT 2025
Bilbao, Spain, June 10–12, 2025
Revised Selected Papers

Springer

Editors
Massimo Mecella
Sapienza University of Rome
Rome, Italy

Arend Rensink
University of Twente
Enschede, The Netherlands

Leszek Maciaszek
Wroclaw University of Economics
and Business
Wroclaw, Poland

Macquarie University
Sydney, Australia

ISSN 1865-0929 ISSN 1865-0937 (electronic)
Communications in Computer and Information Science
ISBN 978-3-032-37352-6 ISBN 978-3-032-37353-3 (eBook)
https://doi.org/10.1007/978-3-032-37353-3

This Springer imprint is published by the registered company Springer Nature Switzerland AG
The registered company address is: Gewerbestrasse 11, 6330 Cham, Switzerland

Preface

The present book includes extended and revised versions of selected papers from the 20th International Conference on Software Technologies (ICSOFT 2025), held in Bilbao, Spain, from 10 to 12 June.

The purpose of the International Conference on Software Technologies is to bring together researchers, engineers and practitioners interested on software development technologies and methodologies. The conference has several tracks including aspects such as "Software Engineering and Systems Development", "Software Systems and Applications" and "Foundational and Trigger Technologies".

ICSOFT 2025 received 78 paper submissions from 29 countries, 46 of which were accepted for presentation at the conference, resulting in a lively, 3-day event with a mixture of in-person and online sessions. The review process was double blind, and submissions received three reviews each on average. The 9 papers in this book are the result of a further selection by the event chairs, based on a number of criteria that included the classifications and comments provided by the program committee members, the session chairs' assessment and also the program chairs' global view. The authors of selected papers were invited to submit revised and extended versions with at least 30% innovative material.

The papers in this book contribute to the understanding of relevant trends of current research on Software Technologies, including: Quality Management, Intelligent Systems and Applications, Automated Software Engineering, Big Data and Data Science, Data Mining and Data Analysis, Process Modeling, Software Engineering Tools, Testing and Testability, Agile Development, Natural Language Technologies and Mobile Apps, Cyber-Physical Systems and Cybersecurity Technologies.

We would like to thank all the authors for their contributions and also the reviewers who helped ensure the quality of this publication.

June 2025

Massimo Mecella
Arend Rensink
Leszek Maciaszek

Organization

Conference Chair

Leszek Maciaszek	Macquarie University, Australia and Wroclaw University of Economics and Business, Poland

Program Co-chairs

Massimo Mecella	Sapienza University of Rome, Italy
Arend Rensink	University of Twente, Netherlands

Program Committee

Jens Albrecht	Technische Hochschule Nürnberg, Germany
Davide Ancona	Università di Genova, Italy
Doo-Hwan Bae	Korea Advanced Institute of Science and Technology, South Korea
Davide Basile	ISTI CNR Pisa, Italy
Bernhard Bauer	University of Augsburg, Germany
Jorge Bernardino	Polytechnic University of Coimbra, Portugal
Lorenzo Bettini	University of Florence, Italy
Dominique Blouin	Télécom Paris, France
Christoph Bockisch	Philipps University of Marburg, Germany
Jan Bosch	Chalmers University of Technology, Sweden
Alessio Bucaioni	Mälardalen University, Sweden
Alena Buchalcevova	Prague University of Economics and Business, Czechia
Alejandro Calderón	University of Cádiz, Spain
Rafael Capilla	Universidad Rey Juan Carlos, Spain
Ana Castillo	Universidad de Alcalá, Spain
Anis Charfi	Carnegie Mellon University in Qatar, Qatar
DeJiu Chen	KTH Royal Institute of Technology, Sweden
Yoonsik Cheon	University of Texas at El Paso, USA
Alberto Coen-Porisini	Università degli Studi dell'Insubria, Italy
Estrela Cruz	Instituto Politecnico de Viana do Castelo, Portugal

João Cunha	Polytechnic Institute of Coimbra, Coimbra Institute of Engineering, Portugal
Sergiu Dascalu	University of Nevada, USA
Cléver Ricardo de Farias	University of São Paulo, Brazil
Giuseppe Di Lucca	University of Sannio Benevento, Italy
Davide Di Ruscio	University of L'Aquila, Italy
Morgan Ericsson	Linnaeus University, Sweden
Letha Etzkorn	University of Alabama in Huntsville, USA
Ernesto Exposito	University of Pau and the Adour Region, France
João Ferreira	University of São Paulo, Brazil
Hector Florez	Universidad Distrital Francisco José de Caldas, Colombia
Maria Ganzha	Warsaw University of Technology, Poland
Kehan Gao	Eastern Connecticut State University, USA
Vinicius Garcia	Federal University of Pernambuco, Brazil
Baltasar García Perez-Schofield	University of Vigo, Spain
Cigdem Gencel Ambrosini	Independent Researcher, Italy
Sébastien Gérard	IRT Jules Verne, France
Claudio Geyer	Universidade Federal do Rio Grande do Sul, Brazil
Paola Giannini	University of Piemonte Orientale, Italy
Jose Gonzalez	University of Seville, Spain
Wahab Hamou-Lhadj	Concordia University, Canada
Jean Hauck	Universidade Federal de Santa Catarina, Brazil
Mercedes Hidalgo-Herrero	Universidad Complutense de Madrid, Spain
Andreas Holzinger	Medical University Graz, Austria
Jang-Eui Hong	Chungbuk National University, South Korea
Hermann Kaindl	TU Wien, Austria
Jun Kong	North Dakota State University, USA
Rob Kusters	Open Universiteit Nederland, Netherlands
Giuseppe Lami	Consiglio Nazionale delle Ricerche, Italy
Claude Laporte	École de Technologie Supérieure, Canada
Konstantin Läufer	Loyola University Chicago, USA
Luigi Lavazza	Università dell'Insubria; CEFRIEL, Italy
Paul Leger	Universidad Católica del Norte, Chile
Patricio Letelier	Technical University of Valencia, Spain
Peng Liang	Wuhan University, China
David Lorenz	Open University, Israel
Daniel Lucrédio	Federal University of São Carlos, Brazil
Ivan Lukovic	University of Belgrade, Serbia
Ivan Machado	Federal University of Bahia, Brazil
Yashwant Malaiya	Colorado State University, USA

Frederic Mallet	Université Côte d'Azur, France
Federico Mari	University of Rome Foro Italico, Italy
Manuel Mazzara	Innopolis University, Russian Federation
Antoni Mesquida Calafat	Universitat de les Illes Balears, Spain
Ali Mili	New Jersey Institute of Technology, USA
Mª Ángeles Moraga	University of Castilla-La Mancha, Spain
Elisa Nakagawa	University of São Paulo, Brazil
Paolo Nesi	University of Florence, Italy
Alex Norta	Tallinn University of Technology, Estonia
Marc Oriol	Universitat Politècnica de Catalunya - BarcelonaTech, Spain
Marcin Paprzycki	Polish Academy of Sciences, Poland
Andras Pataricza	Budapest University of Technology and Economics, Hungary
Gabriel Pestana	Polytechnic Institute of Setúbal, Portugal
Dana Petcu	West University of Timisoara, Romania
Ernesto Pimentel	University of Málaga, Spain
Giuseppe Polese	Università degli Studi di Salerno, Italy
Mohammad Mehdi Pourhashem Kallehbasti	University of Science and Technology of Mazandaran, Iran
Christian Prehofer	DENSO Automotive Germany, Germany
Rosario Pugliese	Università di Firenze, Italy
Francesco Quaglia	Sapienza Università di Roma, Italy
Stefano Quer	Politecnico di Torino, Italy
Andres Rodriguez	Universidad Nacional de La Plata, Argentina
Colette Rolland	Université Paris 1 Panthéon-Sorbonne, France
Chanchal Roy	University of Saskatchewan, Canada
Gunter Saake	Institute of Technical and Business Information Systems, Germany
Johannes Sametinger	Johannes Kepler University Linz, Austria
Ichiro Satoh	National Institute of Informatics, Japan
Christian Schlegel	Technische Hochschule Ulm, Germany
Peter Schneider-Kamp	University of Southern Denmark, Denmark
Eva-Maria Schön	University of Applied Sciences Emden/Leer, Germany
Abdelhak-Djamel Seriai	University of Montpellier, France
Istvan Siket	Hungarian Academy of Science, Research Group on Artificial Intelligence, Hungary
Hiroki Suguri	Miyagi University, Japan
Rosa Sukamto	Universitas Pendidikan Indonesia, Indonesia
Thanwadee Sunetnanta	Mahidol University, Thailand
Porfirio Tramontana	University Federico II of Naples, Italy

Enrico Tronci	Università Di Roma "la Sapienza", Italy
Tullio Vardanega	University of Padua, Italy
László Vidács	University of Szeged, Hungary
Tony Wasserman	Software Methods and Tools, USA
Dietmar Winkler	Vienna University of Technology, Austria
Stefan Zander	Hochschule Darmstadt – University of Applied Sciences, Germany

Additional Reviewers

Aissam Belghiat	University of Jijel, Algeria
Anish Bhobe	Télécom Paris, Institut Polytechnique de Paris, France
Hossein Jamali	University of Nevada, Reno, USA
Vinh Le	University of Nevada, Reno, USA
Levi Scully	University of Nevada, Reno, USA

Invited Speakers

Giancarlo Guizzardi	University of Twente, Netherlands
Wojciech Samek	TU Berlin, Germany
Bjoern Schuller	University of Augsburg, Germany and Imperial College London, UK

Contents

Software Engineering and Systems Development

Efficient Adversarial Generation Through Selective SBFL Guidance and Automated Sub-model Strategy

Daniel Rashedi(✉) and Sibylle Schupp

Institute for Software Systems, Hamburg University of Technology, Schwarzenbergstraße 93D, 21073 Hamburg, Germany
{daniel.rashedi,schupp}@tuhh.de

Abstract. Fast Gradient Sign Method (FGSM) is an effective method for generating adversarial inputs for neural networks, but it is memory-intensive. DeepFault reduces the memory costs of FGSM by transferring Spectrum-Based Fault Localization (SBFL) to neural networks. SBFL is a technique traditionally using the execution trace of a program to identify suspicious code locations that are likely to contain faults. DeepFault employs SBFL to identify neurons in a neural network that are likely to be responsible for misclassifications to guide FGSM.

We propose an adjustable SBFL-guided adversarial input generation approach that addresses both memory and runtime efficiency challenges for sequential classification models. Our contributions include: (1) an automated and adjustable sub-model strategy that selects smaller model configurations for input synthesis, reducing both memory overhead and computational effort, (2) vector-based hit-spectrum computation using GPU-accelerated operations to significantly reduce computation time, (3) targeted adversarial input generation enabling modifications in favor of specific target classes, and (4) comprehensive experimental evaluation on contemporary sequential neural network architectures.

Our evaluation demonstrates substantial improvements over existing methods: up to 4.7× memory reduction compared to FGSM and up to 301× speedup over DeepFault while maintaining comparable adversarial input quality. All experiments complete within tens of seconds, demonstrating practical scalability for contemporary models.

Keywords: Fault Localization · Neural Networks · Adversarial Input Generation · Model Pruning

1 Introduction

Fault localization in neural networks leverages techniques from traditional software fault localization to identify problematic characteristics in neural network models. This domain is gaining increasing importance due to the growing reliance of diverse applications on neural networks, particularly in safety-critical areas

M. Mecella et al. (Eds.): ICSOFT 2025, CCIS 3144, pp. 3–32, 2027.
https://doi.org/10.1007/978-3-032-37353-3_1

where reliability is paramount. Among various addressed problems, one prominent research direction focuses on identifying network components that contribute disproportionately to incorrect outputs or misclassifications. These identified network regions can then guide targeted improvement efforts. Building on fault localization techniques, adversarial input generation has emerged as a related domain that aims to identify neural network vulnerabilities. These approaches generate samples that closely resemble legitimate inputs while causing models to produce adversary-desired outputs, thereby exposing potential security weaknesses.

The Fast Gradient Sign Method (FGSM) [7] is a well-established approach for generating adversarial inputs in neural network classification tasks. Given a model's loss function and an input sample to modify, the FGSM computes the gradient of the loss function with respect to the input. This process essentially reverses the standard model training procedure by using gradient information to perturb inputs rather than adjust model weights in order to maximize the model's loss function. While the FGSM demonstrates computational efficiency, it faces substantial memory limitations when applied to large-scale models due to the expensive gradient computations required across the entire network.

To address FGSM's memory inefficiency, Eniser et al. [4] proposed DeepFault, which incorporates classical fault localization techniques for sequential neural network architectures. Specifically, DeepFault employs Spectrum-Based Fault Localization (SBFL) to identify suspicious neurons within the network. Traditional SBFL techniques analyze code regions executed by test cases and their associated outcomes to compute hit-spectra for each region. These hit-spectra allow ranking of code regions based on their correlation with failures using various suspiciousness metrics. DeepFault adapts this approach by computing hit-spectra for individual neurons based on their activation values on a test set, then applies SBFL suspiciousness metrics to rank neurons according to their activation frequency and relationship to classification outcomes. By focusing adversarial generation on the most suspicious neurons, DeepFault reduces memory overhead compared to standard FGSM. However, this memory efficiency comes at the cost of increased computational runtime due to additional hit-spectrum computation, neuron ranking steps, and sequential CPU-only execution in their implementation.

Both FGSM and DeepFault have limitations that hinder their application to contemporary sequential neural networks with millions or billions of parameters. In this work we propose an adjustable approach that addresses both memory and runtime efficiency by refining existing methods for sequential classification models. Our contributions are fourfold:

1. An automated and adjustable sub-model strategy allowing to select network portions up to a specified layer in sequential architectures, reducing both memory overhead and computational effort for hit-spectrum computation and adversarial input generation.

2. Vector-based hit-spectrum computation using GPU-accelerated vectorized operations to significantly reduce computation time compared to traditional methods.
3. Targeted adversarial input generation enabling controlled output manipulation toward specific target classes, allowing for more precise control over adversarial sample outputs.
4. An experimental evaluation of our approach on various contemporary sequential neural network architectures.

The experiments demonstrate substantial improvements over existing methods, achieving up to 4.7× memory reduction compared to FGSM, and up to 88× runtime improvements in hit-spectrum computation and up to 301× speedup in input synthesis over DeepFault while maintaining competitive adversarial input quality. Our parameter sensitivity analysis reveals that parameter configurations exhibit model- and dataset-dependent effects on both runtime efficiency and generation quality. Additionally, our automated cutoff detection successfully identifies optimal sub-model boundaries, with gradient-based metrics enabling aggressive pruning (1/6 to 1/2 of layers) and activation-based metrics supporting conservative strategies (5/6 to all layers).

Our paper is structured as follows: Sect. 3 provides background on neural networks, fault localization techniques and importance analysis, and Sect. 2 discusses related work applying a variety of fault localization techniques on neural networks. Section 4 details our proposed adjustable sub-model approach, including hit-spectrum computation and targeted adversarial generation. Section 5 presents our experimental evaluation and results. Finally, Sect. 6 concludes with future research directions.

To ensure reproducibility and facilitate further research, we provide an extended open-source implementation supporting both manual and automated sub-model selection mechanisms, along with complete experimental scripts.[1]

This paper is an extended version of our contribution to the 20th International Conference on Software Technologies (ICSOFT25) [20]. We introduce an automated sub-model detection mechanism using greedy importance analysis that uses various importance analysis metrics to automatically determine optimal cut-off points within sequential model layers, eliminating manual selection requirements while preserving critical layers necessary for maintaining adversarial input generation quality. This enhancement significantly improves the usability of our approach in automated adversarial input generation pipelines for sequential models without requiring specialized knowledge for sub-model configuration.

Additionally, we have expanded our experimental evaluation to include additional sequential model architectures and real-world datasets, providing a more comprehensive assessment of our automated approach. Moreover, we analyze the cutoff points selected by our automated mechanism, demonstrating its effectiveness in identifying good sub-model configurations.

[1] The implementation and experiment scripts are available at https://github.com/IDahera/fast-hs-adversarial-input-gen.

2 Related Work

Fault localization in neural networks serves multiple goals: identifying improvable parameters during training, locating components that contribute to undesired outputs, and discovering exploitable vulnerabilities. Established techniques include SBFL [4,9], which executes models and applies statistical measures to identify problematic regions, and Mutation-Based Fault Localization (MBFL) [5,28], which modifies parameters to analyze their impact. These approaches either guide developers toward actionable improvements [23,26,27] or perform automatic repair [22,29].

Our work specifically focuses on improving runtime and memory efficiency of SBFL for adversarial input generation guidance, which is a related but distinct goal compared to model repair. Eniser et al. [4] proposed DeepFault, a fault localization approach for sequential neural networks that transfers traditional code SBFL techniques to neural networks. DeepFault serves as the primary basis for our work, which we seek to improve upon. Traditional SBFL techniques rely on executing the test suite of a software project and tracking the frequency of code regions executed by passing and failing test cases. This information is then used to compute hit spectra for each code region, revealing a relationship between execution frequency and test outcomes. DeepFault adapts this approach by mapping code regions to individual neurons and test cases to input samples with corresponding classification outcomes. From this information, the hit spectrum for each neuron is computed and used to rank neurons based on their suspiciousness using various SBFL metrics. Finally, the most suspicious neurons guide adversarial input generation by applying FGSM [7] only on these neurons instead of the entire network.

Since DeepFault's introduction, several works have extended or refined this approach. Duran et al. [3] investigate the impact of different dataset sizes on the effectiveness of fault analysis in neural networks. The approach NP-SBFL by Hashemifar et al. [9] extends DeepFault by expanding SBFL from individual neurons to paths of neurons. Although NP-SBFL conducts optimizations such as search space reduction, it primarily addresses runtime and memory usage for path analysis rather than individual neuron analysis.

Our work addresses the runtime and memory efficiency limitations of SBFL at the granularity of individual neurons to make the approach applicable to contemporary large-scale sequential neural networks. Specifically, SBFL requires hit spectrum computation and application of suspiciousness metrics for all the model's neurons. For contemporary models with millions of parameters, this computation cost becomes a significant bottleneck that must be addressed to make the approach practical. To the best of our knowledge, our work is the first to specifically address these efficiency challenges for neuron-level SBFL in large-scale networks.

To address the efficiency challenges of neuron-level SBFL, we leverage model pruning and importance analysis techniques. These techniques allow us to identify and remove less critical components of the model, thereby reducing the computational cost of our fault localization approach. We adapt approaches that conduct importance analysis to identify layers that are less important for the model's predictions. These layers are candidates for removal to obtain sub-models that can be analyzed faster without significant loss in adversarial input generation quality. Several state-of-the-art pruning and importance analysis methods exist [2]. However, most are not well-suited for our specific requirement. We need to analyze trained sequential networks efficiently at the layer level to obtain executable sub-models. While approaches such as SNIP [16] and GraSP [25] provide fine-grained importance analysis at the connection level, they are computationally expensive for our use case of analyzing large-scale sequential models. Instead, we employ importance metrics computed at the granularity of entire layers, which can be evaluated efficiently and applied to complete layers rather than individual connections. We apply the importance metrics described in Sect. 3: gradient norms [8,17], Taylor importance [18], and activation variance [19,25] for our greedy layer pruning strategy.

3 Background

To understand what SBFL in neural networks entails, we first need to define the structure of a neural network. Section 3.1 provides an overview of neural network architectures relevant to our work. SBFL techniques seek to statistically identify suspicious components in software code based on their execution and corresponding correlation with failures. Section 3.2 describes how SBFL is adapted to neural networks, including the computation of hit spectra and suspiciousness metrics for neurons. Beyond activation-based fault localization, we employ layer importance metrics to quantify each layer's contribution to the model and guide a greedy pruning strategy that reduces model complexity while preserving essential functionality for adversarial input generation. Section 3.3 introduces these layer importance metrics and explains how they provide complementary information to the hit spectrum by capturing different aspects of layer behavior.

3.1 Neural Networks

We focus the scope of our work on sequential neural networks, which are an established choice for various tasks including image classification and natural language processing [6]. First, we consider the basic building block of neural networks: the neuron.

Definition 1 (Neuron [6]). *We define a neuron $\phi : \mathbb{R}^m \rightarrow \mathbb{R}$ as a function mapping m-dimensional real values to a single real value $\phi(\mathbf{x}) = \sigma(\mathbf{w}^T\mathbf{x} + b)$, where σ is an activation function, $\mathbf{w} \in \mathbb{R}^m$ is the weight vector, and $b \in \mathbb{R}$ is the neuron's bias.*

The activation function σ is typically a non-linear function. Established choices for activation functions include the ReLU function $\sigma(x) = \max(0, x)$ or the sigmoid function $\sigma(x) = \frac{1}{1+e^{-x}}$.

We say that a neuron ϕ is activated by an input $\mathbf{x} \in \mathbb{R}^m$ if $\phi(\mathbf{x}) > \delta$ for a given threshold $\delta \in \mathbb{R}$. For our approach, $\delta = 0$ is sufficient, though other threshold values might be relevant for more diverse model architectures beyond sequential networks. Neuron activation is central to SBFL, as it determines the hit spectrum of a neuron, which forms the basis for computing its suspiciousness value.

The weight vector $\mathbf{w}$ and the bias b are parameters learned during neural network training. They are typically initialized randomly and then updated through backpropagation using gradient descent to optimize the model's loss function on a given dataset. Intuitively, they reflect the model's learned knowledge.

Definition 2 (Neural Network [6]). *We define a neural network as a 3-tuple* $\mathcal{M} = (\mathbf{N}, \mathbf{E}, \mathbf{L})$ *where* $\mathbf{N}$ *is a set of neurons,* $\mathbf{E}$ *is a set of edges, and* $\mathbf{L} = \{\mathbf{l}_1, \ldots, \mathbf{l}_k\}$ *is a set of* k *layers where each* $\mathbf{l}_i \subset \mathbf{N}$ *is a subset of neurons, and layers are pairwise disjoint:* $\mathbf{l}_i \cap \mathbf{l}_j = \emptyset$ *for* $i \neq j$*. Each layer* $\mathbf{l}_i \in \mathbf{L}$ *consists of a set of* n_i *neurons* $\{\phi_{(i,1)}, \ldots, \phi_{(i,n_i)}\}$*. Each edge* $e = (\phi_{(i,j)}, \phi_{(i+1,k)}) \in \mathbf{E}$ *represents a connection between neuron* $\phi_{(i,j)} \in \mathbf{l}_i$ *and a neuron in an adjacent layer* $\phi_{(i+1,k)} \in \mathbf{l}_{i+1}$*, defining the flow of information through the network.*

Without loss of generality, we consider sequential neural networks with its layers being labeled according to their index within the sequence, e.g., we assume layer $\mathbf{l}_1$ to be the input layer, layer $\mathbf{l}_k$ to be the output layer, and layers $\mathbf{l}_2, \ldots, \mathbf{l}_{k-1}$ to be hidden layers. The edges $\mathbf{E}$ in a neural network represent the connections between neurons in adjacent layers and indicate the input provided to each neuron. We refer to the output of the last layer $\mathbf{l}_k$ as the model's prediction or classification result given $\mathbf{x}$ provided to layer $\mathbf{l}_1$, which is typically a vector of real values. Next, we consider the loss function of a neural network which reflects the deviation between model's predictions and the ground truth values.

3.2 Spectrum-Based Fault Localization for Neural Networks

Traditionally, SBFL techniques statistically identify suspicious code regions based on their execution frequency in passing and failing test cases [12]. SBFL techniques adapted to neural networks [4] transfer the idea of code execution to individual neuron activations and test cases to input samples with corresponding classification outcomes. Given a neural network $\mathcal{M} = (\mathbf{N}, \mathbf{E}, \mathbf{L})$ with a set $\mathbf{X} = \{x_1, \ldots, x_n\}$ of input samples for $\mathcal{M}$, the hit spectrum of a neuron $\phi \in \mathbf{N}$ is defined as the 4-tuple $HS_{\mathbf{X}}(\phi) = (a_s, a_f, n_s, n_f)$ as follows:

- $a_s \in \mathbb{N}$ is the number of samples $\mathbf{x}_i \in \mathbf{X}$ that activate ϕ and are correctly classified by the model.
- $a_f \in \mathbb{N}$ is the number of samples $\mathbf{x}_i \in \mathbf{X}$ that activate ϕ and are misclassified by the model.
- $n_s \in \mathbb{N}$ is the number of samples $\mathbf{x}_i \in \mathbf{X}$ that do not activate ϕ and are correctly classified by the model.

- $n_f \in \mathbb{N}$ is the number of samples $\mathbf{x}_i \in \mathbf{X}$ that do not activate ϕ and are misclassified by the model.

In practice, the hit spectrum is used to compute a suspiciousness value for each neuron $\phi \in \mathbf{N}$ using established suspiciousness metrics. To evaluate our approach and compare it to DeepFault [4], we use the Tarantula [12] and Ochiai [1] metrics:

$$\text{Tarantula}(a_s, a_f, n_s, n_f) = \frac{\frac{a_f}{a_f+n_f}}{\frac{a_f}{a_f+n_f} + \frac{a_s}{a_s+n_s}} \tag{1}$$

$$\text{Ochiai}(a_s, a_f, n_s, n_f) = \frac{a_f}{\sqrt{(a_f + n_f) \cdot (a_f + a_s)}} \tag{2}$$

Tarantula computes suspiciousness by dividing the proportion of failed tests where the neuron activated by the sum of two proportions: the proportion of failed tests where it activated and the proportion of passed tests where it activated. A neuron that activates frequently in failed tests but rarely in passed tests will have a high suspiciousness score.

Ochiai measures suspiciousness as the count of failed tests with neuron activation (a_f) divided by the geometric mean of the total failed tests ($a_f + n_f$) and the total activations across all tests ($a_f + a_s$). This metric emphasizes neurons that activate in many failed tests while accounting for both the total failure rate and the neuron's overall activation frequency.

3.3 Layer Importance Metrics

We employ three complementary layer importance metrics from the literature that capture different aspects of layer criticality while remaining computationally efficient. These metrics capture different components' importance to classification outcomes by quantifying sensitivity to parameter changes (gradient norm), quantifying the impact of parameter removal (Taylor importance), or quantifying information flow (activation variance). This selection provides complementary perspectives on layer importance while aligning with our efficiency objectives, as more computationally expensive alternatives such as Hessian-based or Fisher information methods [10,21] would contradict our goal of reducing computational overhead.

Given a neural network $\mathcal{M} = (\mathbf{N}, \mathbf{E}, \mathbf{L})$ with loss function $\mathcal{L}_{\mathcal{M}} : \mathbb{R}^p \times \mathbb{R}^p \to \mathbb{R}$ that measures the discrepancy between predicted outputs and expected output, we compute importance metrics over a set of samples $\mathbf{X} = \{(x_1, y_1), \ldots, (x_n, y_n)\}$.

Gradient Norm [8,17]. The gradient norm captures the magnitude of the loss function's gradient with respect to a layer's parameters, indicating how sensitive the model's loss function is to changes in that layer:

$$I_{\text{grad}}(\mathbf{l}_i) = \frac{1}{|\mathbf{X}|} \sum_{(x,y)\in\mathbf{X}} \|\nabla_{\boldsymbol{\theta}_i} \mathcal{L}_{\mathcal{M}}(x, y)\|_2$$

where $\boldsymbol{\theta}_i$ denotes the parameters of layer $\mathbf{l}_i$ and $\|\cdot\|_2$ denotes the L2 norm. Layers with high gradient norms have a more significant impact on the loss and are therefore candidates for preservation in a sub-model.

First-Order Taylor Importance [18]. The first-order Taylor importance expresses the impact on the loss function when removing or perturbing layer parameters, combining both the gradient and the current parameter values:

$$I_{\text{Taylor}}(\mathbf{l}_i) = \frac{1}{|\mathbf{X}|} \sum_{(x,y)\in\mathbf{X}} \|\boldsymbol{\theta}_i \odot \nabla_{\boldsymbol{\theta}_i} \mathcal{L}_{\mathcal{M}}(x,y)\|_1$$

where $\odot$ denotes element-wise multiplication and $\|\cdot\|_1$ is the L1 norm. The product $\boldsymbol{\theta}_i \odot \nabla_{\boldsymbol{\theta}_i} \mathcal{L}_{\mathcal{M}}$ provides element-wise estimates of how removing each parameter would affect the model's loss function. The L1 norm sums these contributions to quantify overall layer importance. Therefore, layers with high Taylor importance are those we seek to preserve to maintain the model's learned knowledge.

Activation Variance [19,25]. While the prior metrics measure parameter sensitivity, activation variance captures the diversity of representations produced by a layer across different inputs:

$$I_{\text{act}}(\mathbf{l}_i) = \frac{1}{d} \sum_{j=1}^{d} \text{Var}\left(\{a_{i,j}(x) : x \in \mathbf{X}\}\right)$$

where $\mathbf{a}_i(x) \in \mathbb{R}^d$ is the vector of activations produced by layer $\mathbf{l}_i$ for input x provided to the model, and $a_{i,j}(x)$ is the j-th activation component. High activation variance indicates that a layer produces diverse representations across inputs, indicating its relevance in the model's decision-making process and thereby providing a reason to keep this particular layer.

4 Approach

Our work enhances the DeepFault approach [4] by addressing memory and runtime efficiency limitations while expanding its capabilities from general to targeted adversarial input generation. Furthermore, a greedy layer importance analysis approach specifically designed for sequential neural networks, allows to automate sub-model extraction to reduce computational overhead during fault localization.

Figure 1 illustrates the workflow of our approach. The process consists of two preprocessing branches that operate on the full model $\mathcal{M}$ and a set of test samples $\mathbf{X}$: First, layer importance analysis applies the layer importance metrics covered in Sect. 3 to determine individual layer's importance on model classification results. Second, hit spectrum computation (Sect. 4.1) analyzes neuron activation patterns across the full model using vector arithmetic that enables GPU-accelerated computation. Sub-model selection (Sect. 4.2) determines a cut-off layer to obtain the sub-model $\mathcal{M}'$ by comparing gradient norms, Taylor

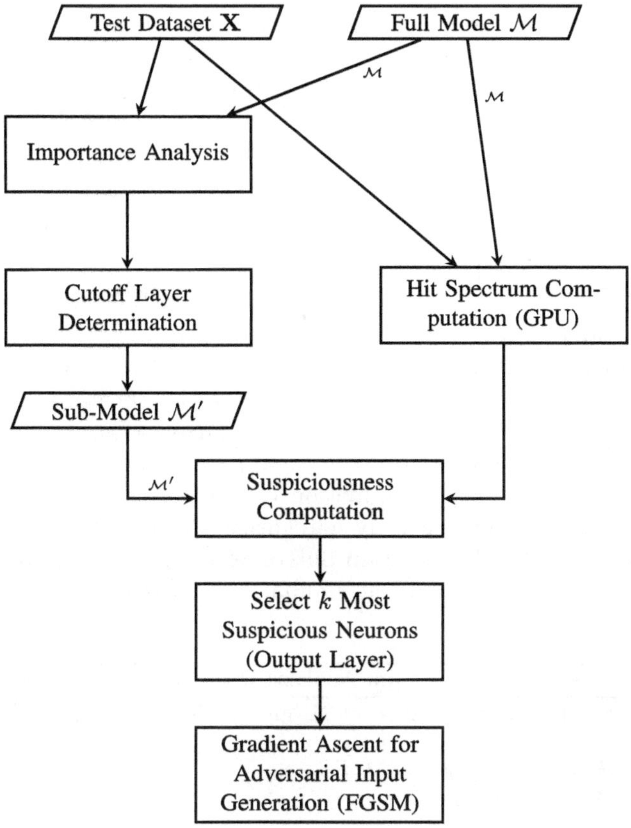

Fig. 1. Flowchart of our approach for adversarial input generation.

importance, or activation variance metrics between layers. Once both branches complete, suspiciousness computation applies Tarantula or Ochiai metrics exclusively to the sub-model's hit spectrum. It then uses these suspiciousness values to identify its output layer's k most suspicious neurons. Finally, these suspicious neurons guide the gradient ascent method (Sect. 4.3) for targeted adversarial input generation using the Fast Gradient Sign Method (FGSM).

4.1 Targeted Hit Spectrum Computation

Our method improves hit spectrum computation efficiency through vectorized operations, as shown in Algorithm 1. We seek to replace neuron-by-neuron iteration with computationally parallelized vector arithmetic over all neurons in layer $\mathbf{l}_i$ simultaneously.

The hit spectrum computation depends on samples of a selected target class t: $\mathbf{X}_t = \{(\mathbf{x}_1, \mathbf{y}_1), \ldots, (\mathbf{x}_n, \mathbf{y}_n)\}$. For each sample $\mathbf{x}_j$, we obtain two key vectors: the model's output $\mathbf{y}'_j$ and the binary activation vector $\mathbf{a}_i(\mathbf{x}_j)$ for each layer

$\mathbf{l}_i$. Note that vectors $\mathbf{y}_1$ to $\mathbf{y}_n$ may represent one-hot encoded vectors with 1 at the index of class t and 0 elsewhere. Accordingly, activation vectors $\mathbf{a}_i(\mathbf{x}_j)$ can also be binarized using a given threshold even if layers output continuous values, indicating neuron activations. To evaluate classification correctness, we use element-wise equality between predicted and expected outputs. Given vectors $\mathbf{a}$ and $\mathbf{b}$ of dimension m, the operator $=_e$ yields a binary vector $\mathbf{c} = (\mathbf{a} =_e \mathbf{b})$ defined by:

$$\forall i \in \{1, \ldots, m\} : \mathbf{c}_i = \begin{cases} 1 & \text{if } \mathbf{a}_i = \mathbf{b}_i \\ 0 & \text{if } \mathbf{a}_i \neq \mathbf{b}_i \end{cases} \tag{3}$$

Applying this operation produces the hit vector $\mathbf{h} = (\mathbf{y}'_j =_e \mathbf{y}_j)$, where $\mathbf{y}_j$ represents the expected output. Note that without loss of generality, we can assume model output is also a binary vector for classification tasks as we can always apply a threshold to convert continuous outputs into binary predictions. The hit spectrum components—$\mathbf{a_s}$, $\mathbf{a_f}$, $\mathbf{n_s}$, and $\mathbf{n_f}$—accumulate through element-wise logical operations. Using conjunction ($\wedge$) and negation ($\neg$) on the binary vectors $\mathbf{h}$ and $\boldsymbol{\alpha}$, we simultaneously categorize all neurons according to their activation state and the classification outcome. Integer casting of these binary results enables vector addition for accumulation across samples.

Algorithm 1. Targeted Hit Spectrum Analysis Using Vector Arithmetic.

Input: model $\mathcal{M}$, layer $\mathbf{l}_i$, sample set $\mathbf{X}_t$ and set $\mathbf{Y}_t = \{\mathbf{y}_1, \ldots, \mathbf{y}_n\}$ of expected outputs
Result: hit spectrum hs_i of layer $\mathbf{l}_i$ over $\mathbf{X}_t$.
$(\mathbf{a_s}, \mathbf{a_f}, \mathbf{n_s}, \mathbf{n_f}) \leftarrow (0, 0, 0, 0)$;
for $\mathbf{x}_j \in \mathbf{X}_t$ **do**
  $\mathbf{y}'_j \leftarrow$ output of $\mathcal{M}$ for $\mathbf{x}_j$;
  $\boldsymbol{\alpha} \leftarrow \mathbf{a}_i(\mathbf{x}_j)$; `// activation vector`
  $\mathbf{h} \leftarrow (\mathbf{y}'_j =_e \mathbf{y}_j)$; `// hit vector`
  $\mathbf{a_s} \leftarrow \mathbf{a_s} + \mathbf{h} \wedge \boldsymbol{\alpha}$;
  $\mathbf{a_f} \leftarrow \mathbf{a_f} + \neg\mathbf{h} \wedge \boldsymbol{\alpha}$;
  $\mathbf{n_s} \leftarrow \mathbf{n_s} + \mathbf{h} \wedge \neg\boldsymbol{\alpha}$;
  $\mathbf{n_f} \leftarrow \mathbf{n_f} + \neg\mathbf{h} \wedge \neg\boldsymbol{\alpha}$;
return $hs_i = (\mathbf{a_s}, \mathbf{a_f}, \mathbf{n_s}, \mathbf{n_f})$

Our approach restricts computation to samples $\mathbf{X}_t$ belonging to class t rather than the complete dataset. This approach focuses the hit spectrum on neurons contributing to misclassifications specifically to class t, as opposed to capturing general misclassification patterns. When generating adversarial examples for arbitrary classes rather than a specific target, one can naturally extend this to samples from any class as is done by DeepFault. Additionally, we compute hit spectrums exclusively for the sub-model's output layer, contrasting with DeepFault's approach of analyzing all neurons throughout the network.

The vectorized implementation achieves computational efficiency by leveraging hardware parallelization available in modern frameworks like TensorFlow and PyTorch. DeepFault [4] employs scalar iteration over individual neurons. For n neurons in layer $\mathbf{l}_i$ and p processing units, our parallelized vector operations yield time complexity:

$$\textbf{Time complexity: } \mathcal{O}(n/p) \tag{4}$$

The scalar approach exhibits $\mathcal{O}(n)$ complexity due to sequential processing of individual operations. This efficiency gain comes at the cost of increased memory requirements. Rather than maintaining scalar values, we store complete vectors of length n, yielding space complexity:

$$\textbf{Space complexity: } \mathcal{O}(n) \tag{5}$$

This reflects the simultaneous storage of input vectors and operation results during parallel computation.

4.2 Automated Sub-model Selection with Importance Analysis

Selecting explicit layer configurations demands expertise regarding the model's internal structure. To reduce this requirement, improve accessibility, and simplify usage, we employ two strategies for automated cutoff layer detection preceding the pruning process and adversarial input generation, namely a simple percentage-based and a slightly more sophisticated importance-aware greedy approach. The first strategy is semi-automated, allowing users to adjust sub-model selection manually and specify a target percentage of parameters to remove, while the second strategy is fully automated, relying solely on layer importance metrics to guide cutoff selection without user intervention.

Percentage-Based Cutoff Selection. The first strategy allows users to specify a target percentage of parameters to remove from the model. The implementation traverses the model from the output layer toward the input layer, accumulating the parameter count of each traversed layer. When the cumulative parameter count of traversed layers surpasses a specified threshold, the current layer becomes the cutoff point. Although this approach provides a straightforward mechanism for model reduction, it does not account for the relative importance of individual layers in contemporary models. Thus, the next strategy expands upon this by incorporating layer importance metrics to guide cutoff selection.

Importance-Aware Greedy Cutoff Selection The second strategy employs a more sophisticated greedy selection approach guided by layer importance metrics previously described in Sect. 3. When no prior knowledge about a model is available, we cannot immediately determine which components are critical for prediction accuracy. A purely percentage-based approach may remove significant learned knowledge if important layers happen to fall within the pruning region on contemporary models. Therefore, our importance-aware approach additionally considers each layer's contribution to the model's predictive capacity while traversing the sequential model.

Recall from Sect. 3 that we consider three layer importance metrics: gradient norm, Taylor importance, and activation variance and that

- the gradient norm $I_{\text{grad}}(\mathbf{l}_i)$ quantifies how modifications on a layer's parameters impact the model's loss function,
- the Taylor importance $I_{\text{Taylor}}(\mathbf{l}_i)$ estimates the impact on the loss function when removing a layer's parameters, and
- the activation variance $I_{\text{act}}(\mathbf{l}_i)$ captures the diversity of information represented in a layer's outputs.

Although the above metrics each provide different measures of layer importance, they all indicate the impact of a layer on the model's output. Therefore, we have chosen to use more than one metric as the different metrics capture different aspects of layer importance. We take peak values in any of these metrics as indicators of transition points where significant learned knowledge is concentrated relative to adjacent layers. By selecting the peak closest to the output layer as our cutoff point, we preserve all layers from the input up to and including this knowledge-dense layer, while removing subsequent layers that contribute less to the model's predictive capacity.

Note that layers without learnable parameters (e.g., MaxPooling, Flatten, Dropout) are skipped during importance metric computation, as these operations do not contribute trainable knowledge to the model.

In practice, we apply the cutoff detection algorithm independently for each of the three importance metrics, yielding up to three candidate cutoff layers. The final cutoff selection depends on the specific application requirements: for maximum parameter reduction while preserving model performance, we select the cutoff closest to the output layer among all candidates; for conservative model reduction prioritizing accuracy preservation, we select the cutoff closest to the input layer. When metrics agree on the same cutoff layer, this provides additional confidence in the selection. Our evaluation in Sect. 5 systematically compares the performance of cutoffs derived from each metric to provide guidance on metric selection for different model architectures and tasks.

Our greedy approach leverages these metrics through a rolling average peak detection mechanism, as illustrated in Fig. 2. Algorithm 2 formalizes this procedure. The method traverses layers in reverse order, from the output layer toward the input layer, analyzing importance values within a sliding window of size w. For each position i in the sequential model, we compute the rolling average $\bar{I}_i$ for the importance function $I : \mathbf{L} \to \mathbb{R}$ over the window:

$$\bar{I}_i = \frac{1}{w} \sum_{j=i-w+1}^{i} I(\mathbf{l}_j) \tag{6}$$

where edge values are padded using constant padding to handle boundary conditions: $I(\mathbf{l}_j) = I(\mathbf{l}_1)$ for $j < 1$, ensuring consistent window sizes throughout the traversal.

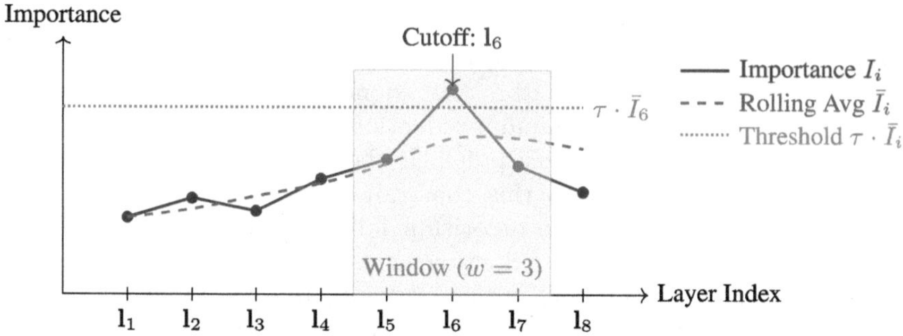

Fig. 2. Rolling average peak detection example with window size $w = 3$ and threshold factor $\tau = 1.2$. Layer $\mathbf{l}_6$ is selected as the cutoff because its importance value exceeds 1.2× the rolling average. Layers $\mathbf{l}_7$ and $\mathbf{l}_8$ (beyond the cutoff) are removed, while layers $\mathbf{l}_1$ through $\mathbf{l}_6$ are retained.

Finally, a layer qualifies as a cutoff candidate if its importance value exceeds the rolling average by a threshold factor τ:

$$I(\mathbf{l}_i) > \tau \cdot \bar{I}_i \tag{7}$$

The threshold factor τ controls the sensitivity of peak detection: lower values (e.g., $\tau = 1.1$) detect more peaks and result in less aggressive pruning, while higher values (e.g., $\tau = 1.5$) require more pronounced peaks and enable more aggressive reduction. In our experiments, we use $\tau = 1.2$. Among all qualifying candidates, we select the layer closest to the output as the cutoff point, as this maximizes the preservation of high-level learned features while achieving parameter reduction.

Algorithm 2. Importance-Aware Cutoff Layer Detection.

```
Input: layer importance function I : L → ℝ for layers L = {l_1, ..., l_n}, window
       size w, threshold factor τ, minimum reduction threshold ρ
Result: cutoff layer index c
i_min ← largest layer index satisfying ρ reduction;
for i ← i_min to 1 do
    Ī_i ← (1/w) Σ_{j=max(1,i−w+1)}^{i} I(l_j);
for i ← i_min to 1 do
    if I(l_i) > τ · Ī_i then
        c ← i;
        return c;
return i_min;
```

To accommodate diverse sequential models and prevent premature termination, our implementation applies a minimum parameter reduction threshold

ρ (e.g., $\rho = 0.1$ for 10% reduction). That is, the reduction threshold ensures that the selected cutoff layer must lead to at least ρ reduction in total model parameters. Therefore, the algorithm first identifies the maximum layer index for a layer that satisfies this minimum reduction requirement, then restricts the search space to layers beyond this index. If the greedy peak detection fails to identify a suitable cutoff within this constrained space (i.e., no layer satisfies $I(\mathbf{l}_i) > \tau \cdot \bar{I}_i$ for $i \leq i_{min}$), the algorithm falls back to selecting $\mathbf{l}_{i_{min}}$ itself, ensuring at least the minimum reduction threshold ρ is achieved. Conversely, when multiple peaks exist, the algorithm's reverse traversal naturally selects the first qualifying peak encountered, which corresponds to the layer closest to the output, maximizing preservation of high-level features. By applying these two constraints, the approach ensures to conduct successful model reduction even when importance metrics exhibit no clear peaks, while preventing meaningless model pruning when peaks occur near the output layer.

Note that Algorithm 2 deliberately employs two separate loops rather than combining rolling average computation with peak detection. While a single-pass approach may appear more efficient, the two-loop design offers two practical advantages. First, modern tensor libraries provide highly optimized vectorized operations that compute rolling averages across all layers simultaneously. For our use case, the additional computation overhead was more than acceptable compared to the overall pruning and adversarial generation process. Second, and more importantly, this design enables pre-computing and caching rolling averages for all three importance metrics (gradient norm, Taylor importance, and activation variance) in a single batch operation. Since different metrics may identify different optimal cutoff points, this separation facilitates systematic comparison and analysis during both development and evaluation phases without redundant recomputation.

4.3 Gradient Ascent Method Leveraging Sub-model Strategy

Contemporary neural network models present substantial computational costs even during their standard inference process. Considering that our approach relies on gradient computation through backpropagation for adversarial input generation, these costs increase further in both time and memory consumption. Our sub-model approach addresses this by restricting backpropagation to a selected subset of layers, thereby reducing computational requirements significantly. In the following, we present our sub-model-based gradient ascent technique for adversarial input generation.

Figure 3 demonstrates how a sub-model can be extracted from a complete network. The visualization highlights neurons belonging to the sub-model in red, showing that only 3 of the 9 total neurons have to be executed for the gradient ascent method. While we focus on sequential architectures in our examples, this sub-model strategy generalizes to arbitrary network topologies.

The procedure detailed in Algorithm 3 operates on a neural network $\mathcal{M} = (\mathbf{N}, \mathbf{E}, \mathbf{L})$ and requires the following inputs:

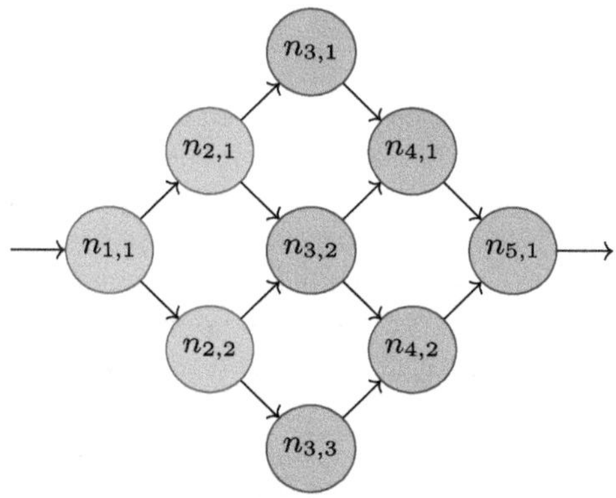

Fig. 3. Example of a sub-model highlighted in red color [20] (Color figure online).

- a set of samples $\mathbf{X}_{\bar{t}}$ from classes other than target class t,
- the pre-computed hit spectrum hs_i for selected layer $\mathbf{l}_i$,
- a suspiciousness metric $\sigma \in \{\texttt{Tarantula, Ochiai}\}$,
- sub-model $\mathcal{M}' = (\mathbf{N}', \mathbf{E}', \mathbf{L}')$ where $\mathbf{N}' \subset \mathbf{N}$, $\mathbf{E}' \subset \mathbf{E}$ containing only edges between retained neurons such that $\forall e \in \mathbf{E}' : e = (n_{pre}, n_{post})$ it holds $n_{pre}, n_{post} \in \mathbf{N}'$, and $\mathbf{L}' \subset \mathbf{L}$ such that $\forall \mathbf{l}_i \in \mathbf{L}'$ it holds $\mathbf{l}_i \subset \mathbf{N}'$

Since the hit spectrum analysis already incorporates target class information, adversarial input generation would not benefit from modifications on samples of the target class.

Algorithm 3. Adversarial Input Generation Using Sub-Model Strategy.

Input: model $\mathcal{M}'$, hit spectrum hs_i of layer $\mathbf{l}_i$, suspiciousness function $\sigma \in \{\texttt{Tarantula}, \texttt{Ochiai}\}$, sample set $\mathbf{X}_{\bar{t}}$ to modify
Result: modified sample set $\mathbf{X}'$
$\mathbf{s}_i \leftarrow \sigma(hs_i)$;
$\Omega \leftarrow \texttt{top\_sus\_indices}(\mathbf{s}_i, k)$;
$\mathbf{X}' \leftarrow \mathbf{X}$;
for $t \in$ *iterations* **do**
  $\mathbf{Y}' \leftarrow$ output of $\mathcal{M}'$ for input $\mathbf{X}'$;
  $\nabla \leftarrow \frac{\partial(\sum_{i \in \Omega} \mathbf{Y}'_k[i])}{\partial \mathbf{X}'}$;
  $\mathbf{X}' \leftarrow \mathbf{X}' + \nabla * \epsilon$

The algorithm begins by applying the suspiciousness metric σ to the hit spectrum, yielding suspiciousness scores for all neurons in layer $\mathbf{l}_i$. From these scores, we identify the k neurons of the sub-model's output layer exhibiting the highest suspiciousness values. Section 5 presents our experimental results and the selection of appropriate parameter values. The algorithm also initializes $\mathbf{X}'$ as a working copy of the input samples that will be iteratively modified.

Following DeepFault's framework [4], each iteration begins by propagating the current sample batch $\mathbf{X}'$ through the sub-model to produce outputs $\mathbf{Y}'$. We then calculate the gradient ∇ as the partial derivative of the summed activation values from the k most suspicious neurons (indexed by Ω) with respect to the input samples. Recall that layer $\mathbf{l}_i$ serves as the sub-model's output layer and contains these high-suspiciousness neurons. The update rule $\mathbf{X}' \leftarrow \mathbf{X}' + \nabla * \epsilon$ perturbs the samples in the direction that maximizes activation of the suspicious neurons, where ϵ controls the perturbation step size. This process repeats for a fixed number of iterations to progressively obtain adversarial inputs.

5 Evaluation

This section is dedicated to the experimental evaluation of our proposed approach. As part of the first research question, we investigate our approach's sub-model strategy. Specifically, we examine how it allows trading off runtimes and memory usage for quality of adversarial input generation on public contemporary models. As part of the second research question, we compare efficiency of our approach against the related work, DeepFault, and the original FGSM method. Then, we evaluate how various parameters impact both quality of adversarial input generation and runtime efficiency, identifying configurations that improve results while maintaining short execution times. Finally, we investigate the outcome of our proposed sub-model strategy for sequential models.

All experiments were conducted on a system specified by Table 1. For our experiments, we have implemented our approach in Python 3.12 using the PyTorch (`torch`) library and the `torchvision` library for creating instances of publicly available image classification models.

We evaluate our approach on a selection of simpler custom models, namely small DenseLayer model and a small convolutional layer model based on LeNet [15] and larger contemporary models, namely AlexNet [14], EfficientNet-B0 [24], and MobileNet [11]. Table 2 lists the models' specifications. These models were trained either on the `mnist`, `fashion-mnist`, `cifar10`, or `svhn` datasets depending on the model's complexity. Every model was trained for 3 epochs on the corresponding training dataset using the Adam optimizer [13].

Table 1. System Specifications

Software	
OS	Ubuntu 22.04 (Jammy)
Python	3.12
PyTorch	2.17.0
Hardware	
CPU	AMD Ryzen 2990WX 32-Core
GPU	RTX 2080 Ti (11.8 GB)
RAM	116 GB

Table 2. The models and the associated datasets used for evaluation.

Model	Dataset	Parameters	Layers	Size (MB)	Acc.
LeNet	`mnist`	28,534	15	0.11	98.67%
DenseNet	`mnist`	576,810	12	2.20	95.82%
LeNet	`f-mnist`	28,534	15	0.11	87.24%
DenseNet	`f-mnist`	576,810	12	2.20	85.52%
MobileNet	`cifar10`	1,528,106	208	5.88	73.91%
EfficientNet-B0	`cifar10`	4,020,358	336	15.50	77.66%
AlexNet	`cifar10`	57,044,810	23	217.61	55.27%
MobileNet	`svhn`	1,528,106	208	5.88	93.19%
EfficientNet-B0	`svhn`	4,020,358	336	15.50	93.78%
AlexNet	`svhn`	57,044,810	23	217.61	88.61%

5.1 RQ1: Trading Off Runtimes and Memory Usage for Adversarial Input Generation Quality

The first research question investigates the trade-off between runtime performance and memory usage for adversarial input generation quality enabled by our sub-model strategy. We emphasize that this work is driven by efficiency improvements while accepting small decreases in adversarial input generation quality. In this section, we particularly evaluate the selected contemporary models AlexNet, EfficientNet-B0, and MobileNet due to their significance for the research question as opposed to the aforementioned smaller-scale models.

The experimental parameters for RQ1 are configured as follows: we process the samples in batches of 32, apply 10 iterations of gradient ascent, and use a gradient factor of 1.0. We selected 5,000 non-class-0 samples to be modified into adversarial samples, which represents a substantially higher number than the tens of samples used in the reference work DeepFault [4]. We employ 25 of the most suspicious neurons for gradient ascent, demonstrating that even small numbers of neurons can produce desired results for contemporary models containing millions of parameters.

Table 3 presents the complete results of our experiments. For each model and dataset combination, we evaluated two sub-model configurations: a smaller sub-model configuration with fewer parameters and a larger sub-model variant with a greater number of parameters.

MobileNet demonstrates the highest susceptibility to adversarial modifications, with target accuracy increasing significantly from 22.08% to 95.50% for `cifar10` and 7.10% to 87.60% for `svhn`. Correspondingly, overall accuracy on modified samples drops from 67.72% to 10.50% for `cifar10` and 94.22% to 11.38% for `svhn`, indicating successful adversarial generation. Even the small sub-model with only 464 parameters produces notable results, though runtime nearly doubles (24.26 s to 49.94 s for `cifar10`) for the larger sub-model configuration.

Table 3. Adversarial input generation results for different sub-model configurations across models and datasets. Target accuracy denotes the percentage of modified samples classified as the target class and is a number our work seeks to increase, while overall accuracy denotes the overall classification accuracy of the model on the modified samples and is a number we seek to decrease.

Model	Parameters	Ratio	Target (%)	Overall (%)	Time
CIFAR-10					
MobileNet-SubA	464	0.03%	22.08%	67.72%	24.26 s
MobileNet-SubB	576,464	37.72%	95.50%	10.50%	49.94 s
			(+73.42pp)	(-57.22pp)	(+25.68 s)
AlexNet-SubA	40,222,528	70.51%	11.76%	58.80%	21.21 s
AlexNet-SubB	57,003,840	99.93%	16.96%	56.98%	21.93 s
			(+5.20pp)	(-1.82pp)	(+0.72 s)
EfficientNet-B0-SubA	928	0.02%	13.88%	76.96%	36.97 s
EfficientNet-B0-SubB	308,660	7.68%	63.34%	21.84%	55.63 s
			(+49.46pp)	(-55.12pp)	(+18.66 s)
SVHN					
MobileNet-SubA	464	0.03%	7.10%	94.22%	24.12 s
MobileNet-SubB	576,464	37.72%	87.60%	11.38%	50.32 s
			(+80.50pp)	(-82.84pp)	(+26.20 s)
AlexNet-SubA	40,222,528	70.51%	22.56%	76.98%	20.33 s
AlexNet-SubB	57,003,840	99.93%	17.60%	81.24%	21.20 s
			(-4.96pp)	(+4.26pp)	(+0.87 s)
EfficientNet-B0-SubA	928	0.02%	7.16%	95.42%	36.14 s
EfficientNet-B0-SubB	308,660	7.68%	1.68%	37.86%	55.18 s
			(-5.48pp)	(-57.56pp)	(+19.04 s)

AlexNet shows modest improvements on `cifar10` (+5.20pp) but surprisingly degrades on `svhn` (-4.96pp), suggesting the largest model tested may be less prone to adversarial generation or that layer importance varies by dataset. Runtime differences remain marginal (21.21 s to 21.93 s for `cifar10`) due to both sub-models retaining 70–99% of parameters.

EfficientNet-B0 exhibits pronounced dataset-dependent behavior: target accuracy improves substantially on `cifar10` (+49.46pp) but degrades on `svhn` (-5.48pp). This observation suggests that optimal sub-model configurations are dataset-specific and may require a systematic search process. Runtime scales consistently with sub-model size (36.97 s to 55.63 s for `cifar10`).

From our experiments, we draw two key conclusions. First, sub-model size critically affects adversarial generation quality, with effects varying by architecture: the smallest model tested (MobileNet) shows significant improvements (up to +80.50pp) with deeper sub-models, while the largest model tested (AlexNet) exhibits dataset-dependent behavior. However, meaningful adversarial input generation can still be achieved with sub-models covering various portions of the architecture. For instance, even very small sub-models (0.03% of MobileNet's parameters) can produce promising results on corresponding architectures.

Second, runtime and memory requirements scale predictably with sub-model size. Across all models, runtime approximately doubles when moving from minimal to deep sub-models (24.26 s to 49.94 s for MobileNet on `cifar10`, 36.97 s to 55.63 s for EfficientNet-B0 on `cifar10`). This confirms that our approach enables practitioners to make explicit, quantifiable trade-offs between generation quality and computational efficiency.

5.2 RQ2: Comparison of Runtimes and Memory Usage Against FGSM and DeepFault

This research question compares the runtime and memory usage between our approach, DeepFault, and the standard FGSM method. In particular, we compare:

- Hit-spectrum computation runtimes between a modified version of DeepFault and our approach.
- Input synthesis runtimes between FGSM and our approach. Note that hit-spectrum computation is not conducted by FGSM at all.

The modified version of DeepFault represents a minimal upgrade we conducted to port DeepFault to TensorFlow 2.x. We consider TensorFlow 1.x as outdated because the updates from 1.x to 2.x include many fundamental performance improvements, making a comparison more meaningful. We did not exchange TensorFlow for PyTorch, as this modification would have required too many changes in the program's logic, and we seek a fair comparison.

First, we examine the hit-spectrum computation times of DF@TF2.x and our approach. We use two dense-layer models with `reLU` activation functions: 8x20-DenseNet (8 layers, 20 neurons per layer) and 10x100-DenseNet (10 layers, 100 neurons per layer), both trained on `mnist`. We selected this dense-layer model architecture because it was also used by [4] for experimental evaluation, and it is natively supported by their implementation without further modifications. Moreover, we chose two different models to better capture the applications' behavior on different model sizes.

Table 4 provides an overview of the determined hit-spectrum computation times of DF@TF2.x and our approach. The results show that our approach is significantly faster than DF@TF2.x for both models. Our approach takes 0.26 s and 0.25 s for the 8x20-DenseNet and 10x100-DenseNet models, respectively. In contrast, DF@TF2.x takes 4.82 s and 22.02 s for the same models. That is, our approach computes the hit spectrum for 8x20-DenseNet roughly 19× faster and for 10x100-DenseNet roughly 88× faster than DF@TF2.x. Implementing the hit-spectrum computation using tensors leads to a significant runtime improvement.

Table 4. Computation times for hit-spectrum generation using 20 batches each of 64 samples.

Approach	DenseNet	
	8x20	10x100
DF@TF2.x	4.82 s	22.02 s
Our Work	**0.26 s**	**0.25 s**

Table 5. Input synthesis times (in seconds) for different approaches and sample sizes.

Model	Approach	Samples	Time	Ratio
8x20-DenseNet	Our Work	10	0.10 s	1.0×
	Our Work	100	0.04 s	1.0×
	Our Work	1000	0.27 s	1.0×
	FGSM	10	0.11 s	1.1×
	FGSM	100	0.03 s	0.8×
	FGSM	1000	0.19 s	0.7×
	DF@TF2.x	10	0.77 s	7.7×
	DF@TF2.x	100	7.50 s	187.5×
	DF@TF2.x	1000	73.27 s	271.4×
10x100-DenseNet	Our Work	10	0.01 s	1.0×
	Our Work	100	0.03 s	1.0×
	Our Work	1000	0.29 s	1.0×
	FGSM	10	0.01 s	1.0×
	FGSM	100	0.02 s	0.67×
	FGSM	1000	0.20 s	0.69×
	DF@TF2.x	10	0.89 s	89.0×
	DF@TF2.x	100	8.60 s	286.7×
	DF@TF2.x	1000	87.47 s	301.6×

Next, we examine the input synthesis times across different sample sizes. The experiments reported in this section consider the full models 8x20-DenseNet and 10x100-DenseNet. Table 5 presents the input synthesis times for our approach, FGSM, and DF@TF2.x across 10, 100, and 1000 samples.

We consider our work as the baseline and examine the factors of input synthesis times relative to it. When comparing our approach to DF@TF2.x for the 8×20-DenseNet and 10×100-DenseNet models, the most apparent improvements become visible. The runtime ratios range from 7.7× to 301.6×, demonstrating substantial performance gains. What is particularly interesting is that while DF@TF2.x appears to scale more linearly in runtime with increasing sample sizes, our approach appears to benefit from larger numbers of samples being batched and processed sequentially. For instance, in the 10 × 100-DenseNet model, processing time increases from 0.01 s for 10 samples to 0.29 s for 1000 samples—despite having 100 times more samples, the runtime increases by only 29×. We take this as an indicator that our implementation may include overhead that is executed during data setup or breakdown phases. The observation that processing 10 samples takes 0.10 s while 100 samples takes only 0.04 s in the 8x20-DenseNet model can also be related to some data setup overhead associated with PyTorch and GPU initialization processes.

When considering FGSM, our approach closely matches its performance numbers, although FGSM slightly outperforms our approach. While this difference is of small magnitude, it could be related to processing steps in our implementation reserved for handling sub-models. By expectation, our approach should achieve lower runtimes than FGSM, as it considers only selected neurons from the target layer for input synthesis. However, for larger sample sizes, our approach slightly outperforms FGSM as expected. In additional runs we conducted for larger sample sizes of 5000 samples, our approach takes 1.24 s and 1.32 s for the 8 × 20-DenseNet and 10 × 100-DenseNet models respectively, while FGSM requires 1.16 s and 1.51 s for the same configurations. For the 10 × 100-DenseNet model, these runs demonstrate that our efficiency gains from processing fewer neurons increasingly dominate over setup overheads as sample sizes grow.

To investigate runtimes and memory usage when considering sub-models of contemporary architectures, we compare FGSM operating on entire models against our approach targeting specific sub-models. Figure 4 presents the peak GPU memory utilization for three contemporary models when generating 1000 adversarial samples: MobileNet, AlexNet, and EfficientNet-B0, all trained on `cifar10`.[2]

Memory consumption decreases significantly across all three models: MobileNet (3604 to 1238 MB, 2.9× reduction), AlexNet (3418 to 730 MB, 4.7× reduction), and EfficientNet-B0 (8200 to 5652 MB, 1.5× reduction). This reduction substantially enlarges the safety margin against memory overflow for EfficientNet-B0, which approaches the GPU's 11.8 GB limit.

Notably, EfficientNet-B0 exhibits the highest memory usage and longest runtimes despite having fewer parameters than AlexNet. This reflects architectural differences where varying layer types and neural connectivity patterns disproportionately contribute to memory consumption regardless of parameter numbers.

From these results, we draw two key conclusions. First, our sub-model strategy consistently reduces peak GPU memory consumption by 1.5× to 4.7× across diverse architectures, demonstrating broad applicability. Second, memory usage depends on architectural complexity beyond parameter count. Different architec-

[2] Due to the nature of our development environment, which relies on both Python and underlying libraries that leverage GPU APIs, we ran a second script in parallel to the applications that captures GPU usage values at fixed intervals. This approach was necessary to accurately measure peak memory consumption during adversarial input generation, as PyTorch's internal memory management does not directly expose this information.

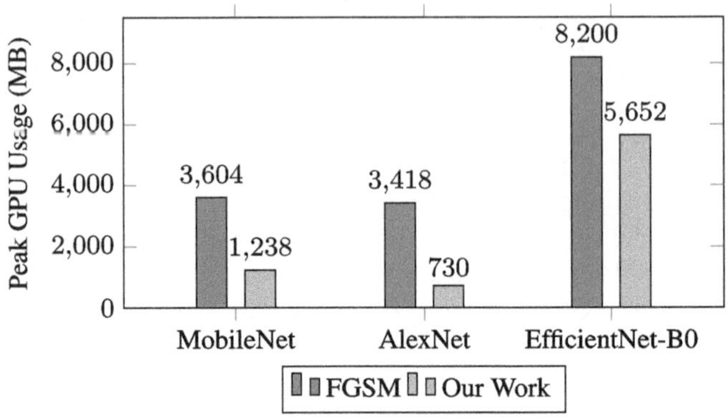

Fig. 4. Peak GPU memory usage comparison between FGSM and our approach on SubB configurations (batch size 32) when generating 1000 adversarial samples.

tures exhibit distinct memory patterns, and their sub-models inherit these characteristics. This underscores the value of our approach, which provides practitioners explicit control over the computational efficiency versus generation quality trade-off.

5.3 RQ3: Impact of Parameter Configuration on Adversarial Input Generation

For this research question, we investigate the impact of the three main parameters, namely gradient factor, iterations, and number of neurons, on the selected models. Our goal is to understand the depth of modifications necessary to obtain meaningful adversarial input while maintaining reasonable runtimes. While we expect that increasing parameter values generally improves adversarial input generation by enabling more significant modifications, the degree of impact on both quality and runtime is of particular interest.

Table 6 summarizes the results of varying the gradient factor (ε) across three contemporary models: AlexNet, EfficientNet-B0, and MobileNet. As expected, the gradient factor demonstrates a notable impact on results across almost all models. This aligns with expectations, as the gradient factor determines the extent of modification within each iteration. Recall from prior sections that we consider increases in target accuracy (the ratio of modified samples identified as the target class) and decreases in overall accuracy (the ratio of samples identified as the target class) as positive outcomes.

For the most part, increasing the gradient factor from 1.0 to 5.0 helps to decrease overall accuracy of the models, except for `cifar10` MobileNet. On some models like AlexNet, the difference is less pronounced as observable in Table 6. However, AlexNet also exhibits the least significant reduction in overall accuracy on modified samples. The results for target accuracies are more varied. A gradient factor of 2.5 shows improvements across all `cifar10` models, with the effect being most observable in EfficientNet and least pronounced in MobileNet. However, a gradient factor of 5.0 leads to decreased performance on MobileNet and EfficientNet. AlexNet shows significant improvement with factor 5.0, indicating that more aggressive modifications were needed for this model.

These observations indicate that while a suitable gradient factor heavily impacts success in targeted adversarial input generation, using a fixed value may not be optimal. The ideal gradient factor appears to depend on both the model and dataset under investigation. However, as runtime variations remain within a small window, ranging from a decrease of 1.14 s to an increase of 0.42 s (see Table 6), we consider it a useful parameter to improve adversarial input generation while mitigating runtime increases.

Table 6. Impact of gradient factor (ε) on adversarial input generation. All experiments use SubB configuration with iter=10, $|N| = 10$, and Ochiai metric. Target: ratio of modified samples classified as target class. Overall: ratio of all samples classified as target class. Differences show changes from baseline ($\varepsilon = 1.0$).

Model	Target (%)	Δ_t	Overall (%)	Δ_o	Time (s)	Δ_{time}
CIFAR-10						
AlexNet ($\varepsilon = 1.0$)	14.60	–	56.10	–	11.11	–
AlexNet ($\varepsilon = 2.5$)	18.40	(+3.80)	55.40	(-0.70)	9.97	(-1.14)
AlexNet ($\varepsilon = 5.0$)	21.90	(+7.30)	52.90	(-3.20)	10.15	(-0.96)
EfficientNet-B0 ($\varepsilon = 1.0$)	63.70	–	26.00	–	17.35	–
EfficientNet-B0 ($\varepsilon = 2.5$)	78.90	(+15.20)	15.90	(-10.10)	16.96	(-0.39)
EfficientNet-B0 ($\varepsilon = 5.0$)	37.40	(-26.30)	13.60	(-12.40)	17.28	(-0.07)
MobileNet ($\varepsilon = 1.0$)	86.70	–	12.20	–	14.27	–
MobileNet ($\varepsilon = 2.5$)	86.80	(+0.10)	10.40	(-1.80)	14.21	(-0.06)
MobileNet ($\varepsilon = 5.0$)	63.10	(-23.60)	11.40	(-0.80)	14.47	(+0.20)
SVHN						
AlexNet ($\varepsilon = 1.0$)	7.40	–	88.40	–	11.61	–
AlexNet ($\varepsilon = 2.5$)	8.30	(+0.90)	87.70	(-0.70)	11.18	(-0.43)
AlexNet ($\varepsilon = 5.0$)	7.80	(+0.40)	87.50	(-0.90)	10.98	(-0.63)
EfficientNet-B0 ($\varepsilon = 1.0$)	4.10	–	63.30	–	18.28	–
EfficientNet-B0 ($\varepsilon = 2.5$)	0.80	(-3.30)	30.90	(-32.40)	18.70	(+0.42)
EfficientNet-B0 ($\varepsilon = 5.0$)	0.00	(-4.10)	14.50	(-48.80)	18.14	(-0.14)
MobileNet ($\varepsilon = 1.0$)	24.10	–	24.30	–	15.48	–
MobileNet ($\varepsilon = 2.5$)	18.10	(-6.00)	15.00	(-9.30)	15.50	(+0.02)
MobileNet ($\varepsilon = 5.0$)	9.60	(-14.50)	11.60	(-12.70)	15.64	(+0.16)

Table 7 summarizes the results of varying the number of iterations across the selected contemporary models. For all `cifar10` models, improvements in target accuracies are observable when varying iteration numbers from 10 to 15 to 20. The improvements are less pronounced for AlexNet and more pronounced for EfficientNet and MobileNet. Notably, overall accuracy decreases as expected, though target accuracy also decreases for some configurations on EfficientNet and MobileNet models, indicating reduced effectiveness.

The increases in runtimes are significantly more pronounced compared to variations in gradient factor values. All models experience runtime increases as expected due to the additional iterations performed. EfficientNet experiences the largest increases, while changes for AlexNet appear rather negligible (ranging from 0.4 s to 2.54 s) considering the model's size. A possible explanation for AlexNet's modest runtime increases may be its architecture, which may require different data types for storage and execution regardless of actual parameter numbers.

Increasing iterations appears to be a safe choice for improving adversarial input generation success, though dependence on the dataset persists. More importantly, the impact on runtimes is continuously present and likely dependent on the architecture under investigation.

Finally, we investigate the impact of varying the number of neurons selected for gradient ascent. Table 8 summarizes the results across the selected contemporary models. The number of neurons proves to be extremely important for certain models. MobileNet shows increases of up to 71.80pp. Overall, this parameter is more likely to improve results notably without increasing runtimes as significantly as iterations do. Nevertheless, the observed results indicate a high dependence on both the dataset and model.

Finding a proper configuration for targeted adversarial input generation proves to be a non-trivial problem requiring further research to identify correlations across a more diverse set of models and datasets.

- Increasing iterations leads to overall better results but may increase runtimes significantly.
- Increasing the number of neurons leads to better input generation results on all models except EfficientNet-B0, while achieving better runtimes than iteration increments.
- Varying the gradient factor leads to more diverse results, with our observations implying that small increments may be useful in improving results.

5.4 RQ4: Automated Cutoff Detection Performance

As part of the last research question, we evaluate the effectiveness of automated cutoff detection in sequential model pruning using three importance metrics: gradient, activation variance, and Taylor expansion. For evaluation, we employ the detection algorithm with a rolling average with threshold factor $\tau = 1.2$ and window size $w = 4$ to identify good cutoff layers for pruning. It is important to note that only layers with learnable parameters are considered in this analysis, which is why some layer indices do not appear in the results. We focus our analysis on the `mnist` models and omit reporting the `fashion-mnist` counterparts, as

Table 7. Impact of iteration count (iter) on adversarial input generation. All experiments use SubB configuration with ε=1.0, $|N| = 10$, and Ochiai metric. Differences show changes from baseline (iter = 10).

Model	Target (%)	Δ_t	Overall (%)	Δ_o	Time (s)	Δ_{time}
CIFAR-10						
AlexNet (iter = 10)	14.60	–	56.10	–	11.11	–
AlexNet (iter = 15)	16.20	(+1.60)	56.20	(+0.10)	11.51	(+0.40)
AlexNet (iter = 20)	17.50	(+2.90)	56.10	(+0.00)	12.82	(+1.71)
EfficientNet-B0 (iter = 10)	63.70	–	26.00	–	17.35	–
EfficientNet-B0 (iter = 15)	73.60	(+9.90)	18.40	(-7.60)	21.76	(+4.41)
EfficientNet-B0 (iter = 20)	76.60	(+12.90)	15.90	(-10.10)	26.66	(+9.31)
MobileNet (iter = 10)	86.70	–	12.20	–	14.27	–
MobileNet (iter = 15)	93.60	(+6.90)	10.70	(-1.50)	17.90	(+3.63)
MobileNet (iter = 20)	97.10	(+10.40)	10.60	(-1.60)	22.95	(+8.68)
SVHN						
AlexNet (iter = 10)	7.40	–	88.40	–	11.61	–
AlexNet (iter = 15)	8.10	(+0.70)	87.90	(-0.50)	12.34	(+0.73)
AlexNet (iter = 20)	8.30	(+0.90)	87.70	(-0.70)	14.06	(+2.45)
EfficientNet-B0 (iter = 10)	4.10	–	63.30	–	18.28	–
EfficientNet-B0 (iter = 15)	2.90	(-1.20)	48.60	(-14.70)	22.68	(+4.40)
EfficientNet-B0 (iter = 20)	1.10	(-3.00)	34.60	(-28.70)	27.63	(+9.35)
MobileNet (iter = 10)	24.10	–	24.30	–	15.48	–
MobileNet (iter = 15)	23.20	(-0.90)	19.90	(-4.40)	19.61	(+4.13)
MobileNet (iter = 20)	19.90	(-4.20)	16.00	(-8.30)	23.33	(+7.85)

those results strongly resembled the `mnist` findings, indicating that the importance values and detected cutoffs are primarily influenced by model architecture rather than dataset characteristics.

Figure 5 presents the automated cutoff detection results for the `mnist` Dense model across all three importance metrics, and Fig. 6 shows the corresponding results for the `mnist` Conv model. The results reveal distinct patterns in how different metrics identify optimal cutoff points. Gradient-based detection consistently identifies early cutoff points, retaining only the first layer in the Dense model and three layers in the Conv model, suggesting aggressive pruning potential. In contrast, activation-based detection demonstrates the most conservative approach, retaining five layers in the Dense model and all six layers in the Conv model. This indicates that activation variance remains significant throughout the network depth, particularly in convolutional architectures where feature representations continue to evolve across layers. Taylor expansion provides intermediate behavior, balancing between the aggressive gradient approach and the conservative activation strategy, retaining five layers in both models.

Table 8. Impact of number of neurons ($|N|$) on adversarial input generation. All experiments use SubB configuration with iter = 10, $\varepsilon = 1.0$, and Ochiai metric. Differences show changes from baseline ($|N| = 10$).

Model	Target (%)	Δ_t	Overall (%)	Δ_o	Time (s)	Δ_{time}
CIFAR-10						
AlexNet (—N— = 10)	14.60	–	56.10	–	11.11	–
AlexNet (—N— = 25)	17.70	(+3.10)	55.90	(-0.20)	10.07	(-1.04)
AlexNet (—N— = 50)	22.10	(+7.50)	53.10	(-3.00)	11.06	(-0.05)
EfficientNet-B0 (—N— = 10)	63.70	–	26.00	–	17.35	–
EfficientNet-B0 (—N— = 25)	63.80	(+0.10)	22.20	(-3.80)	17.26	(-0.09)
EfficientNet-B0 (—N— = 50)	61.20	(-2.50)	19.00	(-7.00)	19.15	(+1.80)
MobileNet (—N— = 10)	86.70	–	12.20	–	14.27	–
MobileNet (—N— = 25)	96.60	(+9.90)	10.60	(-1.60)	15.55	(+1.28)
MobileNet (—N— = 50)	99.80	(+13.10)	10.20	(-2.00)	17.96	(+3.69)
SVHN						
AlexNet (—N— = 10)	7.40	–	88.40	–	11.61	–
AlexNet (—N— = 25)	15.60	(+8.20)	80.50	(-7.90)	11.15	(-0.46)
AlexNet (—N— = 50)	23.70	(+16.30)	69.30	(-19.10)	11.63	(+0.02)
EfficientNet-B0 (—N— = 10)	4.10	–	63.30	–	18.28	–
EfficientNet-B0 (—N— = 25)	1.20	(-2.90)	36.00	(-27.30)	18.53	(+0.25)
EfficientNet-B0 (—N— = 50)	0.70	(-3.40)	23.90	(-39.40)	19.03	(+0.75)
MobileNet (—N— = 10)	24.10	–	24.30	–	15.48	–
MobileNet (—N— = 25)	85.70	(+61.60)	9.60	(-14.70)	16.24	(+0.76)
MobileNet (—N— = 50)	95.90	(+71.80)	6.60	(-17.70)	19.37	(+3.89)

The visualization in Fig. 5 shows that the Dense model exhibits a clear peak in gradient importance at the first layer, followed by a sharp decline, which explains the early cutoff detection. Activation variance, however, shows a more gradual increase reaching its maximum at intermediate layers before declining, resulting in a much later cutoff. Similarly, the visualization in Fig. 6 shows that the Conv model displays more complex patterns, with gradient importance peaking at layer 6, while activation variance steadily increases throughout the network, never triggering the threshold and thus defaulting to retaining all layers. Taylor importance in both models shows a general declining trend, with occasional fluctuations that result in intermediate cutoff positions.

These observations demonstrate that architecture type plays a crucial role in determining optimal cutoff points, as evidenced by the consistent patterns observed across `mnist` and `fashion-mnist` datasets. Convolutional networks show more uniform importance distributions compared to dense networks, leading to later cutoffs and more conservative pruning recommendations. The automated rolling average peak detection successfully identifies distinct cutoff points

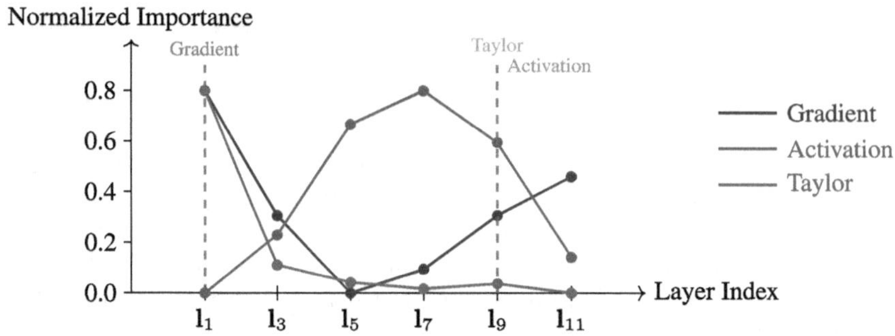

Fig. 5. Automated cutoff detection for `mnist` Dense model. All three importance metrics are shown with normalized values for comparison. Vertical dashed lines indicate the detected cutoff layer for each metric.

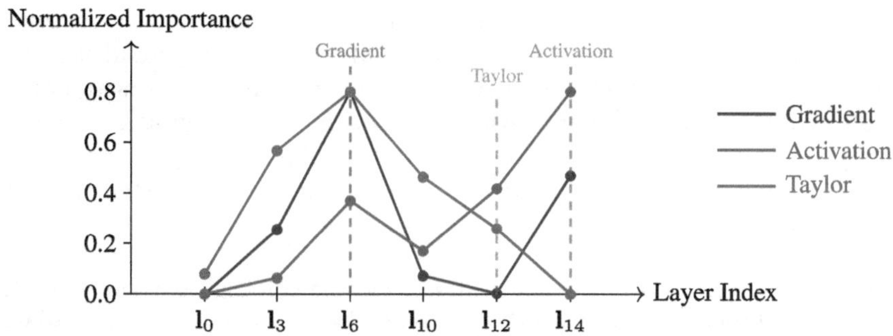

Fig. 6. Automated cutoff detection for `mnist` Conv model. All three importance metrics are shown with normalized values for comparison. Vertical dashed lines indicate the detected cutoff layer for each metric.

without manual intervention, though the choice of importance metric significantly impacts the pruning strategy. For practitioners, this suggests that metric selection should be informed by specific pruning objectives—whether aggressive compression (gradient-based) or conservative accuracy preservation (activation-based) is prioritized.

6 Conclusion

This work presents a novel approach to targeted adversarial input generation that leverages spectrum-based fault localization through a sub-model strategy. Our experimental evaluation across multiple contemporary neural network architectures and datasets demonstrates several significant advantages over existing methods.

First, our approach achieves substantial runtime improvements over DeepFault, with speedups ranging from 19× to 88× for hit-spectrum computation and up to 301.6× for input synthesis. These gains stem from computing hit spectrums on sub-model output layers rather than processing entire models, which significantly reduces computational overhead. Second, our sub-model strategy consistently reduces peak GPU memory consumption by 1.5× to 4.7× across diverse architectures compared to standard FGSM, making adversarial input generation feasible on resource-constrained devices. Third, our approach provides practitioners with explicit control over the trade-off between adversarial input generation quality and computational efficiency through configurable sub-model boundaries. Finally, our automated cutoff detection mechanism successfully identifies suitable sub-model boundaries across different architectures, allowing practitioners to select importance metrics aligned with their specific objectives.

Our experimental evaluation reveals two promising directions for future work. First, the selection of optimal parameters for adversarial input generation remains a complex problem that depends on model architecture, dataset characteristics, and desired adversarial properties. Future research should investigate systematic approaches to identify correlations between these factors and optimal parameter configurations. Second, while our current implementation focuses on feedforward and convolutional architectures, extending the approach to support a broader range of model architectures represents a natural next step that would broaden its applicability.

Acknowledgments. This research benefited from the editorial assistance of Claude 4.5 Sonnet (Anthropic, 2025), which helped refine language and improve readability, and also aided in the development of our implementation through code review and debugging assistance. All intellectual contributions, including methodology, experiments, analyses, and conclusions represent our independent work and original research contributions.

References

1. Abreu, R., Zoeteweij, P., van Gemund, A.J.C.: An evaluation of similarity coefficients for software fault localization. In: Proceedings of the 12th Pacific Rim International Symposium on Dependable Computing. PRDC '06, Riverside, CA, USA, pp. 39–46. IEEE (2006). https://doi.org/10.1109/PRDC.2006.18
2. Cheng, H., Zhang, M., Shi, J.Q.: A Survey on Deep Neural Network Pruning-Taxonomy, Comparison, Analysis, and Recommendations (Aug 2024). https://doi.org/10.48550/arXiv.2308.06767, http://arxiv.org/abs/2308.06767, arXiv:2308.06767 [cs]
3. Duran, M., Zhang, X.Y., Arcaini, P., Ishikawa, F.: What to blame? on the granularity of fault localization for deep neural networks. In: 2021 IEEE 32nd International Symposium on Software Reliability Engineering. ISSRE, Wuhan, China, pp. 264–275. IEEE (2021). https://doi.org/10.1109/ISSRE52982.2021.00034
4. Eniser, H.F., Gerasimou, S., Sen, A.: DeepFault: fault localization for deep neural networks. In: Hähnle, R., van der Aalst, W. (eds.) FASE 2019. LNCS, vol. 11424, pp. 171–191. Springer, Cham (2019). https://doi.org/10.1007/978-3-030-16722-6_10

5. Ghanbari, A., Thomas, D.G., Arshad, M.A., Rajan, H.: Mutation-based fault localization of deep neural networks. In: Proceedings of the 38th IEEE/ACM International Conference on Automated Software Engineering. ASE 2023, Luxembourg, Luxembourg, pp. 1301–1313. IEEE (2023). https://doi.org/10.1109/ASE56229.2023.00171
6. Goodfellow, I., Bengio, Y., Courville, A.: Deep Learning. MIT Press, Cambridge (2016). http://www.deeplearningbook.org
7. Goodfellow, I.J., Shlens, J., Szegedy, C.: Explaining and harnessing adversarial examples (2015). https://doi.org/10.48550/arXiv.1412.6572
8. Han, S., Pool, J., Tran, J., Dally, W.J.: Learning both weights and connections for efficient neural networks. In: Advances in Neural Information Processing Systems. NeurIPS 2015, vol. 28, pp. 1135–1143 (2015)
9. Hashemifar, S., Parsa, S., Kalaee, A.: Path analysis for effective fault localization in deep neural networks. Appl. Soft Comput. **171**, 112805 (2025)
10. Hassibi, B., Stork, D.G., Wolff, G.J.: Optimal brain surgeon and general network pruning. In: IEEE International Conference on Neural Networks. ICNN '93, vol. 1, pp. 293–299. IEEE (1993). https://doi.org/10.1109/ICNN.1993.298572
11. Howard, A., et al.: Searching for MobileNetV3 (2019). https://doi.org/10.48550/arXiv.1905.02244
12. Jones, J.A., Harrold, M.J., Stasko, J.: Visualization of test information to assist fault localization. In: Proceedings of the 24th International Conference on Software Engineering. ICSE '02, Orlando, FL, USA, pp. 467–477. ACM (2002). https://doi.org/10.1145/581339.581397
13. Kingma, D.P., Ba, J.: Adam: a method for stochastic optimization (2017). https://doi.org/10.48550/arXiv.1412.6980
14. Krizhevsky, A., Sutskever, I., Hinton, G.E.: ImageNet classification with deep convolutional neural networks. In: Advances in Neural Information Processing Systems, vol. 25, pp. 1097–1105 (2012)
15. LeCun, Y., Bottou, L., Bengio, Y., Haffner, P.: Gradient-based learning applied to document recognition. Proc. IEEE **86**, 2278–2324 (1998). https://doi.org/10.1109/5.726791
16. Lee, N., Ajanthan, T., Torr, P.H.S.: Snip: single-shot network pruning based on connection sensitivity. In: International Conference on Learning Representations. ICLR 2019 (2019)
17. Li, H., Kadav, A., Durdanovic, I., Samet, H., Graf, H.P.: Pruning filters for efficient convnets. In: International Conference on Learning Representations. ICLR 2017 (2017). originally published as arXiv:1608.08710
18. Molchanov, P., Tyree, S., Karras, T., Aila, T., Kautz, J.: Pruning convolutional neural networks for resource efficient inference. In: International Conference on Learning Representations. ICLR 2017 (2017)
19. Morcos, A.S., Raghu, M., Bengio, S.: Insights on representational similarity in neural networks with canonical correlation. In: Advances in Neural Information Processing Systems. NeurIPS 2018, vol. 31, pp. 5732–5741 (2018)
20. Rashedi, D., Schupp, S.: Efficient hit-spectrum-guided fast gradient sign method: an adjustable approach with memory and runtime optimizations. In: Proceedings of the 20th International Conference on Software Technologies - Volume 1: ICSOFT. pp. 51–62. INSTICC, SciTePress (2025). https://doi.org/10.5220/0013463100003964
21. Singh, S.P., Alistarh, D.A.: Woodfisher: efficient second-order approximation for neural network compression. In: Advances in Neural Information Processing Systems. NeurIPS 2020, vol. 33, pp. 18098–18109 (2020)

22. Sohn, J., Kang, S., Yoo, S.: Arachne: search based repair of deep neural networks. ACM Trans. Software Eng. Methodol. **32**(4), 1–26 (2023)
23. Sun, Y., Huang, X., Kroening, D., Sharp, J., Hill, M., Ashmore, R.: Deepconcolic: testing and debugging deep neural networks. In: Proceedings of the 41st International Conference on Software Engineering: Companion Proceedings. ICSE-Companion '19, Montreal, QC, Canada, pp. 111–114. IEEE (2019). https://doi.org/10.1109/ICSE-Companion.2019.00051
24. Tan, M., Le, Q.V.: EfficientNet: rethinking model scaling for convolutional neural networks. CoRR abs/1905.11946 (2019). http://arxiv.org/abs/1905.11946
25. Wang, C., Zhang, G., Grosse, R.: Picking winning tickets before training by preserving gradient flow. In: Advances in Neural Information Processing Systems. NeurIPS 2020, vol. 33, pp. 2840–2851 (2020)
26. Wardat, M., Cruz, B.D., Le, W., Rajan, H.: Deepdiagnosis: automatically diagnosing faults and recommending actionable fixes in deep learning programs. In: Proceedings of the 44th International Conference on Software Engineering. ICSE '22, Pittsburgh, PA, USA, pp. 561–572. ACM (2022). https://doi.org/10.1145/3510003.3510071
27. Wardat, M., Le, W., Rajan, H.: Deeplocalize: fault localization for deep neural networks. In: Proceedings of the 43rd International Conference on Software Engineering. ICSE '21, Madrid, Spain, pp. 251–262. IEEE (2021). https://doi.org/10.1109/ICSE43902.2021.00034
28. Yin, Y., et al.: Dynamic data fault localization for deep neural networks. In: Proceedings of the 31st ACM Joint European Software Engineering Conference and Symposium on the Foundations of Software Engineering, San Francisco, CA, USA, pp. 1345–1357. ACM (2023). https://doi.org/10.1145/3611643.3616345 ESEC/FSE 2023
29. Zhang, H., Chan, W.K.: Apricot: a weight-adaptation approach to fixing deep learning models. In: Proceedings of the 34th IEEE/ACM International Conference on Automated Software Engineering. ASE '19, San Diego, CA, USA, pp. 376–387. IEEE (2019). https://doi.org/10.1109/ASE.2019.00043

Security Engineering in Product-Line Development: Concept and Practitioner Evaluation

Christian Biermann[1,2](✉), Richard May[1], and Thomas Leich[1]

[1] Harz University of Applied Sciences, Wernigerode, Germany
{rmay,tleich}@hs-harz.de
[2] msg systems ag, München, Germany
christian.biermann@msg.group

Abstract. As modern software systems grow in complexity and configurability, organizations increasingly rely on Product-Line Engineering (PLE) to manage variability and reuse. Yet, security remains insufficiently integrated into these processes and is often treated as an afterthought rather than a core design concern. To address this gap, we propose a dedicated security-engineering extension that systematically embeds security in the PLE framework.
The extension was developed through a structured framework development process and synthesizes insights from 52 existing publications. It aligns with ISO/IEC 27000 to ensure compliance and practical relevance. The resulting framework comprises six processes and twelve activities situated between domain engineering and application engineering, addressing topics such as business processes, incident management, source-code testing, and third-party services.
An initial survey with 36 security practitioners confirmed the framework's necessity, clarity, and usefulness, with over 90% positive responses. However, the feedback indicated a need for finer-grained methodological guidance and more explicit operationalization of activities. Future work will therefore focus on deepening these aspects through case studies and practical evaluation.

Keywords: Product-Line Engineering · Security Engineering · Security · Framework · Evaluation · Practitioner Insights · Survey

1 Introduction

Security incidents caused by (mis)configurations or unintended feature interactions are becoming a critical challenge in today's systems, which comprise increasing configurability [33,54]. However, such systems are ubiquitous in industry: they control manufacturing processes [26], manage enterprise resources [43], or support healthcare workflows [19]. So, their flexibility is valuable, but, unfortunately, it also increases the attack surface by creating a variety of attack

M. Mecella et al. (Eds.): ICSOFT 2025, CCIS 3144, pp. 33–58, 2027.
https://doi.org/10.1007/978-3-032-37353-3_2

vectors. Each additional configuration option may introduce new dependencies or interaction effects that are difficult to predict or generally unwanted, potentially resulting in exploitable vulnerabilities [1,50,59]. Managing the complexity of configurable systems is a main objective of Product Line Engineering (PLE), which systematically distinguishes between shared and variable components to facilitate the derivation of product variants. This approach improves reuse, traceability, and consistency, typically leading to reduced development time, cost, and maintenance effort [6,67].

Problem Statement. Existing research has addressed security in PLE in various ways, but the coverage remains still fragmented and incomplete. Early work primarily investigated secure feature modeling, access control, and policy specification to prevent unsecure configurations [54]. More recently, systematic reviews and mapping studies [35,46,48,49] have analyzed the state of research and found that most contributions are limited to specific process steps, such as variability analysis, feature verification, or testing. For example, CyberSPL [80] provides security checks at the verification stage to identify unsecure feature configurations prior to deployment. While useful, such approaches do not provide guidance for all lifecycle phases, such as requirements elicitation, threat modeling, or security risk assessment, or holistically consider security during PLE (i.e., security by design [40]). In addition, security is frequently treated as a generic non-functional requirement or quality attribute rather than a first-class concern integrated throughout the PLE process [35].

These gaps leads to a predominantly reactive handling of security: issues are detected late, after variability models and configurations have already been defined, which increases the risk of inconsistent mitigations across product variants and raises maintenance costs [44,50]. Another major limitation is the lack of alignment with established security management frameworks, such as the ISO/IEC 27000 series [30]. Only a few existing approaches specify how their activities map to standard-compliant processes, even though such alignment is mandatory in many regulated industries. Without explicit compliance support, the adoption of research results in practice remains challenging, as organizations cannot easily integrate them into their certification or audit workflows [35,46,48,49]. Overall, there is currently no holistic, standard-compliant framework that systematically incorporates security throughout all phases of PLE while remaining adaptable to domain-specific regulations.

Contribution. To address this gap, we developed an extension of the classical PLE framework by Pohl et al. [67], proposing *security engineering* as an additional, cross-cutting layer between domain engineering and application engineering. The layer consists of six processes and twelve activities, derived from the synthesis of 52 existing frameworks and workflows [64], and was explicitly designed to be ISO/IEC 27000-compliant, and is thus highly practice-oriented. We emphasize that our approach remains domain-independent but can be tailored to sector-specific regulations, for example, for safety-critical cyber-physical systems in manufacturing or healthcare.

Note that this article builds on findings of previous research [11] and extends the earlier literature search by three additional publications. Moreover, to obtain early feedback, we asked 36 security practitioners to evaluate the clarity, necessity, and usefulness of the security-engineering extension. The results of our survey show mainly positive perceptions and therefore provide an encouraging indication that the approach is relevant and comprehensible for practitioners. In addition, we got additional ideas based on practitioner feedback that may allow for more practice-oriented improvements for future versions of the security extension. These are presented and discussed in the course of this article. Overall, in this article, we contribute the following to the research community:

- A critical analysis of existing research on security in PLE, identifying key gaps and limitations.
- A novel, ISO/IEC 27000-compliant security engineering layer that extends PLE with six processes and twelve activities.
- Empirical insights from 36 practitioners providing early feedback related to necessity, clarity, and practical usefulness.
- An open-access dataset containing the complete extraction sheet for replication and further studies.[1]

Overall, this work establishes security as a first-class concern in PLE by providing an additional layer between domain engineering and applications engineering. In other words, we present a foundation for systematically addressing security throughout the variability management process of configurable systems in terms of a security by design approach.

Structure. This paper is organized as follows: Sect. 2 provides the necessary background on PLE and security management. Section 3 outlines the applied methodology and summarizes the steps to develop the proposed security-engineering extension and well as to conduct to survey evaluation. In Sect. 4, we present the extension itself, detailing its processes and activities. Section 5 discusses key implications, practical considerations In Sect. 6 we consider potential threats to validity. Section 7 situates our work within the context of related research, and finally, Sect. 8 concludes the paper and outlines directions for future work.

2 Background

The following section presents essential background information on Product Line Engineering (PLE) and security management.

2.1 Product-Line Engineering

PLE is a well-established approach, providing a systematic way to develop software product families that share common characteristics and features, built on

[1] https://doi.org/10.5281/zenodo.17332688.

a shared core architecture and configured for specific stakeholder needs, such as functional requirements, standards, or user needs. In this context, it builds on two main pillars, called domain engineering and applications engineering. Domain engineering focuses on developing reusable assets and architectures, while application engineering derives specific products by configuring and combining these assets [67,75]. The main goal of PLE is to optimize software development by improving efficiency and reusability, reducing costs, and accelerating development [42]. Typically, feature models are used as a de-facto standard to represent both static and dynamic variability, supporting systematic reuse of software artifacts and facilitating automated product (variant) derivation [6,7]. However, PLE introduces complexity, requiring specialized strategies to verify system correctness, typically related to feature-based, product-based, and family-based analyses [75].

Security requirements usually play a special role in PLE as they cross-cut functional variability. This is why holistic strategies are needed that integrate security into both domain engineering and application engineering to ensure product quality, reliability, and security of derived products [24]. However, this common approach presents certain obstacles and can lead to security objectives not being addressed holistically [44].

2.2 Security Management

To achieve high quality, all processes in software development must meet specific quality characteristics. In addition to usability and maintainability, security is considered as a central quality attribute that cross-cuts a variety of components (i.e., assets) and associated processes [29]. So, security management is a business-critical component of software systems that requires robust approaches to successfully protect system assets from threats. Typical threats are data breaches, unauthorized access, or data manipulation [30,66]. Such threats are commonly identified by monitoring systems (e.g., security information and event management system) or vulnerability databases [65] while concrete risks are related to their potential impact and likelihood [30]. A vulnerability represents a concrete point of attack that can be exploited, i.e., weaknesses exploitable by attacks or even system failures.

One of the main pillars of security is the CIA triad, comprising the security objectives confidentiality, integrity, and availability [70]. It also forms the basis of widely recognized standards such as ISO/IEC 27000 [30], which guide organizations in implementing robust security measures in the context of risk management and ensure compliance in practice. At best, effective risk management integrates security activities in all phases of the software development lifecycle to meet defined security requirements (e.g., based on the CIA triad) and ensure an acceptable level of risk [66].

3 Methodology

In the following section, the method of our work is presented (cf. Fig. 1). More precisely, we first go into detail regarding the development of the security-engineering extension. Then, we describe the method related to our practitioner evaluation survey.

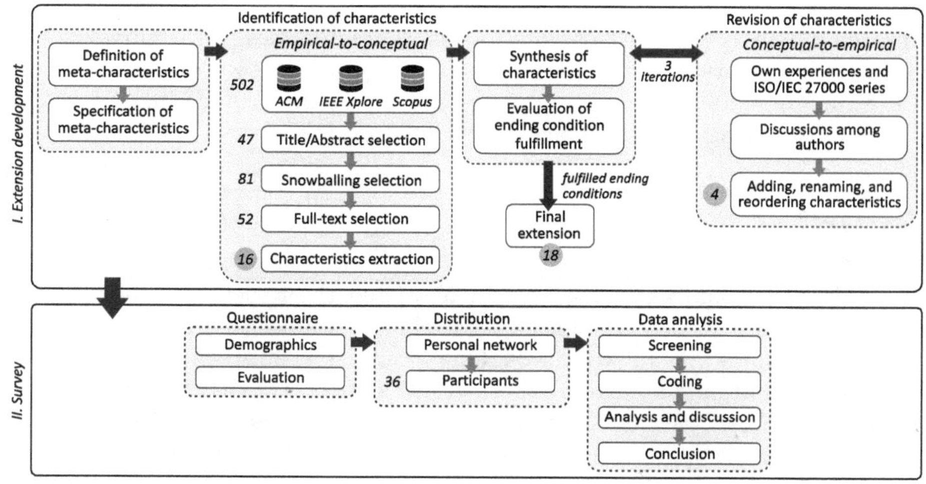

Fig. 1. Method overview, including the extension development and survey; numbers indicate amount of papers/participants or characteristics (dark circled), i.e., processes and activities.

3.1 Extension Development

The extension of the framework is based on the methodology of Nickerson et al. [64], providing structured guidelines for the development of frameworks. Thus, this method is particularly well suited to our context. The method involved three main steps presented in the following:

Meta-characteristics. In the first step, meta-characteristics were formulated to capture engineering processes and activities concerning IT security and PLE. We focus explicitly on security engineering as a third perspective, to extend domain engineering and application engineering. Security engineering builds on domain engineering results and provides requirements and features for application engineering. This ensures equal consideration of functional and secure development. Moreover, we differentiate among three perspectives: the problem space (i.e., domain-specific abstractions such as requirements), the solution space (i.e., realization of these abstractions), and the mapping (i.e., configuration options to adapt abstractions to specific contexts particular situations) [10].

Ending Conditions. In the second step, the ending conditions were determined (E_i) to ensure that the methodological process maintains high quality [64]. Eight conditions were defined: four objective criteria are aimed to ensure unique characteristics (E_1), original context is preserved (E_2), no merging in the last iteration (E_3), and no additions in the last iteration (E_4). Four subjective criteria refer to robustness (E_5), completeness (E_6), adaptability (E_7), and explainability (E_8).

Characteristics Development. In the third step, the empirical-to-conceptual approach was used to iteratively develop the characteristics [64], supported by a systematic literature review (SLR) methodology [38]. Here, we focused on secure PLE frameworks and workflows in preference to specific engineering processes.

The following search string was constructed:

```
("secur*") AND ("framework" OR "taxonomy" OR "engineering" OR
"pattern" OR "process" OR "approach" OR "architecture") AND
("product line")
```

The inclusion and exclusion criteria restricted the review to peer-reviewed work since 2005 with at least four pages, excluding studies that did not focus on secure PLE frameworks or workflows. On November 1, 2024, the second author conducted an automated search across ACM Guide to Computing Literature (21 articles), IEEE Xplore (100 articles), and Scopus (381 articles), yielding 502 results. After title/abstract screening, 47 papers remained. Two iterations of forward and backward snowballing added nine more papers, leading to 49 papers (2005 to 2024). To keep the results up to date (i.e., including latest results in 2024 and 2025), we performed another snowballing iteration on August 23, 2025. In this way, we identified 25 additional peer-reviewed publications. Overall, we included three of theses papers, leading to a final number of 52 papers to be analyzed (cf. Fig. 1 and Table 1).

All selected works were analyzed using the defined meta-characteristics, and processes and activities were abstracted and synthesized. The first and second authors discussed these results in an unrestricted number of discussions, evaluating them against the ending conditions. All conditions except E_1, E_3, E_4, E_5, and E_6 were met. This iteration produced the first extension version, including 14 characteristics (six processes, eight activities).

Subsequent iterations used a conceptual-to-empirical approach [64], relying on the authors' expertise and the ISO/IEC 27000 [30] standards. Four activities related to security testing were iteratively added, reordered, and renamed. Each iteration included discussions using an open-card sorting method and evaluations of ending condition fulfillment. After three iterations, the final extension consisted of six processes and twelve activities (cf. Fig. 1 and Fig. 2).

3.2 Survey Design

Next, we outline the design of our survey to gain initial practitioner feedback. Precisely, we describe the characteristics of the participants, the structure of the questionnaire, and the survey's conduct.

Table 1. Overview of the security-engineering process (italic) and activity fulfillment.

		Security analysis				*Security design*						*Security testing*				
Author(s) and reference	Year	Domain legal regulations	Domain requirements	Domain threats and risks	Third-party services	Security standards	Security requirements	Data protection	Business processes	*Security policy modeling & design*	*Security realization*	Compliance	Configurations & dependencies	Incident management	Source code	*Documentation*
Kanwal and Fokkink [32]	2025	○	●	●	○	○	●	○	○	●	○	●	●	○	○	●
Murphy et al. [60]	2025	●	●	●	○	●	○	○	○	●	○	●	●	○	●	●
Casaluce et al. [12]	2024	○	○	●	○	○	○	○	○	○	●	○	●	●	●	●
Iqbal et al. [28]	2024	○	○	●	●	○	●	●	○	●	●	○	●	○	○	●
May et al. [43]	2023	●	●	●	●	●	●	●	●	●	●	●	●	○	●	●
Varela-Vaca et al. [83]	2023	○	○	●	●	●	●	○	○	●	●	●	●	○	○	●
Tomashchuk et al. [77]	2021	●	●	●	●	○	●	●	○	●	○	●	●	○	○	●
Varela-Vaca et al. [82]	2021	●	●	●	●	●	●	●	○	●	●	●	●	○	○	●
Williams et al. [86]	2020	○	○	●	●	○	●	●	○	●	●	○	○	●	○	●
Navas et al. [63]	2020	○	●	●	●	●	●	○	○	●	○	●	●	○	○	●
Young et al. [90]	2020	○	○	●	●	●	●	○	●	●	○	●	●	○	○	●
Adejokun and Siok [4]	2020	○	○	●	●	●	●	●	○	●	○	●	●	○	○	●
Varela-Vaca et al. [81]	2020	○	○	●	●	●	●	●	○	○	●	●	●	○	●	●
ter Beek et al. [8]	2020	○	○	●	●	○	●	●	○	●	●	○	●	○	○	●
Wilson and Young [87]	2020	●	●	○	●	●	●	●	●	●	●	●	●	●	●	●
Horcas et al. [24]	2019	○	○	●	○	○	●	●	○	○	●	○	●	○	○	●
Varela-Vaca et al. [80]	2019	●	●	●	●	●	●	●	○	●	●	●	●	○	○	●
Horcas et al. [23]	2018	●	○	○	●	○	●	●	●	●	●	●	●	○	○	●
Ya'u et al. [89]	2018	●	○	○	○	○	○	●	○	○	●	●	●	○	○	●
Sprovieri et al. [72]	2017	○	●	●	●	○	●	●	●	●	●	○	●	○	○	●
Alam et al. [5]	2017	○	●	○	●	●	●	●	●	●	●	●	●	●	●	●
Fernandez et al. [18]	2016	○	●	●	●	●	●	●	○	●	●	●	●	○	○	●
Sion et al. [71]	2016	○	○	○	●	○	●	○	○	○	●	○	●	○	○	●
Varela-Vaca and Gasca [84]	2015	○	●	●	●	●	●	●	●	●	●	●	●	○	○	●
Mylläniemi et al. [62]	2015	●	●	●	●	○	○	●	○	●	●	●	●	○	○	●
Achour et al. [3]	2015	○	●	●	●	●	●	●	○	●	●	●	●	○	○	●
Achour et al. [2]	2015	○	●	●	●	●	●	●	○	●	●	●	●	○	○	●
Fernandez et al. [17]	2015	●	●	●	●	●	●	●	○	●	●	●	●	●	○	●
Sánchez et al. [73]	2014	○	●	●	●	○	●	●	○	○	●	○	●	○	○	●
Mellado et al. [54]	2014	○	●	●	●	●	●	●	○	●	●	●	●	○	○	●
Hammani et al. [21]	2014	●	○	●	○	○	●	○	○	○	●	●	●	○	○	●
Horcas et al. [22]	2013	○	●	●	●	○	●	●	○	○	●	○	●	○	○	●
Villela et al. [85]	2012	○	●	●	●	○	●	●	○	○	○	○	●	○	○	●
Tan et al. [74]	2012	○	○	●	●	○	○	●	○	○	○	○	●	○	○	●
Murwantara [61]	2012	○	○	○	●	○	●	○	○	●	●	○	●	○	○	●
Guana and Correal [20]	2012	●	○	●	●	○	●	●	○	●	○	●	●	○	○	●
Yu et al. [91]	2012	○	○	●	○	○	○	○	○	○	○	○	●	○	○	●
Zhang et al. [92]	2011	○	○	○	○	○	●	●	○	○	●	○	●	○	○	●
Achour et al. [27]	2011	○	●	●	●	○	●	●	○	●	●	●	●	●	●	●
Trujillo et al. [79]	2011	●	●	●	●	●	●	●	○	○	●	●	●	○	○	●
Rodríguez et al. [69]	2011	○	●	●	●	●	●	○	○	●	●	●	●	○	○	●
Mellado et al. [53]	2010	○	●	●	●	●	●	●	○	●	●	●	●	○	○	●
Mellado et al. [58]	2009	○	●	●	●	●	●	●	○	●	●	●	●	○	○	●
Mellado et al. [57]	2008	○	●	●	●	●	●	●	○	●	●	●	●	○	○	●
Mellado et al. [52]	2008	○	●	●	●	●	●	●	○	●	●	●	●	○	○	●
Mellado et al. [56]	2008	○	●	●	●	●	●	●	○	●	●	●	●	○	○	●
Mellado et al. [51]	2008	○	●	●	●	●	●	●	○	●	●	●	●	○	○	●
Etxeberria and Sagardui [15]	2008	○	●	●	●	○	●	○	○	○	●	○	●	○	○	●
Kim et al. [37]	2008	○	●	●	●	○	●	●	●	○	●	○	●	○	○	●
Hundt et al. [25]	2007	○	○	○	●	○	●	●	○	●	●	○	●	○	○	●
Mellado et al. [55]	2007	○	●	●	●	●	●	●	○	●	●	●	●	○	○	●
Fægri and Hallsteinsen [16]	2006	●	●	●	●	●	●	●	○	●	●	●	●	●	○	●
ISO/IEC 27000 [30]	2022	●	●	●	●	●	●	●	●	●	●	●	●	●	●	●

● Fulfilled ○ Not fulfilled

Participants. The survey was aimed at practitioners with a background in security. Our goal was to gather initial, practice-oriented feedback on the proposed security-engineering extension. No formal exclusion criteria were set, but the questionnaire was designed for respondents with a basic understanding of software-engineering and security concepts. Recruitment took place via the authors' professional network in industry based on an e-mail list, including the recommendation to share the survey with further interested practitioners (i.e., unknown number of reached persons). Note that we cannot exclude certain response bias because of this distribution channel. Moreover, because distribution focused largely on European networks, the results primarily reflect this regional perspective.

Questionnaire. The survey consisted of a short introduction, a consent statement, and ten questions divided into two parts (cf. Figure 1). It was created in Microsoft Forms to allow easy online participation and automatic data export for later analysis. Completion time was about ten minutes, intentionally keeping the questionnaire concise to encourage participation. All responses were anonymized, stored in encrypted form in a country of the European Union, i.e., providing a sufficient degree of privacy.

Part 1 – Demographics: The first part asked for background information, including the participant's experience in the security field (Q_1, single choice), country of employment (Q_2, free text), and the industry sector of their organization (Q_3, single choice). Where applicable, multiple answers and *other* or *prefer not to say* options were provided.

Part 2—Evaluation: The second part focused on the participants' evaluation of the security-engineering extension. Questions addressed the perceived necessity in the context of the traditional PLE framework (Q_4, single choice), the clarity of its processes (Q_5, single choice), and the potential benefits for research or practice (Q_6, single choice). Note that we provided figures of I.) the traditional PLE framework and II.) the security-engineering extension for Q_4 and Q_5. An open question invited suggestions for improvement (Q_7, free text). Further items explored whether participants found it relevant to include business processes in the framework (Q_8, single choice) and whether they could imagine applying the approach in their own work (Q_9, single choice). At the end, participants could optionally leave their e-mail address for future contact (Q_{10}); these data were removed before analysis to ensure compliance with privacy regulations.

Conduct. The survey was launched on September 09, 2025. Both the first and second authors collaboratively designed the questionnaire and jointly agreed on the distribution strategy. The second author then implemented the questionnaire. All responses were collected centrally using Microsoft Forms, which provided a consistent storage format and allowed direct export to a spreadsheet for further processing. After data collection was completed, the second author performed an initial quality check, proving that each response provided an appropriate quality level. The resulting dataset consisted of 36 valid responses and served as the basis for the subsequent analysis.

Data analysis was done by the second author. For quantitative items (e.g., closed questions with fixed response categories), a descriptive evaluation was conducted. Free-text responses were analyzed qualitatively through open coding and grouping into themes. Here, the second author performed the initial coding, after which the resulting categories were jointly reviewed and refined in two discussion rounds between the first and the second author until consensus was reached.

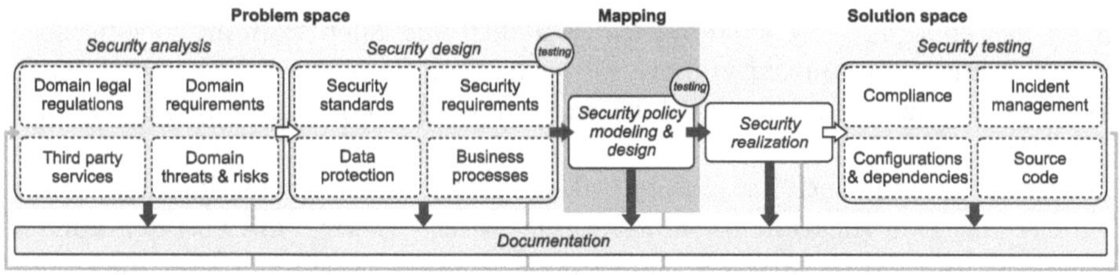

Fig. 2. Overview of iterative security-engineering extension structured according to problem space, mapping, and solution space acc. Biermann et al. [11]; including 18 characteristics, i.e., six processes (italic) and twelve activities.

4 Security-Engineering Extension

To systematically address security concerns throughout PLE development, we introduce our framework extension: *security engineering*. This extension integrates six processes and twelve activities, which are organized along the three key perspectives of the problem space, the mapping between problem and solution, and the solution space (cf. Figure 2).

4.1 Problem Space

The problem space captures the security perspectives of the stakeholders, their concerns, and the requirements. Consequently, the focus lies on understanding (i.e., analyzing) and defining the security landscape and architecture. This perspective is vital, since it sets the foundation for all subsequent security efforts.

Security Analysis. The security analysis constitutes the first step in systematically addressing security concerns within software product lines. It involves a detailed examination of the domain to identify legal requirements, stakeholder expectations, potential risks, and threats.

An activity involved in this process is the analysis of *domain legal regulations*. This activity aims to understand the legal and regulatory frameworks that apply to more general domains, such as the series for information security [30], or specific domains, such as the Health Insurance Portability and Accountability Act [17] in healthcare. One of the central objectives of this activity is to identify the relevant guidelines and restrictions to align the overall security concept with them, ensuring compliance with legal obligations. We emphasize that also non-security or non-privacy standards can be considered here (e.g., safety).

An additional activity within security analysis is the identification of *domain requirements*. While this process is similar to traditional domain engineering approaches [67,68], it explicitly focuses on capturing security-related aspects that shape the domain context. This includes eliciting the specific security needs of stakeholders involved in system development, such as requirements concerning the protection of assets (i.e., features, modules) in cyber-physical systems [82] or the examination of domain-typical interfaces in enterprise-resource-planning

(ERP) systems [43]. By systematically identifying such domain-specific security requirements, potential vulnerabilities and conflicts can be recognized early, allowing for consistent alignment between domain understanding and security objectives.

Another crucial activity closely linked to the definition of domain requirements is the identification of *domain threats and risks.* This activity aims to systematically identify, analyze, and prioritize security threats that may affect the domain. It includes conducting preventive risk assessments and threat modeling to uncover domain-specific vulnerabilities and determine suitable mitigation strategies. Since each industry exhibits its own security challenges, for instance, the financial sector is particularly exposed to hacking attempts, whereas data misuse and loss are critical concerns in healthcare, it is essential to tailor the analysis to the domain context. Established frameworks such as STRIDE, DREAD, SQUARE [3], or Magerit [53] provide structured guidance, while lightweight approaches like UML modeling, activity models [17], or trade-off analyses [73] can serve as practical alternatives in less complex settings.

With the growing integration of *third-party services*, such as cloud infrastructures, these components play an increasingly important role in security analysis. Modern software systems often depend on external services to provide critical functionality, thereby introducing potential security vulnerabilities [43]. Assessing such services for compliance, trustworthiness, and associated risks is essential to ensure that they do not become a weak link in the overall system security. For example, the integration of third-party components, such as data processors in Internet-of-Things devices, requires a careful evaluation of their security mechanisms and adherence to domain-specific standards [77]. Thus, this activity supports informed decision-making regarding the selection and maintenance of external services.

Security Design. The *security design* process ensures that security is integrated into the system from the outset rather than treated as an optional quality attribute or non-functional requirement added later. Building on the results of the security analysis, it focuses on developing detailed specifications and strategies to address the identified security challenges and requirements. Furthermore, this process encompasses comprehensive testing activities, including verification and validation, to ensure the effectiveness of the implemented security measures.

A fundamental activity in security design is the adoption of *security standards*, which relies extensively on the outcomes of security analysis, particularly regarding legal and regulatory requirements. By employing established frameworks such as ISO/IEC 27001 [53], the NIST Cybersecurity Framework [87], or the OWASP guidelines [81], organizations can ensure that their security design aligns with industry best practices and remains auditable. Such standards provide a foundational basis for defining and maintaining security objectives, as well as for evaluating and continuously improving their implementation [16].

Security Requirements represent another key activity within this process. Derived from domain analysis, they define what the system must achieve to protect itself against identified and potential threats and risks. Typical examples include ensuring security objectives [16]. These objectives translate into concrete requirements that can be fulfilled through mechanisms, such as encryption [17], access control [18], or redundancy [16]. Security requirements can be specified, structured, and prioritized in multiple ways, including decision or feature models [53], goal-oriented models [37], reusable security patterns [18], or artifact-based annotations and constraints [85], thereby supporting systematic traceability throughout the engineering process.

Alongside the previously described activities, *data protection* strategies are established as part of the security design process, emphasizing mechanisms that ensure data privacy and compliance with legal requirements. These strategies encompass the use of secure communication protocols with validated certificates [52], as well as the implementation of encryption and authentication techniques [80]. In this regard, a strong connection to regulatory frameworks such as the GDPR [77] is essential to ensure the legal handling, storage and exchange of sensitive data throughout the system lifecycle.

Furthermore, security must also be considered in the context of a system's *business processes*, as they constitute the core operational logic and value creation mechanisms of an organization. Managing these processes, such as controlling and analytics workflows [43] or supply chain replenishment operations [87], is therefore essential to ensure functional reliability, maintain business continuity and strengthen organizational resilience. So, the business process activity focuses on modeling and designing workflows using notations such as the Unified Modeling Language (UML) or the Business Process Model and Notation (BPMN), while integrating security measures in a way that sustains operational efficiency. In this regard, security mechanisms pursue two complementary goals: mitigating risks and maintaining process performance. A representative example is the principle of Segregation of Duty (SoD), which enforces the separation of critical permissions within processes such as sales to ensure that no single person can create orders, modify customer data, and approve invoices simultaneously [39]. The goal here is to make the exploitation of business processes more complex without hindering legitimate operations. To achieve this balance, we emphasize that access management frameworks such as Role-Based Access Control (RBAC) provide an effective means of harmonizing security enforcement with process efficiency.

4.2 Mapping

The *mapping* can be considered as a conceptual bridge between the problem space and the solution space. It translates the results of security analysis and design into actionable models, rules, and policies that guide the consistent and effective implementation of security measures across the (reusable) system development.

At the core of the mapping perspective lies *security policy modeling and design*. This process focuses on developing abstract yet operational models that define a system's security rules, objectives, and constraints, covering aspects, for example, business processes, data flows, or system interfaces. The resulting policies serve as a foundation for translating high-level security goals into enforceable mechanisms within the system architecture. We highlight that different modeling methodologies can be applied for this purpose: from traditional natural-language specifications [80] that enhance comprehensibility for stakeholders, to formal logical representations such as configuration rules [20] that enable automated validation and conflict detection. Graph-based representations, for example, feature models [69] or attack trees used for defining constraints [8], support visualization, traceability, and systematic reasoning about dependencies and potential vulnerabilities.

As an outcome of this phase, concrete reusable security artifacts [53] or architectural patterns [18] can be derived, facilitating the standardization and consistent reuse of proven security solutions across systems and projects. Moreover, integrating these policy models into configuration management or system deployment processes fosters continuous security assurance throughout the lifecycle. Finally, comprehensive testing and validation, both at the model and system level, are essential to ensure that the defined policies are internally consistent, technically enforceable, and aligned with the intended security objectives.

4.3 Solution Space

The *solution space* focuses on the implementation, verification, and validation of the security requirements and associated features defined in the preceding processes and activities. It represents the transition from conceptual design to concrete realization, ensuring that theoretical models and policies are effectively translated into operational system components. This space comprises two primary processes: security realization and security testing.

Security Realization. Security realization involves translating security policies and designs into concrete, operational implementations. This includes mapping abstract security requirements to functional and technical specifications within the domain engineering process [15].

Within this process, existing system features are integrated with the specified security requirements to ensure their practical realization. Typical implementations include mechanisms such as encryption protocols, access control lists, secure logging, and auditing functions, all of which must adhere to the system's security architecture [53]. Business processes defined in UML or BPMN should be converted into XML representations to enable automated processing and promote seamless information exchange among stakeholders. Moreover, categorizing implemented features based on their potential exploitation impact facilitates well-founded risk acceptance and prioritization decisions [15]. Lastly, promoting feature reusability while ensuring valid and consistent configurations is essential to avoid security misconfigurations and to ensure a reliable and maintainable system design [62].

Security Testing. Security testing focuses on verifying and validating the effectiveness, robustness, and resilience of the implemented security design. This process comprises four key activities: compliance, incident management, configurations and dependencies, and source code.

The *compliance* activity ensures that the system conforms to all relevant legal, regulatory, and domain-specific security requirements [55,60]. Compliance testing thus verifies that the implemented security features, for example, data encryption, logging mechanisms, or access control policies [16], are consistent with the obligations identified during the security analysis phase. Moreover, this activity helps ensure that security measures remain up to date as legal frameworks and industry standards evolve [43]. Advanced techniques, for example, statistical model checking or process mining [12] can further support compliance validation by detecting deviations between intended and actual behavior. In early development stages, when real execution logs are not yet available, simulated logs generated from process or behavioral models can be used to verify compliance with legal and sequential security requirements.

Incident Management testing is focused on evaluating the reusability and traceability of core system features that enable the detection, response, and recovery from security incidents. More specifically, this includes verifying and validating mechanisms such as logging, auditing, and alerting functionalities, which form essential components of both vulnerability detection and incident response [27,86]. While incident management is traditionally associated with the post-development phases, namely system deployment and operation [30], integrating corresponding tests already during development can significantly enhance system preparedness. In particular, assessing the reusability and traceability of incident-related functions early on can contribute to a more reliable and maintainable level of security over the long term.

Testing *configurations and dependencies* focuses on verifying that all system configurations and component interdependencies are correctly implemented and free from security vulnerabilities. This activity involves assessing development and deployment environments, tools, and third-party integrations (e.g., cross-configurations) to ensure full alignment with the defined security design [82]. Typical verification tasks include iterative testing of access control lists, encryption protocols, logging and auditing mechanisms, and dependency management systems to detect weak configurations or exploitable vulnerabilities [12,32,53]. Furthermore, external dependencies, for example, third-party APIs, plugins, or libraries, are systematically analyzed to verify their integrity, compatibility, and trustworthiness, ensuring they do not introduce new security risks into the system [23,82].

Testing *source code* represents a fundamental activity in identifying vulnerabilities, particularly those caused by human or procedural errors during software development. Since such mistakes are rarely reported voluntarily, often due to a perceived sense of personal accountability among developers [13,44], it becomes essential to adopt systematic and automated testing strategies that operate across features, products, and entire system families. These strategies not only help uncover recurring weaknesses but also promote secure coding practices and continuous improvement within development teams.

Typical mechanisms include static and dynamic code analysis, complemented by manual reviews, to detect reused or inherited components and verify their compliance with organizational security guidelines and reference architectures [81]. A further challenge arises from clone-and-own development and code planting, where developers reuse snippets or patterns from external platforms such as Stack Overflow, GitHub, or large-language models. While these practices can enhance productivity, they often carry the risk of importing insecure routines, for example, improperly implemented encryption features, unsecure default configurations, or undocumented dependencies, into production systems [44].

4.4 Documentation

Throughout all processes and their corresponding activities, comprehensive documentation should be maintained, ideally managed within a centralized and version-controlled repository to support traceability, reuse, and collaboration [43,82]. The following examples are illustrative and may vary depending on the specific case or domain context.

In the *problem space*, documentation captures the outcomes of security analysis, including domain-specific requirements, compliance obligations, threat models, and risk assessments [77,86]. This serves as a foundational reference for understanding the security context and provides the basis for subsequent design activities, encompassing essential artifacts, for example, security requirements and architectural blueprints [20,62].

During the *mapping phase*, documentation evolves to incorporate security policies, models (e.g., variability or BPMN models), or abstract design structures [22,43]. Ideally, this documentation consolidates empirical findings and artifacts models into a cohesive reference that guides developers, testers, and other stakeholders, thereby promoting consistency, reusability, and efficiency across the PLE process.

In the *solution space*, documentation focuses on implementation and verification artifacts, including detailed records of configurations, dependencies, test cases, results, and incident management procedures [82,87]. Reusable test scripts, verified and validated configurations, and response plans are preserved to streamline maintenance and facilitate auditing. Finally, feedback gathered from testing and monitoring activities is incorporated to enable continuous improvement and sustained alignment between security objectives and system evolution [51,84].

5 Survey

After presenting the security-engineering extension in detail, we describe the results of the survey.

5.1 Demographics

The final sample consisted of 36 valid responses. Table 2 summarizes the key demographic characteristics of the participants. With respect to professional experience in security (Q_1), the majority of respondents reported more than four years of experience, with 42% indicating four to six years and 39% seven to ten years. A smaller group reported more than ten years of experience (17%) or one to three years (3%). The geographic distribution (Q_2) was dominated by participants from Germany (69%), followed by Austria (11%), France (11%), and Ukraine (8%). Regarding the organizational context (Q_3), 58% of participants were employed in the information-technology sector. Consulting (19%), manufacturing (11%), and finance (11%) were also represented, suggesting that the data largely reflect the perspective of information-technology and consulting professionals.

5.2 Evaluation of the Security-Engineering Extension

Table 2 presents the results of the evaluation questions regarding the security-engineering extension. For Q_4 (necessity), 58% strongly agreed and 39% agreed that security should be integrated as a dedicated layer in PLE Only one participant (3%) neither agreed nor disagreed; no disagreement was reported. In Q_5 (i.e., clarity of the proposed processes), 39% strongly agreed and 53% agreed, while 6% selected the neutral option and 3% disagreed. Q_6 (usefulness) yielded similarly positive results, with 36% strongly agreeing and 58% agreeing. Only 6% selected the neutral option, and no disagreement was recorded. The free-text responses (Q_7) provided additional qualitative insights. The most frequent suggestions were to strengthen risk analysis (39%) and threat modeling (36%). Further recommendations included adding privacy considerations (17%), providing better tooling support (14%), and incorporating penetration testing (8%). Individual comments mentioned asset and context identification, impact analysis, security updates, incident response logic, governance integration, KPI-based monitoring, supply-chain security, and architectural guidance. Responses to Q_8 regarding the consideration of business processes were more diverse: 11% strongly agreed, 42% agreed, 33% neither agreed nor disagreed, and 8% disagreed. Finally, Q_9 (i.e., applicability) showed that 58% (strongly) agreed that they could imagine applying the framework or parts of it in their work. One third (33%) selected the neutral option, and 8% disagreed.

6 Implications

In the following, we describe a selection of major implications based on our results as well as challenges that still remain, leading to further research directions.

Additional Security-Engineering Activities. In the survey, participants most frequently highlighted three aspects for strengthening within the extension (Q_7): risk analysis and prioritization (39%), threat modeling (36%), and

Table 2. Distribution of responses for demographics and evaluation questions (n=36); excluding free-text questions (i.e., Q_7).

Category	Question	Response	n (%)
Part 1 – Demographics	Q_1: *Experience*	4–6 years	15 (42%)
		7–10 years	14 (39%)
		>10 years	6 (17%)
		1–3 years	1 (3%)
	Q_2: *Country*	Germany	25 (69%)
		Austria	4 (11%)
		France	4 (11%)
		Ukraine	3 (8%)
	Q_3: *Industry*	Information technology	21 (58%)
		Consulting	7 (19%)
		Manufacturing	4 (11%)
		Finance	4 (11%)
Part 2 – Evaluation	Q_4: *Necessity*	Strongly agree	21 (58%)
		Agree	14 (39%)
		Neither agree nor disagree	1 (3%)
		Disagree	0 (0%)
		Strongly disagree	0 (0%)
	Q_5: *Clarity*	Strongly agree	14 (39%)
		Agree	19 (53%)
		Neither agree nor disagree	2 (6%)
		Disagree	1 (3%)
		Strongly disagree	0 (0%)
	Q_6: *Usefulness*	Strongly agree	13 (36%)
		Agree	21 (58%)
		Neither agree nor disagree	2 (6%)
		Disagree	0 (0%)
		Strongly disagree	0 (0%)
	Q_8: *Business processes*	Strongly agree	4 (11%)
		Agree	15 (42%)
		Neither agree nor disagree	12 (33%)
		Disagree	3 (8%)
		Strongly disagree	0 (0%)
	Q_9: *Applicability*	Strongly agree	5 (14%)
		Agree	16 (44%)
		Neither agree nor disagree	12 (33%)
		Disagree	3 (8%)
		Strongly disagree	0 (0%)

penetration testing (8%). Although these areas are already implicitly covered by the proposed processes and activities, their prominence in the responses highlights a need for more concrete methodological guidance and tool support.

Threat modeling and risk prioritization are integral to the extension's analytical and mapping processes, where threats and vulnerabilities are systematically identified and ranked according to their potential impact. This procedure aligns with standards such as ISO/IEC 27005 [31], but the feedback indicates that practitioners need greater transparency and traceability, especially how risk results feed into design and testing activities. Similarly, the need for stronger emphasis on penetration testing reflects a need for more tangible verification and validation methods. Although already embedded in configuration and source-code testing, explicit inclusion of approaches such as white-box testing could bridge the gap between conceptual assurance and technical testing. Overall, the responses suggest that practitioners perceive the extension as conceptually sound and useful but expect stronger operationalization. Making these activities more explicit is one of our main objectives for future research, for example, by providing concrete case studies.

Consideration of Business Processes. The limited integration of business processes within current security frameworks and workflows implies a significant gap. Modern software systems, especially in enterprise contexts such as ERP environments, depend on process modeling languages like BPMN to define workflows involving tasks, interfaces, and roles [43]. However, security aspects are often only considered after process modeling has been completed, resulting in fragmented or inconsistent protection (cf. Table 1). Integrating security directly into BPMN models by specifying access controls, role permissions, and protected interfaces enables the early incorporation of security measures. When transformed into machine-readable formats such as XML and supported by frameworks like OWASP XML Security, these models become both executable and auditable, ensuring compliance with standards such as ISO/IEC 27000 [30]. We argue that this approach contributes to maintaining operational efficiency while ensuring that business-critical workflows remain secure and compliant throughout their lifecycle.

In our survey, 33% of participants selected "neither agree nor disagree," and 8% disagreed with the inclusion of business processes in the framework (Q_8). This neutrality may indicate that the practical value of process-based security integration is not yet fully recognized or that respondents lacked experience with BPMN modeling. Another possible explanation lies in organizational role separation, where security is typically handled by technical teams, while business processes are managed by business units. To strengthen this connection, we propose the use of business capabilities as linking artifacts in security analyses. Here, capabilities define what an organization must reliably deliver (e.g., order-to-cash), while business processes specify how these services are operationally executed.

Third-Party Dependencies and Services. We argue that preventive rather than reactive security measures are essential to effectively meet the objectives of the CIA triad and reduce exposure to potential vulnerabilities before they can be exploited [70]. In this context, standardized evaluation criteria for third-party components, covering both compliance verification and structured risk assessment, should be an integral part of PLE to ensure consistent and transparent security assurance [66]. This need arises from the increasing reliance on third-party services, which introduces considerable vulnerabilities such as inconsistent authentication mechanisms, insufficient isolation, or the use of legacy systems with inadequate security controls [9]. Nevertheless, only few of the analyzed studies provide comprehensive strategies for managing these dependencies.

Incident Management in Early Development Phases. Incident management is typically considered primarily during system operation and maintenance [78], yet addressing it only post-deployment neglects crucial opportunities for early assurance. Integrating and validating incident management mechanisms already during development, in particular those related to logging, alerting, and recovery, can improve a system's capacity to detect, analyze, and respond to security events before release. This early focus benefits not only security-critical applications, such as ERP systems, but also safety-sensitive domains like cyber-physical systems, for example, in manufacturing.

Equally important is the role of business processes and their models in strengthening early incident management. For example, generating log entries automatically upon completing specific process steps (e.g., order creation) or configuring dependent systems to record synchronized events can enhance traceability and facilitate recovery. Such measures foster a more transparent and auditable process chain, ensuring that incident response actions can be reproduced and verified. Overall, we argue that validating incident response templates and recovery workflows as part of pre-deployment testing promotes reusability, improves organizational preparedness, and ensures that implemented security measures remain robust and consistent throughout the entire development lifecycle.

Comprehensive Source-Code Testing. Although source-code testing is an established research domain [80], it remains underrepresented in the analyzed literature. Existing approaches typically focus on feature-based or product-based testing, yet a family-based perspective, for example, covering cross-configurations and dependencies within larger product portfolios, offers additional potential for identifying systemic vulnerabilities [48]. Moreover, testing must increasingly address emerging risks associated with code planting, where reused or adapted code from external sources (e.g., clone-and-own practices) introduces hidden vulnerabilities [41]. With the rising adoption of large-language models for code generation, this issue is expected to intensify, as automatically generated code may lack rigorous validation and secure implementation practices.

In general, we emphasize that systems incorporating artificial intelligence (i.e., AI systems) pose increasing challenges due to their adaptive and often non-deterministic behavior, which can result in unexpected security vulnerabilities or loss of trust [45]. Thus, extending testing practices to encompass both traditional and AI-driven components is essential for ensuring reliability, transparency, and long-term robustness of modern, configurable software systems.

Standard Adoption and Compliance. Not surprisingly, the adoption of domain-specific legal regulations and standards (e.g., in manufacturing, healthcare, or banking) remains inconsistent, highlighting the persistent difficulty of aligning specialized requirements with established PLE workflows even more [35]. We highly recommend embedding compliance reviews within the PLE process can help ensure ongoing conformity with evolving regulations and industry best practices, thereby facilitating the effective translation of theoretical concepts into practical solutions. Nevertheless, the implementation of standards is often resource-intensive, discouraging their use in smaller or resource-constrained projects. Thus, we argue that lightweight, domain-adapted versions of existing standards, at best supported by automated compliance verification tools, could significantly reduce effort and cost, fostering broader and more sustainable adoption in practice.

7 Threats to Validity

To ensure the robustness of our results, we discuss potential threats to validity along four dimensions: construct validity, internal validity, external validity, and conclusion validity.

Construct Validity. Regarding the framework extension, a potential threat is that our meta-characteristics may not fully represent the space of security-related activities in PLE. To mitigate this, we relied on an established methodology for framework construction [64] and iteratively refined characteristics in multiple discussion rounds between authors. For the survey, construct validity could be threatened by ambiguous wording or too general response categories, which may have led participants to interpret questions differently. Although we carefully formulated items to focus on clarity, necessity, and usefulness, the quite short length of the survey limited the depth of captured insights, and responses may reflect subjective perceptions rather than objective measures.

Internal Validity. One threat related to the internal validity lies in the selection and interpretation of literature. Despite our systematic search and snowballing, relevant studies might have been missed, leading to incomplete coverage. Moreover, terminology differences across papers might have caused misclassification of processes or activities. We mitigated these risks through independent screening by two authors and consensus discussions for ambiguous cases. For the survey, potential threats include selection bias due to convenience sampling (e.g., relying on professional networks) and response bias (e.g., participants with a stronger interest in security might be more willing to respond). Although anonymity and neutral phrasing were used to reduce social desirability bias, we cannot fully exclude its influence.

External Validity. Our framework extension was derived from 52 papers and refined using ISO/IEC 27000 requirements, which increases transferability to various domains. However, its empirical validation was limited to 36 European respondents primarily from the information technology sector. Thus, the findings may not fully represent perspectives from other regions, domain (e.g., manufacturing, healthcare), or organizations with lower maturity levels in security management. We argue that future work should include broader sampling, domain-specific case studies, and longitudinal studies to confirm the applicability of our framework.

Conclusion Validity. Given the descriptive nature of our survey, we refrained from statistical hypothesis testing, focusing instead on frequencies and thematic classification of qualitative feedback. This prevents overinterpretation but obviously also limits the strength of causal claims. To enhance reliability, two authors jointly reviewed and consolidated the coding of free-text responses to ensure consistent interpretation.

Overall, while we adopted several measures to mitigate threats to validity, we acknowledge that the presented extension and survey results represent an initial step and will require further replication and validation in different settings. A concrete case study building on the security-engineering layer is already planned.

8 Related Work

Research on variability and security has increasingly intersected in recent years, reflecting a growing awareness of security as a critical concern in PLE. For example, some publications primarily focused on representing and mitigating security issues within variability models, such as Kenner et al. [34] who used feature models to represent attack vectors. Other work, for example, by Varela-Vaca et al. [81–83] refers to automated security verification and management using feature models. There are also several publications that focus on the characteristics, interactions, and dependencies of security in PLE. For example, Myllärniemi et al. [62] analyzed security variability and Dove [14] referred to variable security issue detection patterns. In addition, some researchers focused on domain-dependent properties of security, such as Tomashchuk et al. [76,77] in healthcare or May and Adler [47] in manufacturing.

Beyond such quite isolated security concerns, some publications explicitly address security in PLE in the context of workflows or frameworks. These include, for instance, a reference architecture for decision support in security-aware domain engineering [16], a framework for structured security-requirements engineering [53,55], or a framework for verification compliance [80].

In contrast to these existing approaches, our work provides a comprehensive, ISO/IEC 27000-aligned PLE extension that integrates security as a dedicated layer within the entire PLE framework [67], offering a domain-independent and empirically validated (i.e., survey with 36 practitioners) framework rather than addressing isolated mechanisms or domain-specific solutions. We note that our earlier work on secure configurable ERP systems [43] also combined PLE with security engineering but represents an earlier, domain-specific version of the security-engineering concept, focusing exclusively on ERP systems. The present study builds on our first domain-independent proposal [11] and extends it by incorporating three additional publications into the SLR as well as by empirically evaluating the extension's clarity, necessity, and usefulness.

9 Conclusion

In this paper, we proposed an extension of the well-known PLE framework [67], namely: *security engineering*. Developed through a systematic development process [64] and aligned with the ISO/IEC 27000 series [30], the extension builds on 52 publications on secure PLE.

The extension is domain-independent but can be tailored to different contexts, such as manufacturing, by incorporating relevant standards and regulations. Beyond six processes and twelve activities, it addresses cross-cutting topics including business processes and capabilities, incident management, source-code testing, security standards, and third-party services. An initial security practitioner survey (36 responses) confirmed the frameworkn's validity and relevance: more than 90% each supported integrating security as a dedicated layer, agreed on the clarity of the processes, and found the extension useful. However, only about half of the respondents considered business processes directly relevant, indicating the need to better connect organizational and technical perspectives.

Future work will focus on strengthening this link and on integrating compliance and standardization aspects more explicitly. Planned case studies will further apply and evaluate the framework using STRIDE [36] for threat analysis and the Cyber Kill Chain [88] for assessing resilience across attack phases, aiming to advance structured, reusable, and verifiable security engineering in PLE.

References

1. Abal, I., Melo, J., Stănciulescu, Ş, Brabrand, C., Ribeiro, M., Wąsowski, A.: Variability bugs in highly configurable systems: a qualitative analysis. Trans. Softw. Eng. **26**(3), 1–34 (2018)
2. Achour, I., Labed, L., Ghezala, H.B.: Formalization of secure service oriented product line. In: ICSOFT, pp, 1–8. IEEE (2015)
3. Achour, I., Labed, L., Ghezala, H.B.: Proposition of secure service oriented product line. In: SIIE, pp. 52–59. IEEE (2015)
4. Adejokun, A., Siok, M.F.: Effective systems security requirements in product line engineering. Insight **23**(3), 26–30 (2020)
5. Alam, M.M., Khan, A.I., Zafar, A.: A secure framework for software product line development. Int. J. Comput. Appl. Found. Comput. Sci. **975**, 33–40 (2017)
6. Apel, S., Batory, D., Kästner, C., Saake, G.: Feature-Oriented Software Product Lines. Springer, Cham (2013). https://doi.org/10.1007/978-3-642-37521-7
7. Batory, D.: Feature-oriented programming and the AHEAD tool suite. In: ICSE, pp. 702–703. IEEE (2004)
8. ter Beek, M.H., Legay, A., Lafuente, A.L., Vandin, A.: Variability meets security: quantitative security modeling and analysis of highly customizable attack scenarios. In: VaMoS, pp. 1–9. ACM (2020)

9. Benaroch, M.: Third-party induced cyber incidents—much ado about nothing? J. Cybersecur. **7**(1), tyab020 (2021)
10. Berg, K., Bishop, J., Muthig, D.: Tracing software product line variability: from problem to solution space. In: SAICSIT, pp, pp. 182–191 (2005)
11. Biermann, C., May, R., Leich, T.: Integrating security into the product-line-engineering framework: a security-engineering extension. In: Proceedings of the 20th International Conference on Software Technologies - Volume 1: ICSOFT, pp. 75–86. SciTePress (2025)
12. Casaluce, R., Burattin, A., Chiaromonte, F., Lafuente, A.L., Vandin, A.: White-box validation of quantitative product lines by statistical model checking and process mining. J. Syst. Softw. **210** (2024)
13. Dietrich, C., Krombholz, K., Borgolte, K., Fiebig, T.: Investigating system operators' perspective on security misconfigurations. In: CCS, pp. 1272–1289. ACM (2018)
14. Dove, R.: Security issue detection and mitigation patterns for product line resource variation. Insight **23**(3), 22–25 (2020)
15. Etxeberria, L., Sagardui, G.: Evaluation of quality attribute variability in software product families. In: ECBS, pp. 255–264. IEEE (2008)
16. Fægri, T.E., Hallsteinsen, S.: A software product line reference architecture for security. In: Käköla, T., Duenas, J.C. (eds.) Software Product Lines, pp. 275–326. Springer, Heidelberg (2006). https://doi.org/10.1007/978-3-540-33253-4_8
17. Fernandez, E.B., Yoshioka, N., Washizaki, H.: Patterns for security and privacy in cloud ecosystems. In: ESPRE, pp. 13–18. IEEE (2015)
18. Fernandez, E.B., Yoshioka, N., Washizaki, H., Syed, M.H.: Modeling and security in cloud ecosystems. Future Internet **8**(2), 13 (2016)
19. Gomes, A.T.A., Ziviani, A., Correa, B.S.P.M., Teixeira, I.M., Moreira, V.M.: Splice: a software product line for healthcare. In: IHI, pp. 721–726. ACM (2012)
20. Guana, V., Correal, D.: Improving software product line configuration: a quality attribute-driven approach. Inf. Softw. Technol. **55**(3), 541–562 (2012)
21. Hammani, F.Z., Rhanoui, M., El Asri, B.: Towards a variable non-functional requirements integration for component-based product line a generic approach. In: WCCS, pp. 146–151. IEEE (2014)
22. Horcas, J.M., Pinto, M., Fuentes, L.: Variability and dependency modeling of quality attributes. In: SEAA, pp. 185–188. IEEE (2013)
23. Horcas, J.M., Pinto, M., Fuentes, L.: Variability models for generating efficient configurations of functional quality attributes. Inf. Softw. Technol. **95**, 147–164 (2018)
24. Horcas, J.M., Pinto, M., Fuentes, L.: Software product line engineering: a practical experience. In: SPLC, pp. 164–176. ACM (2019)
25. Hundt, C., Mehner, K., Pfeiffer, C., Sokenou, D.: Improving alignment of crosscutting features with code in product line engineering. J. Object Technol. **6**(9), 417–436 (2007)
26. Iglesias, A., Lu, H., Arellano, C., Yue, T., Ali, S., Sagardui, G.: Product line engineering of monitoring functionality in industrial cyber-physical systems: a domain analysis. In: SPLC, pp. 195–204. ACM (2017)
27. Ines, A., Khadouma, S., Labed, L., Ghezala, H.B.: Towards a secure service oriented product line. In: SERP, pp, 1–7. Citeseer (2011)
28. Iqbal, M., et al.: Enhancing secure development in globally distributed software product lines: a machine learning-powered framework for cyber-resilient ecosystems. Comput. Mater. Continua **79**(3) (2024)

29. Systems and software engineering - SQuaRE - System and software quality. Standard. In: ISO (2011)
30. Information technology – Security techniques – Information security management systems. Standard, ISO (2022)
31. Information security, cybersecurity and privacy protection - Guidance on managing information security risks, Standard, ISO (2022)
32. Kanwal, S., Fokkink, W.: A framework for model-based specification and verification in feature-oriented software product lines. In: Hojjat, H., Caltais, G. (eds.) FSEN 2025. LNCS, vol. 15593, pp. 61–79. Springer, Cham (2025). https://doi.org/10.1007/978-3-031-87054-5_5
33. Kanwal, S., Fokkink, W.: A framework for model-mased specification and verification in feature-oriented software product lines. In: Hojjat, H., Caltais, G. (eds.) FSEN 2025. LNCS, vol. 15593, pp. 61–79. Springer, Cham (2025). https://doi.org/10.1007/978-3-031-87054-5_5
34. Kenner, A., Dassow, S., Lausberger, C., Krüger, J., Leich, T.: Using variability modeling to support security evaluations: virtualizing the right attack scenarios. In: VaMoS, pp, 1–9. ACM (2020)
35. Kenner, A., May, R., Krüger, J., Saake, G., Leich, T.: Safety, security, and configurable software systems: a systematic mapping study. In: SPLC, pp. 148–159. ACM (2021)
36. Khan, R., McLaughlin, K., Laverty, D., Sezer, S.: Stride-based threat modeling for cyber-physical systems. In: ISGT-Europe, pp. 1–6. IEEE (2017)
37. Kim, J., Park, S., Sugumaran, V.: DRAMA: a framework for domain requirements analysis and modeling architectures in software product lines. J. Syst. Softw. **81**(1), 37–55 (2008)
38. Kitchenham, B.A., Budgen, D., Brereton, O.P.: Evidence-Based Software Engineering and Systematic Reviews. In: CRC Press (2015)
39. Kobelsky, K.W.: A conceptual model for segregation of duties: integrating theory and practice for manual and it-supported processes. Int. J. Account. Inf. Syst. **15**(4), 304–322 (2014)
40. Kreitz, M.: Security by design in software engineering. ACM SIGSOFT Softw. Eng. Notes **44**(3), 23–23 (2019)
41. Krüger, J., Berger, T.: An empirical analysis of the costs of clone-and platform-oriented software reuse. In: ESEC/FSE, pp. 432–444. ACM (2020)
42. van der Linden, F.J., et al.: Software Product Lines in Action. Springer, Cham (2007). https://doi.org/10.1007/978-3-540-71437-8
43. May, R., Biermann, C., Kenner, A., Krüger, J., Leich, T.: A product-line-engineering framework for secure enterprise-resource-planning systems. In: CENTERIS, pp, 1–8. Elsevier (2023)
44. May, R., Biermann, C., Krüger, J., Leich, T.: Asking security practitioners: did you find the vulnerable (MIS)configuration? In: VaMoS, pp. 1–10. ACM (2025)
45. May, R., Krüger, J., Leich, T.: Sok: how artificial-intelligence incidents can jeopardize safety and security. In: ARES, pp. 1–12. ACM (2024)
46. May, R.: A systematic mapping study on security in configurable safety-critical systems based on product-line concepts, pp. 217–224. SciTePress (2023)
47. May, R., Adler, S.: Experiences in developing configurable digital twin-assisted XR applications for industrial environments. In: VaMoS, pp. 107–111. ACM (2025)
48. May, R., Alex, A., Suresh, R., Leich, T.: Product-Line Engineering for Smart Manufacturing: A Systematic Mapping Study on Security Concepts, pp. 323–330. SciTePress (2024)

49. May, R., Biermann, C., Krüger, J., Saake, G., Leich, T.: A systematic mapping study of security concepts for configurable data storages. In: SPLC, pp. 108–119. ACM (2022)
50. May, R., Biermann, C., Zerweck, X.M., Ludwig, K., Krüger, J., Leich, T.: Vulnerably (mis)configured? Exploring 10 years of developers' Q&As on Stack Overflow. In: VaMoS, pp. 112–122. ACM (2024)
51. Mellado, D., Fernández-Medina, E., Piattini, M.: Security requirements engineering process for software product lines: a case study. In: ICSEA, pp. 1–6. IEEE (2008)
52. Mellado, D., Fernández-Medina, E., Piattini, M.: Towards security requirements management for software product lines: a security domain requirements engineering process. Comput. Stand. Interfaces **30**(6), 361–371 (2008)
53. Mellado, D., Fernández-Medina, E., Piattini, M.: Security requirements engineering framework for software product lines. Inf. Softw. Technol. **52**(10), 1094–1117 (2010)
54. Mellado, D., Mouratidis, H., Fernández-Medina, E.: Secure tropos framework for software product lines requirements engineering. Comput. Stand. Interfaces **36**(4), 711–722 (2014)
55. Mellado, D., Fernández-Medina, E., Piattini, M.: Sreppline: towards a security requirements engineering process for software product lines. In: WOSIS, pp. 220–232. SciTePress (2007)
56. Mellado, D., Fernández-Medina, E., Piattini, M.: Security requirements in software product lines. In: SECRYPT, pp. 442–449. SciTePress (2008)
57. Mellado, D., Fernandez-Medina, E., Piattini, M.: Security requirements variability for software product lines. In: ARES, pp. 1413–1420. IEEE (2008)
58. Mellado, D., Rodríguez, J., Fernández-Medina, E., Piattini, M.: Automated support for security requirements engineering in software product line domain engineering. In: ARES, pp. 224–231. IEEE (2009)
59. Mesa, O., et al.: Understanding vulnerabilities in ppugin-based web systems: an exploratory study of wordpress. In: SPLC, pp. 149–159. ACM (2018)
60. Murphy, L., Viger, T., Di Sandro, A., Chechik, M.: PLACIDUS: engineering product lines of rigorous assurance cases. In: Kosmatov, N., Kovács, L. (eds.) IFM 2024. LNCS, vol. 15234, pp. 87–108. Springer, Cham (2024). https://doi.org/10.1007/978-3-031-76554-4_6
61. Murwantara, I.M.: Hybrid ANP: quality attributes decision modeling of a product line architecture design. In: URKE, pp. 30–34. IEEE (2012)
62. Myllärniemi, V., Raatikainen, M., Männistö, T.: Representing and configuring security variability in software product lines. In: QoSA, pp, 1–10. ACM (2015)
63. Navas, J., Voirin, J.L., Paul, S., Bonnet, S.: Towards a model-based approach to systems and cybersecurity: co-engineering in a product line context. Insight **23**(3), 39–43 (2020)
64. Nickerson, R.C., Varshney, U., Muntermann, J.: A method for taxonomy development and its application in information systems. Eur. J. Inf. Syst. **22**(3), 336–359 (2013)
65. Guide to cyber threat information sharing. Standard, National Institute of Standards and Technology (2016)
66. Guide for conducting risk assessments. Standard, National Institute of Standards and Technology (2012)
67. Pohl, K.: Software Product Line Engineering: Foundations, Principles, and Techniques. Springer, Cham (2005). https://doi.org/10.1007/3-540-28901-1
68. Reinhartz-Berger, I., Cohen, S., Bettin, J., Clark, T., Sturm, A.: Domain engineering, Product Lines, Languages and Conceptual Models (2013)

69. Rodríguez, J., Fernández-Medina, E., Piattini, M., Mellado, D.: A security requirements engineering tool for domain engineering in software product lines. In: Non-functional Properties in Service Oriented Architecture: Requirements, Models and Methods, pp. 73–92. IGI Global (2011)
70. Samonas, S., Coss, D.: The CIA strikes back: redefining confidentiality, integrity and availability in security. J. Inf. Syst. Secur. **10**(3) (2014)
71. Sion, L., Van Landuyt, D., Yskout, K., Joosen, W.: Towards systematically addressing security variability in software product lines. In: SPLC, pp. 342–343. ACM (2016)
72. Sprovieri, D., Argyropoulos, N., Souveyet, C., Mazo, R., Mouratidis, H., Fish, A.: Security alignment analysis of software product lines. In: ES, pp. 97–103. IEEE (2017)
73. Sánchez, L.E., Diaz-Pace, J.A., Zunino, A., Moisan, S., Rigault, J.P.: An approach for managing quality attributes at runtime using feature models. In: SBCARS, pp. 11–20. IEEE (2014)
74. Tan, L., Lin, Y., Ye, H.: Modeling quality attributes in software product line architecture. In: SCET, pp, 1–5. IEEE (2012)
75. Thüm, T., et al.: A classification and survey of analysis strategies for software product lines. Comput. Surv. **47**(1), 1–45 (2014)
76. Tomashchuk, O.: Threat and risk management framework for eHealth IoT applications. In: SPLC, pp. 120–126. ACM (2020)
77. Tomashchuk, O., Van Landuyt, D., Joosen, W.: The architectural divergence problem in security and privacy of eHealth IoT product lines. In: SPLC, pp. 114–119. ACM (2021)
78. Tøndel, I.A., Line, M.B., Jaatun, M.G.: Information security incident management: current practice as reported in the literature. Comput. Secur. **45**, 42–57 (2014)
79. Trujillo, S., Alonso, I., Hamid, B., Gonzalez, D., Blanco, M., Zhang, H.: Towards variability support for security and dependability patterns: a case study. In: SPLC, pp. 1–4. ACM (2011)
80. Varela-Vaca, Á.J., Gasca, R., Ceballos, R., Gómez-López, M.T., Bernaldez Torres, P.: CyberSPL: a framework for the verification of cybersecurity policy compliance of system configurations using software product lines. Appl. Sci. **9**(24), 1–28 (2019)
81. Varela-Vaca, Á.J., Gasca, R.M., Carmona-Fombella, J.A., T., G.L.M.: Amadeus: towards the automated security testing. In: SPLC, pp. 1–12. ACM (2020)
82. Varela-Vaca, Á.J., Rosado, D.G., Sánchez, L.E., Gómez-López, M.T., Gasca, R.M., Fernández-Medina, E.: Carmen: a framework for the verification and diagnosis of the specification of security requirements in cyber-physical systems. Comput. Ind. **132**, 103524 (2021)
83. Varela-Vaca, A.J., et al.: Feature models to boost the vulnerability management process. J. Syst. Softw. **195**, 1–22 (2023)
84. Varela-Vaca, A.J., Gasca, R.M.: Formalization of security patterns as a means to infer security controls in business processes. Logic J. IGPL **23**(1), 57–72 (2015)
85. Villela, K., Arif, T., Zanardini, D.: Towards product configuration taking into account quality concerns. In: SPLC, pp. 82–90. ACM (2012)
86. Williams, P., Moss, P., Bataller, S., Hassell, S.: Engineering a cyber resilient product line. Insight **23**(3), 17–21 (2020)
87. Wilson, B., Young, B.: Cyber secure and resilient approaches for feature based variation management. In: SSS, pp, 1–6. IEEE (2020)
88. Yadav, T., Rao, A.M.: Technical aspects of cyber kill chain. In: Abawajy, J.H., Mukherjea, S., Thampi, S.M., Ruiz-Martínez, A. (eds.) SSCC 2015. CCIS, vol. 536,

pp. 438–452. Springer, Cham (2015). https://doi.org/10.1007/978-3-319-22915-7_40
89. Ya'u, B.I., Nordin, A., Salleh, N.: Requirements patterns structure for specifying and reusing software product line requirements. In: ICT4M, pp. 185–190. IEEE (2018)
90. Young, B., Darbin, R., Clements, P.: System security engineering and feature-based product line engineering: a productive marriage. Insight **23**(3), 13–16 (2020)
91. Yu, D., Geng, P., Wu, W.: Constructing traceability between features and requirements for software product line engineering. APSEC **2**, 27–34. IEEE (2012)
92. Zhang, G., Ye, H., Lin, Y.: Modelling Quality Attributes in Feature Models in Software Product Line Engineering, pp. 249–254. SciTePress (2011)

Testing Online Machine Learning Programs: A Scenario-Based Approach and Tools

Maxence Demougeot[1(✉)], Sylvie Trouilhet[1], Jean-Paul Arcangeli[1], and Françoise Adreit[2]

[1] IRIT, Université de Toulouse, Toulouse, France
{maxence.demougeot,sylvie.trouilhet,jean-paul.arcangeli}@irit.fr
[2] IRIT, Université Toulouse Jean Jaurès, Toulouse, France
francoise.adreit@irit.fr

Abstract. Online Machine Learning (ML) programs build and update ML models throughout their execution. As with any program, testing is a solution for verification and validation. Testing allows to measure how well they work, identify favorable or unfavorable use cases, compare different versions or settings, or reveal defects. We analyze the differences between model testing and learning program testing, and focus on testing the behavior of programs that learn online. To address their particular features, we propose a scenario-based approach and a testing process. Next, we present a toolset which supports scenario-based testing of a program that learns online the end-user's preferences in an ambient environment: OCE Scenario Maker is an interactive tool that allows domain experts without ML knowledge to edit test scenarios and save them as JSON files; OCE Scenario Runner is another tool that automates the execution of JSON scenarios by the ML-based solution under test and provides quality measurements on the outputs. For validation purposes, several use cases have been investigated demonstrating the viability of the approach. Based on an analysis of the limitations of the proposed solution, we outline some perspectives for this work.

Keywords: Online Machine Learning · Learning Program · Test · Test Scenario · Testing Process · Testing Toolset

1 Introduction

Machine Learning (ML) consists in processing reference examples called training data by means of a learning algorithm. From these data, the algorithm generalizes a behavior to hold (this may be predicting, deciding, executing a task...) when faced with data other than training data. The **learning program** (LP) is the program that implements the learning algorithm, and a **model** (meaning a trained model) is a product of running the learning program with training data. In production, the model (a program too) transforms input data into outputs

M. Mecella et al. (Eds.): ICSOFT 2025, CCIS 3144, pp. 59–86, 2027.
https://doi.org/10.1007/978-3-032-37353-3_3

(i.e., predictions, decisions...) in accordance with the behavior learned from the training data.

Like any software, LPs and models need to be tested. Testing [2,16] is a way to show how well they work, to identify favorable or unfavorable use cases, to compare different versions or settings, or to reveal defects. It is part of the model development and tuning process, with the aim of assessing its quality, especially its compliance with functional requirements. Upstream, the LP must also be tested as defects can lead to the production of poor models.

This paper addresses the problem of **testing learning programs** in the context of **online ML** (see Sect. 2). It focuses on **functional testing**: the aim is to verify that the machine learns "well", i.e., that the LP builds models whose behaviors are in line with the training data in the various learning situations it may face. Section 3 analyzes these issues with a particular focus on online learning, and highlights the differences between testing a model and testing a learning program.

For LP testing, we propose a **scenario-based approach** and a **process**. Test scenarios[1] are designed by **domain experts** without necessarily skills in ML, based on properties to be controlled, then run to produce quality measurements. We apply this solution to a program called OCE (Opportunistic Composition Engine), which learns online how to build applications for an end-user in an open ambient context [38]. We show how our approach can be used, present a toolset that implements our proposal within the OCE framework, and examine several use cases that show the viability of our solution.

This paper is an extended revised version of the one we presented at the 20th International Conference on Software Technologies (ICSOFT 2025) [13]. It is organized as follows. Section 2 gives a brief overview of ML from a software engineering point of view, and introduces to online ML. Section 3 analyzes the problem of testing learning programs, sets out the research questions we are addressing, then reviews state-of-the-art work on testing ML-based solutions. Section 4 describes the scenario-based approach to test programs that learn online, with a process for carrying it out. Section 5 introduces our case study, the opportunistic composition engine (OCE), and shows how the scenario-based approach applies to OCE's learning program. Section 6 gives a detailed presentation of the toolset we have developed to support implementation and running of test scenarios of OCE's learning program. Our approach has been experimented and validated in the context of OCE across several use cases, four of which are presented in Sect. 7. Section 8 studies the related work. Finally, we draw some conclusions and perspectives in Sect. 9.

[1] In the field of software testing, "test scenario" usually refers to the organization and planning of the testing process within a software development project. Our definition of "test scenario" is different: it means a usage scenario intended to be tested, thus constituting a test case.

2 Machine Learning in a Software Engineering Perspective

ML techniques [25] can be used when a software solution cannot be programmed, either because there is no known algorithm, or because the algorithm is too complex to implement. They consist in building (training) a model by means of a learning program and training data.

2.1 Offline Machine Learning

Offline ML is the most common form of ML. In offline ML, the model is built and tuned by one or more human experts (ML experts and domain experts). They are responsible for choosing an off-the-shelf learning component (i.e., a learning program) and setting the learning parameters (hyperparameters). Alternatively, a specific learning program can be developed with the help of a software expert. ML and domain experts also select and prepare the training data. After construction and fine-tuning, the model is put in production. It can be rebuilt, i.e., revised or adapted, depending on the results obtained in production, however the rebuilt and production phases are separate. The model is thus managed like standard software with maintenance steps.

2.2 MLOps

A recent trend, called MLOps (the term stems from the contraction of "ML" and "DevOps"), aims to build, deploy, monitor, and maintain ML models in production in a reliable and automated way [35]. The principles, components, roles of stakeholders, and workflows are analyzed in [20]. Among the principles, there is continuous training and evaluation. Continuous training (or learning) means training in the post-release phase [5]. The process consists in periodic rebuild of a model by retraining it with new data, evaluation (testing) to assess the quality of the retrained model, and continuous integration and deployment (CI/CD) to put it in production. In accordance with offline ML, rebuild and evaluation are performed offline.

2.3 Online Machine Learning

Sometimes, it is difficult to anticipate the data that the model will face in production, and the model needs to adapt over time according to the data encountered. Online ML addresses this issue. It is similar to Lifelong ML, which aims to mimic the human learning process and capability [21]. According to S. Russell and P. Norvig [31], online ML relies on repeated comparisons between the outputs delivered in production and what they should be (the outputs assumed to be the "right" ones): when the model produces an output for a given input, it is provided with the "right" one as a feedback, what triggers a new learning phase and model evolution; an example of an online learning solution, the

Opportunistic Composition Engine, is presented in Sect. 5.1. In that case, learning and production are intertwined, and learning is lifelong: the learning program updates the model iteratively and incrementally throughout its execution. Thus, compared to MLOps, online ML supports model evolution in a more immediate and automatic way. Besides, since the learning context may be open and unpredictable, online ML has to deal with unanticipated training data arriving on the fly, which may be of poor quality but whose defects cannot be corrected before learning as with offline learning.

3 Testing Learning Programs

Machine learning encompasses learning activities (i.e., building a model by a learning program) and decision-making activities (i.e., using the model), whether learning and decision are interleaved or not. Models and learning programs are distinct software artifacts, each of them requiring testing.

In this test perspective, a common problem is the **non-deterministic nature of machine learning** [33], particularly (but not exclusively) in the case of online learning. Randomness inherent in learning and decision-making mechanisms leads to variable outcomes from one execution to another, even with the same inputs. Thus, it can happen that the expected results are not obtained during tests even though the learning and decision-making mechanisms are working correctly [19]. For example, in reinforcement learning [34], it is normal for the machine to sometimes choose, for exploration purposes, a solution that is neither the best nor the logically expected one. Therefore, it is difficult to determine if an unexpected output results from a random factor or a defect in the learning or the decision mechanisms. Another common problem is the **lack of precise specifications**, which limits the framing of the software behavior and therefore verification possibilities.

Moreover, by browsing the literature, work on ML-based software testing mainly focuses on models resulting from offline supervised learning [39]. Our work focuses on testing learning programs that build models online. In the following, we analyze the differences between model testing and learning program testing, and focus on testing programs that learn online.

3.1 Model Testing

Before deploying a model, testing aims to answer the question: is the model a "good" model? In other words, did the machine "learn" effectively? Model testing shares the same goals as traditional software testing but focuses on quality properties specific to the model such as accuracy, relevance, fairness, or robustness [39]. It consists in **running the model** and **evaluate its behavior** through the decisions it makes. This poses several challenges that we examine below.

Since models result from running a learning program fed by examples, defects in models may arise from the training data, the learning program, or a mismatch between the two (when a program poorly learns from certain data) [39]. However, it is challenging to trace the source of a defect to correct it. Indeed, models do not have the same materiality as traditional software: they do not consist of a simple source code but are composed of more or less tangible various elements (code, parameters, data) and often operate as a "black box".

On the other hand, ML is sometimes used by development teams in situations where the expected results are not known in advance [26]. In this case, predicting and interpreting test results is an additional challenge, and it can be difficult to determine whether a test passes or not. Software exhibiting this problem, known as the oracle problem, is often considered non-testable [37] due to the absence of an oracle or the difficulty in designing one [27].

Interpreting the results can also be tricky, due to the nature of the outputs and their complexity. In this context, it is so challenging to measure the quality of models using common criteria such as precision (ratio of correct answers to given answers), recall (selection rate of correct answers), or F-scores (combination of precision and recall).

3.2 Learning Program Testing

Although the two problems are closely related, testing a learning program is not the same as testing a model. The question is: does the learning program "learn well" across the scope for which it was designed? In other words, does the learning program build "good" models relative to the training data provided to it?

The **correspondence between training data and model** is captured by the formula 1, in which D is a training dataset, *Scope* is the set of all training datasets that the LP might encounter (the application domain of the LP), $P1$ is a property of D, M_D is the model built by the LP from D, and $P2$ is an expected property of M_D:

$$\forall D \in \mathit{Scope}, P1(D) \implies P2(M_D) \quad (1)$$

In other words, this formula means that if the learning program has built a model M_D from training data D that satisfy $P1$, then M_D should satisfy $P2$. For illustration purposes, let's take the example of a robot that learns to move from one point to another in a complex and dynamic physical space. In this case, the LP builds a model to guide the robot from reference routes. We might want to check that **IF** *D contains no routes that use a given corridor C* ($P1$) **THEN** *to go from point A to point B, M_D guides the robot without passing through corridor C* ($P2$). As usual in testing, the goal is to assess (un)satisfaction of the formula 2, that captures the **mismatch between training data and model**, i.e., a poor transformation of training data into a model:

$$\exists D \in \mathit{Scope}, P1(D) \wedge \neg(P2(M_D)) \quad (2)$$

However, identifying $P1$ as well as selecting D is crucial to the overall significance of the tests and demands strong domain expertise. Neither D nor M_D are simple data, as numerical data for example. In the case of online ML, D

is a **sequence** of training data which is required to meet $P1$. Selecting D is all the more delicate since, in production, data arrives in sequence and are not always expected. Hence, the question is not about the presence of a defect in the training data (a common source of defects in models); rather, it's about checking the consistency between training data and the model built from them, possibly concluding that there is a mismatch between the two.

Defining an expected property ($P2$) of the model is another source of complexity: especially, it is not possible to specify expected models for comparisons and accuracy assessment (the oracle problem again). $P2$ is thus a property related to the decisions that a model makes, i.e., to the output of the model given input data.

Thus, to check if the built model satisfies $P2$, and so indirectly evaluate the quality of the learning program, it must be executed. Since LP testing involves model testing, it suffers from the problems associated to model testing. However, in this context, the purpose of model testing is not to evaluate the basic quality of the model, as is usually the case in model testing, but its behavior in relation to what has been learned.

Cross-Validation and K-fold cross-validation [4] are standard methods for testing the performance of models, especially overfitting and underfitting. They are commonly used for comparison and selection of the most appropriate model for a given problem. They consist in putting aside part of the training data to use it as test data. But, in the context of online learning, they are not applicable for assessing the correspondence between the sequence of training data and the model since they do not allow to capture the consequence relationship between data and model expressed by the IF-THEN formula 1.

As a result, to tackle the LP testing problem, testers need to have different models built by the learning program for different use cases, with the aim of subsequently testing each of these models. So, running a test case must **first construct a model then run and evaluate it**. This makes both design and execution of the test cases more complex.

It is noteworthy that the problem of testing learning programs has clear analogies with the problem of testing compilers. LP and compilers are programs which execution produces programs. In [10], the authors review the work on compiler testing, focusing on correctness, i.e., the semantic conformity between the source program and the executable one produced by the compiler. Like learning programs, compilers are complex software with multiple functions and parameters. They lack precise specifications, which makes verification difficult. The oracle problem is also present because it is impossible for testers to provide the expected result (the executable program) to compare with the result obtained during testing. Therefore, as with a learning program, a compiler can only be evaluated indirectly by testing what it produces (the executable program). Furthermore, to verify that it systematically produces the correct executable, the set of inputs used for the tests (the source programs) must cover as much as possible the different types of programs that will be compiled.

3.3 Research Questions

Testing learning programs is costly. It requires significant **expertise** in terms of domain and business and, as much as possible, **automation**. Based on the above analysis, we have identified three research questions regarding the testing of online learning programs:

- **RQ1**: How to design test cases that include learning and evaluation steps and conform to expected properties?
- **RQ2**: How to organize the testing workflow, from the test set design to execution and evaluation?
- **RQ3**: As part of the workflow, how to implement a test case, automate its execution, and determine if the test passes or not?

Before presenting our answers to **RQ1** and **RQ2** in Sect. 4, and to **RQ3** in Sect. 6, we examine state-of-the-art work on testing ML-based solutions in relation to our problem and research questions.

3.4 Review of Work on ML-Based Systems Testing

Several papers address the general problem of developing ML-based software from a software engineering perspective but provide only brief explanations on testing issues [15,22].

Research on testing software based on ML is relatively recent compared to work on software testing in general. However, significant papers have been published in recent years. Research work on testing and formal verification of software systems based on AI (not only ML-based systems) is reviewed in [12]. Zhang *et al.* [39] provided a comprehensive study on testing ML-based software, focusing on model evaluation and properties such as accuracy, robustness, and fairness. Among other things, a testing process is defined which targets the ML model and debugging: it is organized in two phases, offline testing (before deployment) and online testing (after deployment, in a real environment). In [7], Ben Braiek and Khomh reviewed the engineering issues of ML programs and examined the testing practices. Unlike our standpoint, which separates the learning part (the LP) and the decision-making part (the model), models are considered as a whole (including the learning part) for testing, which does not highlight the problem of transforming training data into decision-making models. Riccio et al. [30] systematically analyzed the literature and highlighted the main challenges related to testing, including test case specification, adequacy criteria, cost, and the oracle problem. In [23], the recent literature is surveyed but restricted to the testing of software based on neural networks.

There are works that target model testing with particular concerns. The one by Mazouni *et al.* aims to reveal, not the maximum number of defects, but their diverse natures in the context of reinforcement learning (RL) [24]. Biagiola and Tonella focus on deep RL and the test of models, called agents, by means of surrogate models [6]: for that, they propose to generate environmental configurations likely to be at the origin of agent failures. In a previous work, the same authors examined the problem of plasticity of solutions based on deep RL, i.e., their ability to adapt to environmental conditions that deviate from the training one [5], in the context of continuous learning. Their approach allows to get measures to verify the continuous evolution of models (including their non-regression) and thus to characterize favorable and unfavorable use cases in open environments.

In conclusion, most work on testing ML-based solutions focuses on testing models to verify that they meet the needs for which they were designed, including in the case of dynamic evolution. This objective differs from ours, which is to check the alignment between the training data and the model built by the learning program. The lack of an oracle is one of the main problems addressed, and metamorphic testing [11] is commonly proposed to verify model behavior in the absence of an oracle.

4 Scenario-Based Testing Approach

In this section, we present our approach for testing programs that learn online. We show how it applies to a particular case (OCE's online learning program) in Sect. 5, then we describe a dedicated toolset in Sect. 6.

4.1 Test Scenario

To be evaluated, a learning program must be executed on training data. Then, the resulting model must be evaluated in turn. Since the learning program builds different models depending on the training data, different models must be evaluated. In an iterative and incremental context such as online learning, designing a test case requires defining a sequence of interactions between the learning program and its learning environment to build a model. To check that the built model behaves as expected, other interactions are required for evaluation purposes. Learning and evaluation interactions can be intertwined. We call a sequence of such interactions a **test scenario**.

A **learning phase** consists in a sequence of interactions which must conform to $P1$ with, for each interaction, an output produced by the model from the input data, a feedback, then a learning operation to improve the model. Each interaction is so described by: (i) a learning situation, i.e., the environment in which the model should produce an output, (ii) an output that the model should ideally return in this situation, called **ideal** output. Defining the ideal output for each learning interaction, as well as expected outputs facilitates automation: it avoids the need for the tester to constantly interact with the learning program, which is tedious and costly. Based on the outputs produced by the model and the ideal outputs, the learning program learns and updates the model in the learning phase of the test as it does in normal operation. At the end of this phase, a model is built that is ready for evaluation.

An **evaluation phase** consists of one or several interactions too. An interaction is defined by the description of both the situation in which the model has to deliver an output and a property of this output that must be checked ($P2$). In its simplest form, the property can be the expected output or several possible correct outputs: expected outputs are intended to be compared with the output returned by the model to give a measure of quality. Depending on what the designer expresses in terms of expected property (a single or several expected outputs, or a more general property), they act more or less like an oracle. Thus, our approach tackles the oracle problem but in a different way from metamorphic testing, by expressing $P2$ with a modulable level of abstraction relative to the expected output.

Structured in this way, such scenarios support offline testing of online learning programs, which answers **RQ1**.

4.2 Scenario-Based Testing Process

In the scenario-based testing process (Fig. 1), the first activity is to identify a formula to be tested, namely $P1$ which describes a property of the training data and $P2$ which relates to the expected result.

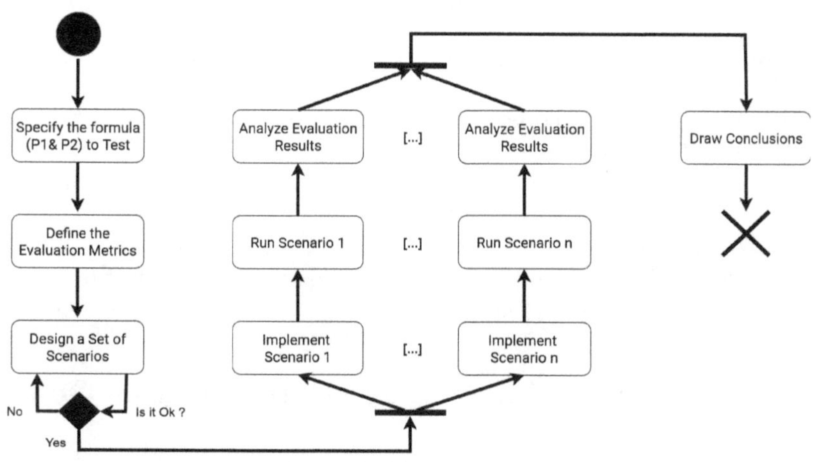

Fig. 1. Activity Diagram of the Scenario-based Testing Process.

Next, it is necessary to define the ways of verifying that $P2$ is satisfied. It may rely on statistical metrics relating to the performance of the model, such as accuracy, recall, or F-score. When $P2$ explicitly specifies the expected output, a function can be defined to measure a distance between the output of the model and the expected one.

Then, an iterative design of the scenario test set begins. Defining scenarios is guided by tactics, *e.g.* limiting the complexity of the training sequence conforming to $P1$ in order to facilitate the analysis of test results. For each scenario, the learning phase is designed to meet $P1$ and the evaluation phase is designed to enable the assessment of $P2$.

Once the set of scenarios is considered to sufficiently cover the scope for which the LP was designed, each scenario is implemented then executed, and the results analyzed (as it stands, the question of the coverage of the application scope by the set of test scenarios is up to the tester - see Sect. 7.5). The metrics previously defined support measures that enable testers to evaluate the model's behavior and determine whether it satisfies $P2$, i.e., whether the test passes or not.

It is then possible to draw general conclusions about the learning program depending on possibly inadequate model behaviors that have been highlighted in the test. Note that the issues related to defect location and their correction are beyond the scope of this paper.

This process (represented in Fig. 1) can be repeated for different formulas, answering so to **RQ2**. Besides, since testing online LP is costly, it is crucial to automate the process as much as possible. In the following, we propose an answer to **RQ3**, which covers the *Implementation*, *Run* and, partially, *Analysis* phases of the testing process.

4.3 Position Relative to MLOps

While MLOps targets the development and operation of (trained) models, our approach targets learning programs (that learn and build models), but not models. It cannot therefore be considered a contribution to MLOps as the latter is currently shaped. Nevertheless, learning programs also demand to be developed and operated, and their delivery process automated. Broadening the scope of MLOps, scenario-based testing of online learning programs could be part of the automated delivery process of ML-based software since it contributes to automation of testing (in Sect. 7.5 and Sect. 9, the reader will find a brief discussion on further automation in the testing process).

5 Application to OCE: A Program that Learns Online

This section first introduces the fundamental principles of our case study, the Opportunistic Composition Engine (OCE), which learns online in interaction with the end user. Then, it shows how our approach for testing applies to OCE's learning program.

5.1 OCE: A Program that Learns Online

OCE is an ambient intelligence [14] prototype solution that dynamically builds applications based on software components present in the ambient environment and knowledge learned online about the user's preferences [38]. Let's start with some background to better understand how OCE operates.

A software component is an executable software entity that provides services and requires others to function [32]. Component-based programming involves assembling components by binding their services to form an application. The Fig. 2 represents in UML [28] a simple example of a text-to-speech application that assembles four components: **TextInput** for text input, **TextToVoice** for text-to-voice conversion, **Speaker**, and **Button. TextInput** uses the *TextProcess* service provided by **TextToVoice** to transmit the text. **TextToVoice** converts the text into an audio signal and passes it to **Speaker** via the *VoiceProcess* service. **Speaker** plays the audio signal, which volume can be adjusted using **Button** and transmitted to **Speaker** via the *SetVolume* service.

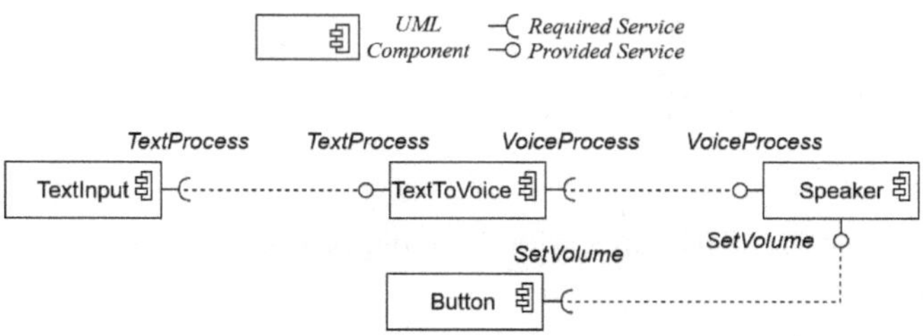

Fig. 2. UML component diagram [28] of the Text-to-Speech application (from [13]).

OCE automates the assembly operation. In ambient environments, characterized by their open and dynamic nature, components may appear or disappear unpredictably. OCE addresses a major challenge: manage the variability of ambient environments and offer the user "right" application at the right time according to their situation and preferences. It consists of **a reinforcement learning** [34] **program and a model** that is permanently trained and evolving. An OCE "cycle" is a sequence of several steps (Fig. 3):

1. OCE detects the available components in the user's ambient environment.
2. Based on the available components and learned knowledge about the user's preferences, OCE's model decides on the assembly to build.
3. OCE presents the assembly proposition to the user through a graphical interface.
4. The user accepts, modifies, or rejects the assembly proposition. These actions translate into positive or negative rewards, which serve as training data for OCE's learning program.
5. OCE learns by reinforcement, i.e., OCE's learning program increments and adapts the model.

Thus, through successive cycles and interactions with the user, OCE learning solution builds and evolves online a model on which the future decisions will be made.

Several working prototypes of OCE have been developed. Do they propose applications to the user that are tailored to their preferences in the current situation? Testing is a way to answer this question and to build trust in OCE.

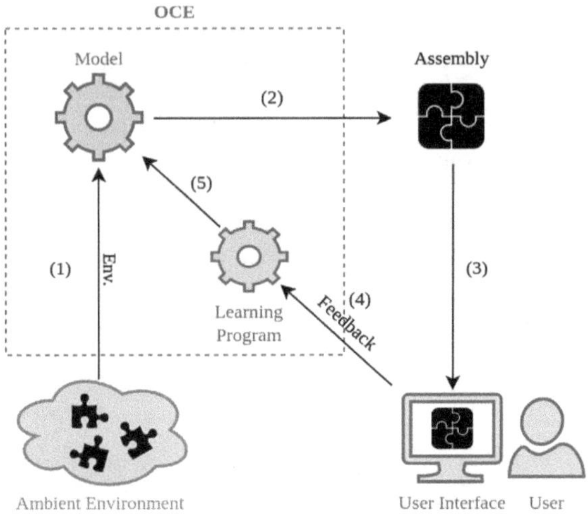

Fig. 3. OCE application building process (from [13]).

5.2 Testing OCE Online Learning Program

For OCE, an interaction corresponds to a cycle, and a test scenario is a sequence of learning and evaluation cycles. A **learning cycle** is described by a list of software components populating the ambient environment and the ideal assembly. The ideal assembly replaces the actions that a user would perform at runtime on the OCE output (i.e., accept, modify, reject). It specifies the user preference in normal use in this situation, and so defines the user feedback. This feedback is used for learning purposes by OCE's learning program, just as normal OCE feedback would be.

An **evaluation cycle** is also defined by a list of software components, this time with a property of the assembly that OCE's model is expected to return. This can be in the form of one or more expected assemblies for comparison, or take the form of more general properties, *e.g.* the presence of certain components or connections in the assembly.

It is possible to define scenarios to test OCE's learning program in different ambient environments, with more or less dynamics according to $P1$ and $P2$. Note that the issues related to users' involvement in the design of scenarios are beyond the scope of this paper.

For instance, as a tester, we seek to verify that **IF** *a user expresses a preference for a component in a certain situation, and that component disappears from the ambient environment* ($P1$) **THEN** *if it reappears in a similar situation, OCE again proposes an assembly with that component (P2)*. To define a scenario, let's take a toy example adapted from [38] and simplified for clarity. Mary is at work. In her ambient environment, there are a software component **Desk** that provides a room booking service called *Order*, and three components, **Text**, **Voice**, and **Tactile**, which allow the user to make a booking request (with different

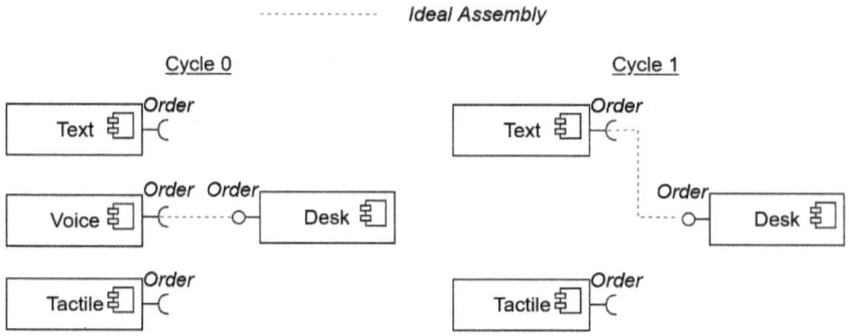

Fig. 4. Learning cycles of the example scenario (from [13]).

interaction modes) and require the *Order* service. Through the *Order* service, these three components may be assembled with **Desk**. Thus, three applications are possible (**Text-Desk**, **Voice-Desk**, **Tactile-Desk**), enabling Mary to book a meeting room. To do so, Mary prefers the component **Voice**. Then, **Voice** disappears and reappears later. We seek to verify that OCE again proposes the assembly **Voice-Desk** when **Voice** reappears.

Let's define a scenario with three cycles. Cycles 0 and 1 (Fig. 4) define the learning phase. Cycle 0 is defined by the list of the four components and the ideal assembly **Voice-Desk** (Mary's preference). For cycle 1, **Voice** has disappeared, so the components are **Desk**, **Text**, and **Tactile**, and the ideal assembly in this case is **Text-Desk**. The composition of the ambient environment and the ideal assemblies in cycles 0 and 1 satisfy the property $P1$.

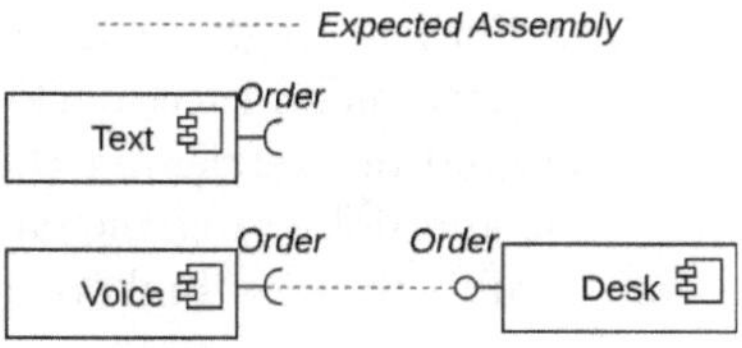

Fig. 5. Evaluation cycle of the example scenario (from [13]).

In the evaluation phase, cycle 2 (Fig. 5) defines a situation (the set of components that compose the ambient environment), different from the two previous ones, in which OCE must provide an assembly: the ambient environment is composed of **Desk**, **Text**, and **Voice** that has reappeared (**Tactile** has disappeared). Here, **Voice-Desk** is specified as the expected assembly in order to be compared with the assembly proposed by OCE. Here, $P2$ is defined at the simplest by a single expected assembly and coupled with a function that computes a distance between the expected assembly and the OCE output. To measure this distance, such a function may, for instance, compute a Jaccard Similarity Index[2].

[2] https://en.wikipedia.org/wiki/Jaccard_index.

6 Toolset

Tools are required to achieve the scenario-based approach. Section 6.1 examines their main features. Section 6.2 presents the application of these principles to the testing of OCE's learning program, in the form of two tools: OCE Scenario Maker and OCE Scenario Runner.

6.1 General Principles

Tools are necessary to make the scenario-based approach operational and usable in practice. They must provide abstractions and facilities to testers, in order to implement scenarios, execute them, and analyze the results obtained.

First, so that domain experts can implement scenarios, they need a scenario editor that allows to describe the training data, i.e., the sequence of learning interactions, each containing a learning situation with its associated ideal output. It must also support the expression of evaluation interactions, i.e., of situations in which the model must produce an output. The editor needs to be expressive enough to allow experts to define their scenarios as closely as possible to the terms of their domain. In order to verify the quality of a model, they have to measure the quality of the results it produces within a scenario. To be able to automatically generate measurements, they need to express measurement functions that can be applied to the outputs.

On the other hand, scenarios must be saveable and executable. Due to their high level of expression, they must be transformed into a lower-level form that can be processed.

Last, the scenarios must be executable with the online LP under test, by running the interactions sequentially. For learning, it consists in interacting with the LP by providing both learning situations and feedback. Running an evaluation interaction involves providing a situation, retrieving the LP's output, applying the measurement function(s) to it and delivering the calculated values. In addition, more advanced functions could produce higher-level analysis results and diagnostics.

6.2 A Toolset for OCE

To apply these principles to the test of OCE's learning program, we have developed two tools: OCE Scenario Maker to edit OCE scenarios and OCE Scenario Runner to automatically run them with the OCE version under test. A short additional video[3] demonstrates their usage in the scenario described in Sect. 5.2.

OCE Scenario Maker. This is an interactive tool for implementing OCE scenarios. It allows the tester to carry out the "Implement Scenario" activity of the testing process depicted in Fig. 1.

[3] https://www.irit.fr/OppoCompo/makerrunnerusecase2025/.

Fig. 6. Maker's interface for scenario implementation (the edited scenario is the one presented in Sect. 5.2).

With Maker, the tester can upload a library of mock components in order to use them later in their scenario. They can also define their own components with a name and services, then record them (Fig. 6, left panel).

From a library of components, the tester can edit a scenario. They can also upload an existing scenario, and possibly modify it. A scenario is a sequence of learning and evaluation cycles (interactions) that comply with $P1$ and $P2$, with a name and a short textual description. To define a learning cycle, the tester can drag and drop components into a panel, defining so the ambient environment. Next, to enable them to specify the ideal assembly in accordance with $P1$, Maker lists the required services of the components present in the environment. For each of them, it proposes the possible provided services to connect (Fig. 6, right panel). The same principle applies for evaluation cycles. In this case, to assess the satisfaction of the property they expect on the assembly built by OCE ($P2$), the tester sets a measurement function with its parameters. For example, the function can measure a distance (*e.g.* a Jaccard Similarity Index) between the output assembly and a specified expected one, or an average distance with several assemblies, or the presence of a specific component or connection in the output assembly.

There are additional features, such as the ability to duplicate any cycle, which reduce the tester's workload. In addition, validity controls are performed on components and assemblies.

From the sequence of cycles, Maker generates a JSON[4] description that implements a scenario, and saves it in a file to be automatically run with the second tool, Runner.

OCE Scenario Runner. This is a Java application that, coupled with OCE, allows the automated execution of OCE scenarios in JSON format, such as those generated by Maker. It allows the tester to carry out the "Run Scenario" activity.

The tester can select the version of OCE to be tested and, to do so, load a scenario or a set of scenarios to be run. Next, they must set various hyperparameters both for learning and evaluation cycles. In particular, the tester can vary the exploration rate and, for example, set it to 0 for the evaluation cycles if they want to neutralize randomness. In any case, non-determinism inherent in ML is present at runtime. To mitigate its impact, Runner allows to repeat the execution of the scenarios, which requires the tester to define the number of repetitions.

Figure 7 shows a screenshot of Runner's interface.

Once the hyperparameter values are set, Runner operates coupled with OCE without further intervention from the tester: for each cycle in the scenario, it provides OCE with the information it extracts from the JSON file (the ambient environment and the ideal assembly for learning); to assess the relevance of OCE's outputs, it runs the specified measurement function at each evaluation cycle, then records the computed values. These measures indicate whether the output assemblies are relevant proposals based on what OCE's learning program learned, i.e., based on the user's preferences.

In practice, Runner produces a spreadsheet that records all the elements of all the interactions with OCE, including calculated measurements. To ease the exploitation of results and automatically create test reports, we have developed a dashboard based on Jupyter Notebook[5], which computes average scores and other various statistical results, and displays them in graphical form as illustrated in Fig. 8 for a simple case.

Architecture. Maker and Runner have been implemented and integrated into the OCE system, which architecture can be represented in the form of a UML component diagram too [28]. Figure 9 represents the configuration of the OCE system in production. When the ambient environment changes, **OCE** receives

[4] https://www.json.org/json-en.html.

[5] https://jupyter.org/.

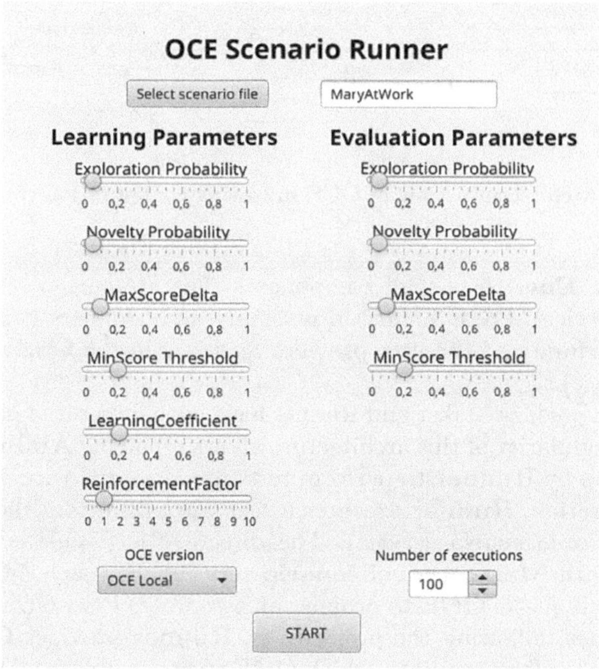

Fig. 7. Runner's interface for scenario execution.

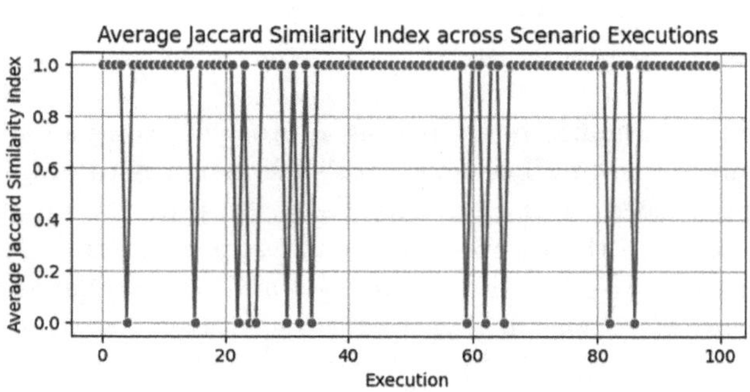

Fig. 8. An excerpt from the dashboard.

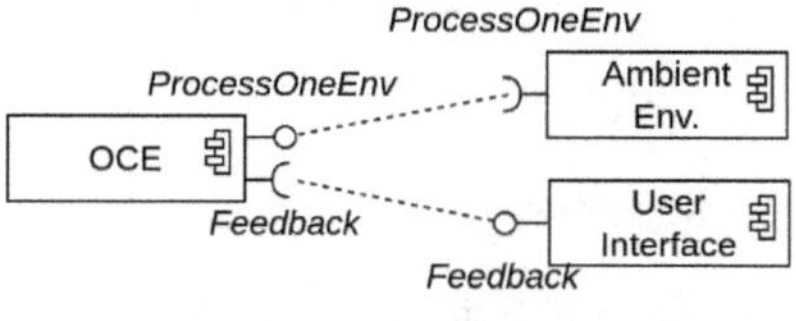

Fig. 9. Architectural view of OCE in production configuration (from [13]).

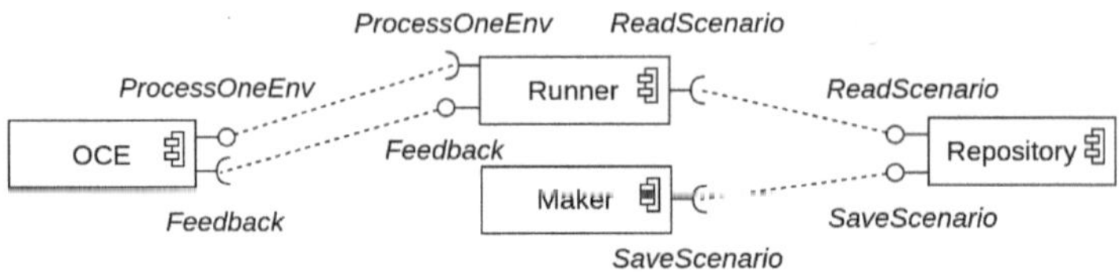

Fig. 10. Architectural view of OCE in testing configuration (from [13]).

from **Ambient Env.** the list of components that are currently present (*ProcessOneEnv* service). **OCE** builds an assembly and proposes it to the user via the **User Interface** and the user provides feedback in the form of an assembly (*Feedback* service).

Figure 10 shows how Maker and Runner have been integrated into OCE architecture. The modularity of this architecture allows replacing **Ambient Env.** and **User Interface** by **Runner** to perform tests implemented with **Maker**. In the testing configuration, **Runner** executes a scenario taken from the **Repository** of scenarios (*ReadScenario* service). The directory is populated by scenarios implemented with **Maker** (**SaveScenario** service). For each cycle of the scenario, **Runner** requests **OCE** to propose an assembly (*ProcessOneEnv* service). In learning cycles, following the proposition, **Runner** provides **OCE** with the ideal assembly (*Feedback* service), which **OCE** treats as user feedback. In evaluation cycles, **Runner** computes quality measurements on the assemblies proposed by OCE.

7 Validation

We have applied the scenario-based testing approach to conduct a test campaign of OCE's learning program. The aim of this campaign is to evaluate its ability to learn user preferences in various use cases. We present four of them, three of which are related to the disappearance and appearance of components that are involved in the user's favorite assemblies, and one is related to changes in user's preferences. More specifically, the testing process described in Sect. 4.2 is applied to:

1. The disappearance and reappearance of a component involved in the user's favorite assembly.
2. The disappearance and appearance of two components used together and preferred by the user.
3. The disappearance and appearance of components in a realistic case of a smart home.
4. A shift in the user's preferences.

For each use case, i.e., for each formula to be evaluated, several scenarios were designed but only one is presented in this paper. The experimental conditions are as follows. We take the standard version of OCE with default settings.

In these settings, the value of the reinforcement learning exploration coefficient is 0.10 (except for the last use case, where it is set to 0). Setting this coefficient to 0.10 means that the OCE's model has a 10% probability of exploring alternative connections between components rather than exploiting knowledge acquired about user preferences. In addition, to smooth out the impact of random factors, each scenario is run 100 times.

7.1 Use Case 1: Disappearance and Reappearance of a Component

Here is the first use case for the scenario-based testing approach: as OCE testers, we want to verify that **IF** *the user expresses a preference for a component in their ambient environment and this component disappears* ($P1$) **THEN** OCE *proposes again an assembly including this component when it reappears* ($P2$).

Different scenarios were designed for this use case (by varying the number of cycles, appearances and disappearances...) using two tactics:

- Limit the complexity of the $P1$-compliant training sequence, i.e., the number of components, services, and cycles.
- Ensure that OCE's model has to make a choice between several possible connections at each cycle (decide), in order to leverage knowledge of user's preferences and make them evolve from user's feedback.

In order to evaluate $P2$, the tester chooses to use the Jaccard Similarity Index between the assembly proposed by OCE and a given expected one.

A scenario designed for this use case is the three-cycle scenario described in Sect. 4.1: the component **Voice**, preferred by Mary in Cycle 0, disappears in Cycle 1 then reappears in Cycle 2. Cycles 0 and 1 are the training data (D) satisfying $P1$. The goal is to verify that OCE's model proposes again the assembly **Voice-Desk** when **Voice** reappears, i.e., $P2(M_D)$.

This scenario was implemented using Maker and run using Runner. Running showed that out of the 100 runs, in about 90 the similarity index calculated between the assembly proposed by OCE and the expected one in the evaluation cycle equals 1.0, indicating that the produced and expected outputs are identical. This means that OCE did actually propose the assembly with the component **Voice** when it reappeared. In the other 10 runs, OCE did not propose this assembly, due to exploration during the evaluation cycle. The other designed scenarios showed the same results. Thus, for this use case, testing did not reveal a value of D such as formula 2 is true, i.e., no incorrect behavior of OCE's learning program was identified.

In the following use cases, test design was based on the same tactics and distance measurement function. So, we do not repeat these points in the text.

7.2 Use Case 2: Disappearance and Reappearance of Two Components Used Together

In this use case, we take component disappearance and reappearance a step further, where two components used together are affected. This time, we want to verify that **IF** *the user expresses a preference for using two components together (P1)* **THEN** *OCE later selects these two components when they are available together again (P2).*

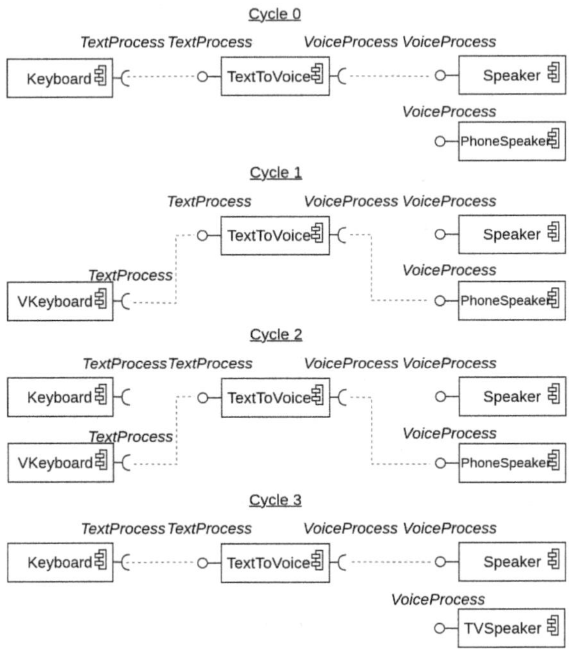

Fig. 11. Learning cycles of the use case 2 (from [13]).

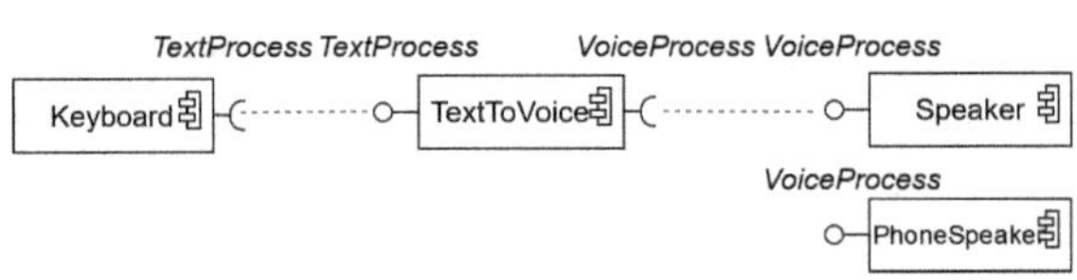

Fig. 12. Evaluation cycle of the use case 2 (from [13]).

Here is a scenario with components for a text-to-speech application. It includes four learning cycles that define D, which satisfies $P1$ (Fig. 11) followed by one evaluation cycle that specifies $P2$ (Fig. 12). When the user uses the keyboard (**Keyboard**), they prefer to use the room's speaker (**Speaker**) at the same time. This preference is expressed by the ideal assemblies of cycles 0 and 3. But when the smartphone's virtual keyboard (**VKeyboard**) is available in the ambient environment, they prefer to use it together with the smartphone's speaker (**PhoneSpeaker**). This is expressed by the ideal assemblies of cycles 1 and 2. In this context, we would like to check that if **VKeyboard** disappears, OCE actually proposes to use **Speaker** together with **Keyboard**.

This scenario yielded some interesting results. In about 90 runs, the similarity index is equal to 0.33. This score means that the produced output is far from the expected one. In these runs, OCE proposed an assembly with **PhoneSpeaker** even though **VKeyboard** was unavailable, thus did not learn well the user's preferences. In the other 10 runs, OCE did propose the expected assembly due to exploration at cycle 4. This result shows a value of D for which the formula 2 is true. This use case thus reveals an unexpected behavior of OCE's learning program, probably requiring further tests and in-depth analysis which could lead to the conclusion that, in such cases, OCE fails to generalize what it has learned.

7.3 Use Case 3: Towards a More Comprehensive and Realistic Use Case

In this use case, we want to test the behavior of OCE's learning program in a more realistic context of a smart home. The aim is to verify that **IF** *the user moves around several rooms in their home, involving a series of appearances and disappearances of components in their surrounding environment (P1)* **THEN** *when the user returns to these rooms, OCE proposes their favorite assemblies in the room, despite slight variations in the ambient environment (P2).*

To do so, we designed a scenario where the user navigates between the bedroom, kitchen, and living room. As a result, several components become available or unavailable in their ambient environment depending on the room. Besides, the user has a smartphone providing a button (**Button**) for switching a device on or off, and a plus-minus button (**PMButton**) for adjusting a device (*e.g.* the volume of a speaker). Embedded in the user's phone, which they keep close at all times, these two components are permanently available.

The scenario comprises three learning cycles (Fig. 13) followed by three evaluation cycles (Fig. 14). When the user wakes up, they are in their bedroom. Here, there are three components: a heater (**Heater**), a treadmill (**Treadmill**) and a lamp (**Lamp1**). In this context, the user prefers to use the first button provided by the smartphone to turn on the lamp, and the plus-minus button to turn down the heating. In the cycle 0 of the scenario (see Fig. 13), these preferences are translated into the ideal assembly. Next, the user heads for the kitchen to make a coffee. On the way, they find their headphones and want to listen to the news on the radio. The user then uses the two buttons on their smartphone to switch on the coffee machine and adjust the volume of the headphones, which corresponds to the ideal assembly in Cycle 1. Finally, the user sits down in the living room to watch an episode of their favorite show. To do this, the user uses their smartphone's streaming application (**StreamApp**) to project the show onto the TV (**TV**), using the second speaker (**Speaker2**), which is represented in the ideal assembly of Cycle 2.

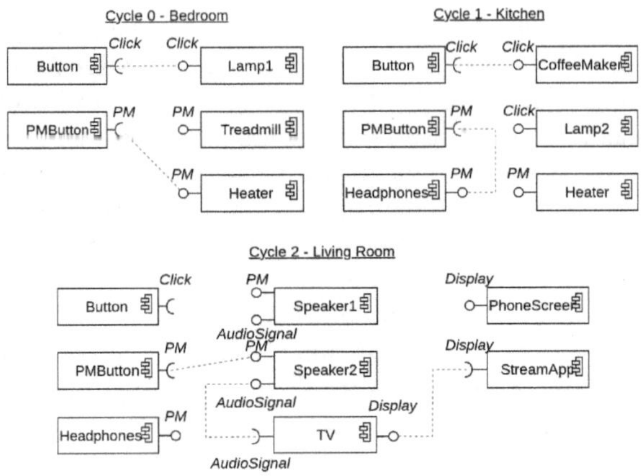

Fig. 13. Learning cycles of the use case 3 (from [13]).

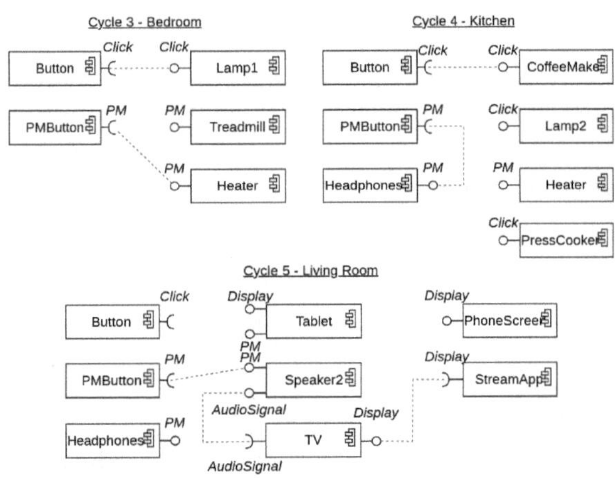

Fig. 14. Evaluation cycles of the use case 3 (from [13]).

This sequence is repeated the next day. In the scenario, it is defined by the three evaluation cycles, to check that OCE's learning program learned the user's preferences in each room of the home. However, a few changes took place: the user has received their brand-new pressure cooker (**PressCooker**), which they store in the kitchen. This new component can be turned on/off via the button of the smartphone. Besides, in the living room, the battery of their tablet (**Tablet**) is fully recharged. The user might now project shows on it and adjust the volume using the plus-minus button. Lastly, the first speaker in the living room is broken thus is no longer available in the ambient environment. These changes have an impact on the composition of ambient environments of the evaluation cycles, but as the user preferences remain unchanged, the expected assemblies are the same as the ideal ones that have been stated in the learning phase.

For each evaluation cycle, in about 90% of runs, we got an average similarity score equals to 1.0, which means that OCE's model proposed the right assembly. In the remaining 10%, the score is lowered (between 0.33 and 0.5) because OCE's model explored one or several connections in its proposition. Here, as for the use case 1, testing did not reveal an incorrect behavior of OCE's learning program.

7.4 Use Case 4: A Shift in the User's Preferences

The previous use cases mainly target the dynamics of the ambient environment. In this use case, the dynamics come from user preferences that evolve over time.

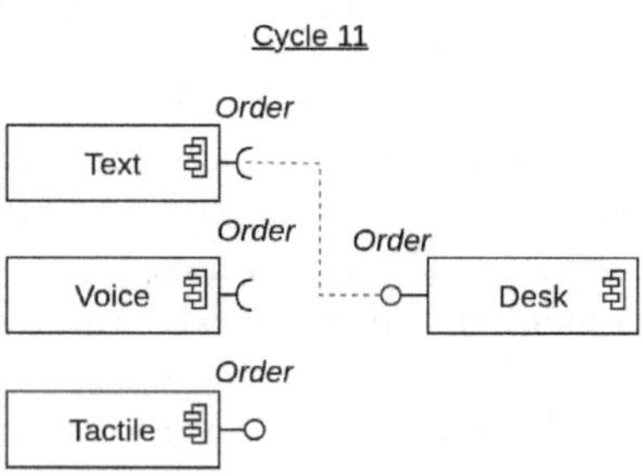

Fig. 15. Eleventh learning cycle of the use case 4.

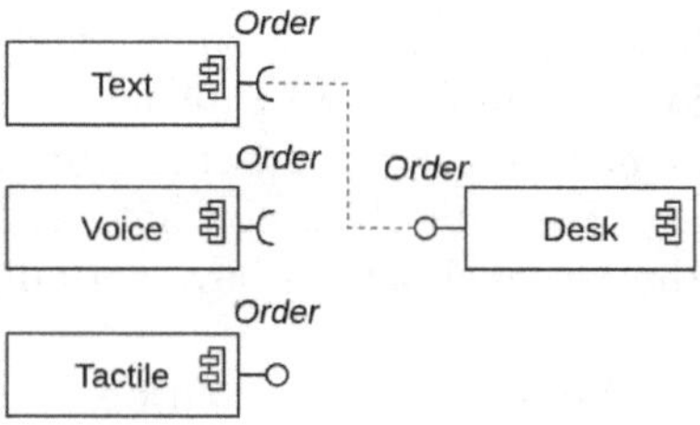

Fig. 16. Evaluation cycle of the use case 4.

Here, the problem is to check that **IF** *the user expresses repeatedly a preference for a component C1 in their ambient environment then changes their preference for another component C2* ($P1$) **THEN** OCE *proposes an assembly including C2 when the situation happens again* ($P2$).

To do so, we designed a scenario using the same components as in Use Case 1. Here, the ambient environment is stable and permanently contains the components **Text**, **Voice**, **Tactile** and **Desk**. The user expresses a preference for the **Voice-Desk** connection 10 times in a row, i.e., the cycle 0 of Fig. 4 is repeated 10 times. Next, in the 11th learning cycle (Fig. 15), their preference changes to **Text-Desk**. This satisfies $P1$. The scenario continues with an evaluation cycle (Fig. 16), for which the expected assembly is **Text-Desk** ($P2$). In order to study how many times the new preference must be indicated to OCE for it to be taken in account in the decision, this two-cycles sequence (Fig. 15 and Fig. 16) is repeated five times.

As previously done, the scenario was run 100 times. To facilitate the analysis of the results, the exploration rate in evaluation cycles was set to 0 to ensure that OCE exploits its knowledge but does not explore when making a decision. As in the previous use cases, to check that P2 is satisfied, a Jaccard similarity index is computed between the assembly proposed by OCE and the expected one for each evaluation cycle. The results showed that, once OCE has integrated the new preference into its decision (i.e., when the similarity index is equal to 1), the following proposed assemblies remain stable and correct, i.e., OCE proposes the **Text-Desk** connection. However, the number of cycles needed to integrate this preference into OCE's decision is quite low and varies from one execution to another (despite the exploration rate being 0). Other similar scenarios (*e.g.* with 20 cycles that expresses of the preference for **Voice-Desk** next a shift to **Text-Desk** were implemented and executed, producing similar results. This observation raises questions about the correctness of OCE's behavior, which these tests cannot answer. Therefore, to answer these questions, further tests are required.

7.5 Experiment and Feedback

The scenario-based testing approach has been applied beyond the few use cases previously presented. It made possible to test both simple and more complex cases, with a greater number of cycles, components and services. The test campaign highlighted situations where OCE's LP behaves as expected, but also the presence of some defects, *e.g.* in the way the user feedback was taken into account by the learning program. Despite its black-box nature, making default location and correction difficult, the revealed defects have actually been corrected by the OCE development team.

However, at this stage of our work, our solution for LP testing suffers from certain limitations. Since domain experts have to define test cases by hand, designing a scenario-based test set (see Fig. 1) is rather cumbersome and costly. Besides, they must imagine the scenarios they believe to be the most significant, which can easily lead to oversights and insufficient coverage of the application domain. This point argues for more automation within the scenario design process to further answer **RQ1** (see Sect. 9).

8 Related Work

8.1 Scenario-Based Approaches

C. Kaner [9] defines a scenario as a story of a person trying to accomplish something with the tested product. Hussain et al. [18] propose a similar definition, but not directly tied to testing: a scenario is an informal description of a specific use of software, or of a part of it, by a user. Here, scenarios are defined from user needs (use cases) and are used to derive test cases. According to these definitions, a scenario is described as a sequence of interactions between the software and a user. This is precisely how we use scenarios to test OCE. Indeed, a scenario describes a sequence of ambient environments (where an environment is represented by a list of software components) as well as ideal assemblies that model interactions between the user and OCE.

In the domain of autonomous vehicles, the concept of scenario is used to evaluate vehicle behaviors based on machine learning. For instance, Ulbrich et al. [36] describe a scenario as a temporal sequence of scenes, where each scene represents a configuration of the physical environment in which one or more autonomous vehicles operate. A scenario details the scenes, the transitions between scenes, and the evaluation criteria. In this context, a scenario specifies sequences of physical environments rather than user-software interactions.

The scenario-based approach enables the comprehensive description of a use case, thereby facilitating end-to-end (system level) testing. This makes it particularly suitable for evaluating machine learning-based software due to their black-box nature. We have tailored this approach for online learning by interleaving learning and evaluation phases within a scenario.

8.2 Tools

Tools like Gymnasium [8], DotRL [29], and Cogment [1] are designed for the development and experimentation of reinforcement learning solutions. Evaluation of a solution typically involves comparing it against other algorithms in predefined environments. However, these tools do not include the notion of scenario. They only offer benchmarks to compare algorithms, providing the tester raw result data that need to be analyzed. In contrast, Runner provides facilities such as tester-specified quality measures of outputs, thereby making analysis easier.

9 Conclusion and Perspectives

In this paper, we define a scenario-based approach for functional testing of online learning programs, i.e., of programs which iteratively build and update ML models. Using test scenarios designed by domain experts without ML knowledge, this approach makes them able to show how well the learning program works, identify favorable or unfavorable use cases, compare several versions or setting, or reveal the presence of defects. A testing process accompanying the approach is also defined, where the activities of implementation, execution and result analysis can be automated, at least in part. This solution has been applied to OCE, a ML-based solution that learns online human user preferences in an ambient environment. It helped to better delimit the application scope of OCE, and revealed several defects. Although the scenario-based testing approach has only been experimented with OCE using OCE-specific toolset, we believe that the general principles, which are independent of OCE and the application domain, are transferable to other online learning systems.

As explained in Sect. 7.5, it is desirable to automate the scenario design step as much as possible. To do so, we are exploring an approach to automatically generate and select scenarios. In the case of OCE, scenarios could be generated from formulas to satisfy and sets of software components. They should take the same form as scenarios constructed using OCE Scenario Maker so that they can be executed by OCE Scenario Runner. However, the number of test scenarios obtained automatically can be very large and not all of them can be tested. Consequently, a selection must be made so that the test set is representative of the domain. Sampling can be done randomly or guided by domain coverage criteria. Adaptive Random Testing [17] is a possible approach, alternative to Random Testing [3]: it enables the random selection of test cases within an input space by means of strategies aimed at ensuring a good distribution of these cases.

References

1. AI Redefined, Gottipati, S.K., Kurandwad, S., Mars, C., Szriftgiser, G., Chabot, F.: Cogment: open source framework for distributed multi-actor training, deployment & operations. CoRR abs/2106.11345 (2021). https://arxiv.org/abs/2106.11345
2. Ammann, P., Offutt, J.: Introduction to Software Testing. Cambridge University Press (2016)
3. Arcuri, A., Iqbal, M.Z., Briand, L.: Random testing: theoretical results and practical implications. IEEE Trans. Software Eng. **38**(2), 258–277 (2012). https://doi.org/10.1109/TSE.2011.121
4. Berrar, D., Ranganathan, S., Gribskov, M., Nakai, K.: Cross-validation. In: Schönbach, C. (ed.) Encyclopedia of Bioinformatics and Computational Biology, pp. 542–545. Academic Press, Oxford (2019). https://doi.org/10.1016/B978-0-12-809633-8.20349-X
5. Biagiola, M., Tonella, P.: Testing the plasticity of reinforcement learning-based systems. ACM Trans. Softw. Eng. Methodol. **31**(4) (2022). https://doi.org/10.1145/3511701
6. Biagiola, M., Tonella, P.: Testing of deep reinforcement learning agents with surrogate models. ACM Trans. Softw. Eng. Methodol. **33**(3) (2024). https://doi.org/10.1145/3631970
7. Braiek, H.B., Khomh, F.: On testing machine learning programs. J. Syst. Softw. **164**, 110542 (2020). https://doi.org/10.1016/j.jss.2020.110542
8. Brockman, G., et al.: OpenAI Gym. CoRR (2016). https://arxiv.org/abs/1606.01540
9. Cem Kaner, J.: An Introduction to Scenario Testing, pp. 1–13. Florida Institute of Technology, Melbourne (2013)
10. Chen, J., et al.: A survey of compiler testing. ACM Comput. Surv. **53**(1) (2020). https://doi.org/10.1145/3363562
11. Chen, T.Y., Cheung, S.C., Yiu, S.M.: Metamorphic testing: a new approach for generating next test cases. arXiv preprint arXiv:2002.12543 (2020)

12. De Angelis, E., De Angelis, G., Proietti, M.: A classification study on testing and verification of AI-based systems. In: 2023 IEEE Int. Conf. on Artificial Intelligence Testing (AITest), pp. 1–8 (2023). https://doi.org/10.1109/AITest58265.2023.00010
13. Demougeot, M., Trouilhet, S., Arcangeli, J.P., Adreit, F.: Scenario-based testing of online learning programs. In: Proceedings of the 20th Int. Conf. on Software Technologies - Volume 1: ICSOFT, pp. 99–110. INSTICC, SciTePress (2025). https://doi.org/10.5220/0013503100003964
14. Dunne, R., Morris, T., Harper, S.: A survey of ambient intelligence. ACM Comput. Surv. (CSUR) **54**(4), 1–27 (2021)
15. Giray, G.: A software engineering perspective on engineering machine learning systems: state of the art and challenges. J. Syst. Softw. **180**, 111031 (2021)
16. Graham, D., Black, R., van Veenendaal, E.: Foundations of Software Testing: ISTQB Certification, 4th edn. Cengage (2020)
17. Huang, R., Sun, W., Xu, Y., Chen, H., Towey, D., Xia, X.: A survey on adaptive random testing. IEEE Trans. Software Eng. **47**(10), 2052–2083 (2021). https://doi.org/10.1109/TSE.2019.2942921
18. Hussain, A., Nadeem, A., Ikram, M.T.: Review on formalizing use cases and scenarios: scenario based testing. In: 2015 Int. Conf. on Emerging Technologies (ICET), pp. 1–6. IEEE (2015)
19. Khomh, F., Adams, B., Cheng, J., Fokaefs, M., Antoniol, G.: Software engineering for machine-learning applications: the road ahead. IEEE Softw. **35**(5), 81–84 (2018)
20. Kreuzberger, D., Kühl, N., Hirschl, S.: Machine learning operations (MLOps): overview, definition, and architecture. IEEE Access **11**, 31866–31879 (2023). https://doi.org/10.1109/ACCESS.2023.3262138
21. Liu, B.: Lifelong machine learning: a paradigm for continuous learning. Front. Comp. Sci. **11**(3), 359–361 (2017)
22. Martínez-Fernández, S., et al.: Software engineering for AI-based systems: a survey. ACM Trans. Softw. Eng. Methodol. (TOSEM) **31**(2), 1–59 (2022)
23. Mazouni, Q., Spieker, H., Gotlieb, A., Acher, M.: A review of validation and verification of neural network-based policies for sequential decision making (2023). https://arxiv.org/abs/2312.09680
24. Mazouni, Q., Spieker, H., Gotlieb, A., Acher, M.: Testing for fault diversity in reinforcement learning. In: Proceedings of the 5th ACM/IEEE Int. Conf. on Automation of Software Test (AST 2024), pp. 136–146. ACM, New York (2024). https://doi.org/10.1145/3644032.3644458
25. Mitchell, T.: Machine Learning. McGraw-Hill, New York (1997)
26. Murphy, C., Kaiser, G.E., Arias, M.: An approach to software testing of machine learning applications. In: Int. Conf. on Software Engineering and Knowledge Engineering (SEKE). Knowledge Systems Institute Graduate School (2007)
27. Nakajima, S.: Generalized oracle for testing machine learning computer programs. In: Cerone, A., Roveri, M. (eds.) SEFM 2017. LNCS, vol. 10729, pp. 174–179. Springer, Cham (2018). https://doi.org/10.1007/978-3-319-74781-1_13
28. OMG: Unified Modeling Language, Version 2.5.1, chap. 11.6 (2017). https://www.omg.org/spec/UML/2.5.1/PDF
29. Papis, B., Wawrzyński, P.: dotRL: a platform for rapid Reinforcement Learning methods development and validation. In: Federated Conf. on Computer Science and Information Systems (FEDCSIS), pp. 129–136. IEEE Press (2013)
30. Riccio, V., Jahangirova, G., Stocco, A., Humbatova, N., Weiss, M., Tonella, P.: Testing machine learning based systems: a systematic mapping. Empir. Softw. Eng. **25**, 5193–5254 (2020)

31. Russell, S.J., Norvig, P.: Artificial Intelligence: A Modern Approach. Inc, Pearson Education (2010)
32. Sommerville, I.: Component-based software engineering. In: Software Engineering, 10th edn., pp. 464–489. Pearson Education (2016)
33. Sugali, K.: Software testing: issues and challenges of artificial intelligence & machine learning. Int. J. Artif. Intell. Appl. **12**(1), 101–112 (2021)
34. Sutton, R., Barto, A.: Reinforcement Learning: An Introduction, 2nd edn. MIT Press (2018)
35. Symeonidis, G., Nerantzis, E., Kazakis, A., Papakostas, G.A.: MLOPs-definitions, tools and challenges. In: 12th IEEE Annual Computing and Communication Workshop and Conference (CCWC), pp. 0453–0460. IEEE Press (2022)
36. Ulbrich, S., Menzel, T., Reschka, A., Schuldt, F., Maurer, M.: Defining and substantiating the terms scene, situation, and scenario for automated driving. In: 18th IEEE Int. Conf. on Intelligent Transportation Systems, pp. 982–988. IEEE (2015)
37. Weyuker, E.J.: On testing non-testable programs. Comput. J. **25**(4), 465–470 (1982)
38. Younes, W., Trouilhet, S., Adreit, F., Arcangeli, J.P.: Agent-mediated application emergence through reinforcement learning from user feedback. In: 29th IEEE Int. Conf. on Enabling Technologies: Infrastructure for Collaborative Enterprises (WETICE), pp. 3–8. IEEE Press (2020)
39. Zhang, J.M., Harman, M., Ma, L., Liu, Y.: Machine learning testing: survey, landscapes and horizons. IEEE Trans. Softw. Eng. **48**(1), 1–36 (2020)

Towards a Maturity Model for AI Software Processes with International Standards

Rubén Márquez[1,2(✉)], Javier Verdugo[1,2], Moisés Rodríguez[1,2], and Mario Piattini[1,2]

[1] AQCLab Software Quality, C/ de Moledores s/n., 13071 Ciudad Real, Spain
[2] Instituto de Tecnologías y Sistemas de Información (UCLM), Paseo Universidad, 4, 13071 Ciudad Real, Spain
Ruben.Marquez@alu.uclm.es, {Javier.Verdugo,Moises.Rodriguez,Mario.Piattini}@uclm.es

Abstract. Artificial intelligence (AI) has become a key driver of innovation across multiple sectors, increasing the need to ensure not only functional performance but also the quality and reliability of AI systems. New regulations directly focused on the field of AI are emerging, such as the EU AI Act, along with new international standards such as ISO/IEC 5338:AI system life cycle processes, which attempt to address the importance of the quality of AI development processes; however these lack a company-oriented approach. This paper proposes the Artificial Intelligence Software Maturity Model (MMSIA), a standardized framework designed to assess and improve the capability and maturity of AI system development processes. The MMSIA integrates the life cycle processes of ISO/IEC 5338 with the assessment framework of the ISO/IEC 33000 family, enabling organizations (especially SMEs) focused on AI system development to assess and continuously improve their AI development practices. The model defines a total of 24 processes required in the AI development lifecycle, divided into five maturity levels, enabling a structured approach that promotes advancement toward the development of reliable and trustworthy AI systems.

Keywords: Maturity Model · Artificial Intelligence · Software Processes · ISO/IEC 5338

1 Introduction

Artificial intelligence (AI) has swiftly evolved from a specialised area of research to become a fundamental technological enabler in almost every sector of contemporary society. Over the past decade, improvements in data accessibility, computational power, and algorithmic complexity have elevated AI from a primarily experimental field to a driver of economic, social, and scientific innovation. Today, AI-based systems assist decision-making in a variety of areas, including

M. Mecella et al. (Eds.): ICSOFT 2025, CCIS 3144, pp. 87–104, 2027.
https://doi.org/10.1007/978-3-032-37353-3_4

healthcare [2], finance [18], education [7], manufacturing [1], and public services, among others. This widespread adoption has increased the need for organisations to ensure not only the operational effectiveness of AI solutions, but also their quality, reliability, and compliance with emerging ethical and regulatory standards.

The dominant global push towards establishing trustworthy and responsible AI highlights that quality management in AI must encompass more than just the evaluation of algorithms or models; it must encompass the entire software lifecycle involved in the design, development, implementation, and maintenance of AI systems [19]. As AI systems become increasingly relevant in high-stakes decision-making, concerns are growing about critical issues such as bias, explainability, robustness, and data governance. In response to these concerns, several governments and international organisations have introduced governance regulations, including the EU Artificial Intelligence Act [4]. This regulation emphasise the principles of accountability, traceability, and continuous improvement. However, it is important to note that this initiative provides general guidance on governance, it does not delineate specific software process standards for the development of AI systems.

Simultaneously, various organisations, such as the International Organisation for Standardisation (ISO) and the International Electrotechnical Commission (IEC), are already working on developing new international standards of good practice to accompany and support these new regulations. International standards such as ISO/IEC 25059 'Quality model for AI systems' [15] or works to incorporate them into industry, such as [20], which proposes a framework for assessing the quality of AI products, are making progress in this area. However, it is also important to focus on the evolution and improvement of the processes necessary for the development of AI systems. For this reason, the ISO has published a new standard, ISO/IEC 5338 'AI system lifecycle processes' [16], which represents a significant advance, as it provides a complete reference model for AI system software processes. In addition, the ISO/IEC 33000 family [8] provides a well-established framework for assessing software process capability and organisational maturity. Together, these standards establish a fundamental basis for organisations to assess and improve their AI development practices. However, despite these advances, many companies, especially small and medium-sized enterprises (SMEs), still lack practical tools and models for applying these standards in a structured and quantifiable manner.

The need for systematic evaluation of processes in the development of AI systems is emphasised by the distinctive characteristics inherent in AI software projects. Unlike conventional software, AI systems rely on data-driven learning components, exhibit probabilistic behaviour, and undergo continuous retraining cycles that evolve after implementation. As a result, traditional software process models, such as ISO/IEC/IEEE 12207 'Software life cycle processes' [10] and CMMI (Capability Maturity Model Integration) v3.0 [3], are insufficient to address the dynamic, data-centric, and risk-sensitive aspects of AI development. Numerous studies [5,20,22] indicate that organisations developing or adopting AI technologies often face challenges in establishing consistent development processes, managing the quality of model lifecycles, and ensuring traceability between datasets, models, and system requirements.

To address these challenges, this document presents the Artificial Intelligence Software Maturity Model (MMSIA), which serves as a framework for assessing maturity and capability adapted to organisations engaged in the development of AI systems. This model incorporates the process reference model described in ISO/IEC 5338, together with the assessment structure of the ISO/IEC 33000 family, thus offering a systematic approach to assessing the maturity of AI-related software processes. The main objective of this study is to help organisations, through a cohesive framework, to evaluate, compare, and improve their AI development processes. By implementing the MMSIA model, organisations can improve performance levels of their ability to implement AI systems that are not only functionally effective but also robust, transparent, and compliant with the ever-evolving standards for trustworthy AI.

The remainder of this document is structured as follows: Sect. 2 provides a comprehensive review of current advances in assessing the quality of AI systems, with an emphasis on recently published international standards and frameworks. Section 3 examines the relationship and differences between ISO/IEC 5338 and traditional software lifecycle standard processes. Section 4 presents the MMSIA model, detailing its structure, maturity levels and the phases of which it is composed. Finally, Sect. 5 describes the conclusions reached, lessons learned and possible directions for future research.

2 State of the Art

The rapid incorporation of AI in various sectors has led to a corresponding increase in standards, frameworks and maturity tools designed to help organisations manage, evaluate and improve their AI initiatives. Two aspects are essential when evaluating software quality: processes and product. In the case of improving the quality of AI products, progress is already being made, as evidenced by the ISO/IEC 25059 standard [15], which modifies four of the eight essential characteristics that a quality product must have, as established in ISO/IEC 25010 [14], and incorporates new sub-characteristics to be considered for AI products, such as transparency, functional adaptability and interoperability. In addition, work such as [20] is making progress in improving the quality of AI products through environments and tools directly focused on companies.

On the other hand, progress made to improve quality in the life cycle processes of AI system development is scarcer. However, certain initiatives are being undertaken that can be classified into three main categories: (a) AI regulations that set out general expectations for trustworthy AI; (b) technical and process quality standards that articulate the quality attributes and lifecycle processes of AI systems; and (c) practical maturity models and benchmarking reports used by organisations to assess progress and implement improvements. The following parts of this section provide a summary of notable examples from each category and identify a number of gaps to be mitigated by the proposed model.

2.1 AI Regulations

Policymakers and standardisation organisations have emphasised the importance of adopting reliable, risk-based approaches to AI. The European Union AI Act [4] establishes a regulatory framework characterised by a system of risk levels for AI applications, which imposes specific obligations on high-risk systems. This law came into force in August 2024 and sets out phased deadlines for the implementation of specific obligations. Compliance with the law requires adherence to clearly defined lifecycle practices, including documentation, traceability, risk assessment and post-market surveillance over the AI project.

In addition, other countries, such as Canada [6] or United Kingdom [23], have already drafted laws related to the use and development of AI, which seek to regulate AI systems by establishing obligations related to risk management, bias monitoring, or impact assessment.

Collectively, these global initiatives mark a transition from high-level ethical principles to applicable, process-oriented governance. However, despite their geographical and regulatory diversity, they share common expectations, from traceability and documentation to continuous improvement. These regulations depend on the correct definition of mature software and AI lifecycle processes. This convergence reinforces the need for assessment tools that can translate these regulatory expectations into measurable process maturity objectives applicable across all AI-oriented organisations.

2.2 Technical and Process-Quality Standards for AI

Standardization efforts specifically targeting the engineering and quality of AI systems have advanced rapidly in recent years. The ISO/IEC 5338 [16] standard defines a reference model for the AI system lifecycle process (based on ISO/IEC/IEEE 12207 [10], ISO/IEC/IEEE 15288 [17], and AI-specific norms such as ISO/IEC 22989 [12] and ISO/IEC 23053 [13]). The standard lists a set of processes necessary to carry out AI system development, explicitly identifies a number of modifications to traditional standardized software development processes, and proposes new AI-specific processes.

Therefore, this international standard provides standardized categories of processes and lifecycle activities for incorporation into AI system development. However, this standard is largely a normative reference; many organizations struggle to put it into practice and translate it into viable process improvements and measurable capability goals.

On the other hand, there are other widely used international standards that provide mechanisms for evaluating these processes, such as the ISO/IEC 33000 family of standards [8]. This set of standards replaces the previous ISO/IEC 15504, also known as Software Process Improvement and Capability dEtermination (SPICE), and provides a framework for assessing organizational maturity. The structured approach offered by this set of standards gives organizations the opportunity to achieve various organizational objectives. These standards were originally developed for traditional software engineering, and their generic nature makes them unsuitable for incorporation into AI environments without prior adaptation.

2.3 Practical and Industry Maturity Models

Despite the remarkable growth of governance frameworks, standards, and industry benchmarks for AI, there remains a critical gap in how organizations assess the maturity of their internal AI development processes. Traditionally, there are widely used approaches in the industry, such as CMMI v3.0 [3], which consist of a framework for assessing and improving process performance capability by identifying weaknesses and opportunities for improvement through a generalist structure. Or, for example, the MMIS (Maturity Model for Software Engineering) v2.0 model [21], also developed by the authors of this article, which builds a maturity model based on the international standards ISO/IEC 12207 and ISO/IEC 33000, with the aim of assisting in the assessment and improvement of traditional software processes for small and medium-sized enterprises.

Nevertheless, these models do not include specific AI processes, or the incorporation of possible particularities that may arise in the development of such systems.

On the other hand, there are also other solutions, such as the SMMT maturity model [22] or the AI and Big Data Maturity Model [5], which seek to assess an organization's capability to incorporate AI solutions and tools into its manufacturing production systems and business operations, respectively. However, their focus is strategic and operational, lacking granularity for technical processes and focusing more on their use than on the actual development of an AI system.

To conclude, the following Table 1 provides a clear summary comparing the AI regulatory frameworks, technical standards, and maturity models discussed above in the literature, along with their objectives and main limitations in relation to the needs raised in this paper.

Table 1. Comparison of AI regulations, standards and practical approach.

Category	Framework/Standard	Primary Focus	Scope	Disadvantages and Limitations
AI Regulations	EU Artificial Intelligence Act [4]	Regulatory governance	First legally binding framework defining risk tiers, conformity assessment, and post-market monitoring and development for AI systems.	Lacks detailed guidance on the processes necessary to carry out the development of an AI system and improve its corresponding quality.
	Other AI Regulations [6,23]	Bills and guides	Promote the responsible and secure development and use of AI through guidelines and codes of conduct.	Regulations under development that are not yet focused on end companies, with practices and best practices that can be incorporated.
Technical Standards	ISO/IEC/IEEE 12207 [10]	Process reference model for software systems	A process reference model focused on the processes required in the traditional software development lifecycle.	Directly focused on traditional software development, it does not include the particularities involved in AI system development.
	ISO/IEC 25059 [15]	Product quality attributes for AI systems	Extended version of ISO/IEC 25010, which modifies and adds specific AI characteristics.	Focused on product quality, not on improving organizational processes for AI development.
	ISO/IEC 33000 family [8]	International Standards for process assessment	A software process assessment framework and continuous process improvement.	Generic framework, that does not include specific details about the field of AI, as it is very general.
	ISO/IEC 5338 [16]	Process reference model for AI systems	A process reference model focused on AI lifecycle processes, which expands on those included in the ISO/IEC/IEEE 12207 standard with new processes.	Does not include an evaluation and measurement process for the proposed processes.
Practical models	CMMI v3.0 [3]	General process capability and improvement	A process assessment framework that helps organizations understand their current level of capability and performance, providing a roadmap for optimizing business outcomes.	A generalist model with high costs in terms of effort and money, focused on large companies due to its long implementation times.
	MMIS v2.0 [21]	Software engineering process capability and improvement	Framework for evaluating and improving the quality of software development processes, in accordance with ISO/IEC 33000 and ISO/IEC 12207 standards.	Focused on traditional software development, excluding the specific processes used in the development of AI systems.
	SMMT maturity model [22]	AI adoption capability in manufacturing	Evaluates ability to integrate AI into industrial operations.	Focuses on AI adoption, not AI system development lifecycle.
	AI and Big Data Maturity Model [5]	Data analytics and AI integration maturity	Measures organizational readiness and strategy for AI-driven decision-making.	Lacks process-level assessment and mainly oriented toward business integration.

3 Analysis of the ISO/IEC 5338 Standard

The definition of structured processes for software development has historically been based on standards such as ISO/IEC/IEEE 12207, which has established itself as a fundamental framework for traditional software engineering. This standard provides best practices for managing software systems through a series of clearly defined processes covering the acquisition, development, operation, maintenance and disposal of software products. However, the growing integration of AI has introduced new aspects and artefacts, such as data sets, models and knowledge bases, which work and need to be treated differently from conventional software components. These artefacts exhibit non-deterministic behaviour, depend on data quality and have continuous learning cycles, aspects that the traditional life cycle processes described in ISO/IEC 12207 are not prepared to address effectively.

As a response to the identified gap, ISO has established the ISO/IEC 5338 standard 'AI system lifecycle processes'. This standard adapts and expands on the ISO/IEC/IEEE 12207 and ISO/IEC/IEEE 15288 standards to address the best practices and processes needed for developing systems under an AI lifecycle. ISO/IEC 5338 retains the fundamental structure framework of its predecessors, while incorporating AI-specific processes, modifying existing processes, and redefining certain outputs to better adapt to the characteristics inherent in AI development, through the use of AI-specific, such as ISO/IEC 22989 'Concepts and terminology of artificial intelligence', incorporating the relevant concepts for AI development, and ISO/IEC 23053 'Framework for artificial intelligence (AI) systems using machine learning (ML)', providing a framework that describes the essential components and functions for the development of AI systems.

The AI systems referred to in the standard are primarily based on those that use machine learning techniques and/or heuristic system development. This indicates that these systems explicitly exploit data or expert knowledge in order to train models and, consequently, infer the necessary knowledge or results. The ISO/IEC 5338 standard describes a comprehensive framework that consists of a set of 33 different processes. As with the ISO/IEC/IEEE 12207 standard, these processes are classified into 4 main groups based on a set of critical factors that organisations involved in the development of AI systems must take into account. These factors cover the management of various components that make up the development process, as well as support mechanisms, including the evaluation of the performance of the processes themselves. These 4 groups are as follows:

- Agreement Processes: involve managing relationships and contracts between customers and suppliers of AI products or services.
- Organizational Project-Enabling Processes: provide the governance, resources, and infrastructure essential for the successful execution of AI projects and objectives.

- Technical Management Processes: encompass the planning, monitoring, evaluating and controlling of activities related to project development and the lifecycle of AI systems.
- Technical Processes: handle the definition, analysis, implementation, AI model training, integration, and validation of components within AI systems.

Although this classification has similarities with the ISO/IEC/IEEE 12207 standard, an analysis has been carried out on the modifications, additions and exclusions introduced in the ISO/IEC 5338, with the aim of defining the most important processes required in the reference process model for the proposed MMSIA model. This analysis has revealed three types of processes:

- Generic Processes [G], processes adopted from ISO/IEC/IEEE 12207 standards without significant modifications, are equally applicable to AI development (e.g., measurement, infrastructure management).
- Modified Processes [M], existing processes that have been redefined or expanded in their elements (purpose, outcomes or activities) to accommodate specific aspects of AI, such as the inclusion of dataset quality criteria, considerations regarding algorithmic bias, and model retraining activities.
- AI-Specific Processes [AI], newly introduced processes that are unique and specific to AI systems development.

This classification emphasises the conceptual transition from static software artefacts to dynamic, data-dependent systems that evolve throughout their lifecycle. A summary of the processes included in the ISO/IEC 5338 standard is presented in Fig. 1, classified by groups and highlighting those that have been modified or newly included.

According to the analysis summarised in the above table, it identifies 7 generic processes, 23 processes modified to adapt them to the AI particularities and 3 AI-specific processes. Below Table 2 there are more details of the changes and new processes that make up the modified processes together with the AI-specific ones.

In this way, a reference model for processes for creating AI systems can be defined, which can be used for the proposed MMSIA maturity model and its incorporation into its maturity scales. The AI-specific processes described in ISO/IEC 5338 are fundamental elements for assessing AI development capabilities. Their integration ensures that assessments go beyond compliance with procedures and cover the reliability, adaptability and sustainability of AI systems.

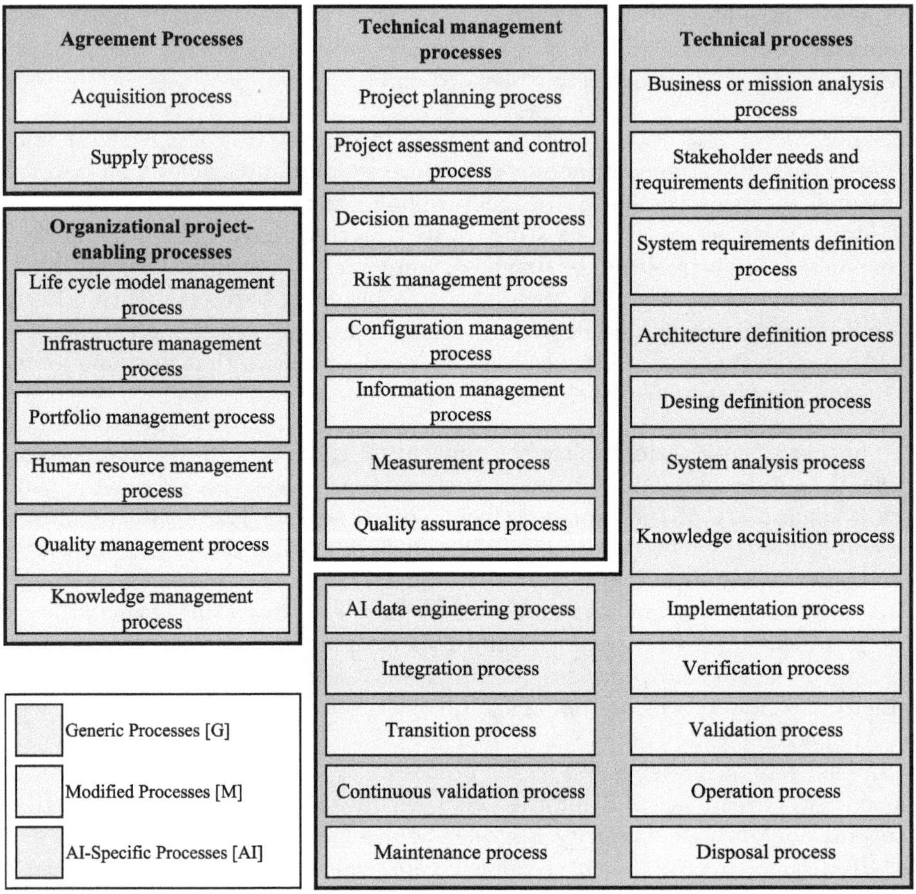

Fig. 1. Software lifecycle process groups according to ISO/IEC 5338. Source: [25].

Table 2. Processes Modified and Specific for AI development according to ISO/IEC 5338.

Category	Process	AI Particularities
Generic	Project planning process	Allow some flexibility concerning model creation, including plans for experiment iteration, strategies, tactics (machine learning), and models for knowledge acquisition and retrieval (knowledge engineering).
Processes	Implementation process	Build an AI model and prepare documentation on the modelling process. Select and execute the appropriate learning algorithm, using optimisation techniques (machine learning) and formalise a heuristic model.
(G)	Supply process	Take into account proof-of-concept, datasets, AI system intervention if its performance varies with production data, or analysis and improvement of the system as part of the agreement of the product/service.
	Quality assurance process	Include specific quality characteristics of AI systems (transparency, fairness, accountability, robustness). In addition, more thorough quality control.
	Project assessment and control process	Include intervals for updating the AI system, due to its iterative and experimental nature.
	Configuration management process	Include version control for the datasets and models developed, as well as their correct traceability.
	Stakeholder needs and requirements definition process	Include performance measures related to biases and identify new stakeholders.
	Human resource management process	Consider new specific roles in AI such as data scientists, data engineers, knowledge engineers, etc.
	Decision management process	Include new types of decisions, such as withdrawing, refactoring, updating specifications or documentation to reflect the learned behavior of the AI system.
	Risk management process	Include fairness, privacy, reliability, transparency, explainability, accountability, availability, and maintainability in risk management.
	Verification process	Use of verification datasets to measure the accuracy and robustness of the developed model, validation datasets to choose the best model, and test datasets to verify the model's performance.
	Validation process	Perform proof-of-concept. Consider model updates and perform continuous monitoring, validating its performance in production.
	System requirements definition process	Consider new AI-specific requirements, such as correction levels (precision, accuracy), autonomy levels, performance (response time) or continuous validation.
	Portfolio management process	Consider AI as a business opportunity to innovate in new projects, the exchange of knowledge between projects for reuse, and the specific risks of AI.
	Knowledge management process	Include datasets or scripts in knowledge management, document experiments and models implemented along with lessons learned.
	Business or mission analysis process	Consider specific risks that may influence the achievement of certain business objectives.
AI-Specific	AI data engineering process	Ensures that data can be used in the model through acquisition, correct processing, extract metadata and documentation, traceability, maintenance, and analysis of datasets, as well as incorporating automated processes.
Processes	Knowledge acquisition process	Provides the knowledge necessary for the development of AI models through the correct identification, storage, and traceability of expert knowledge.
(AI)	Continuous validation process	Ensure that the AI models developed will continue working correctly once the system has been moved into production, as the behavior of a model or its performance may be affected, by incorporating validation logs and considering retraining the model.

4 Artificial Intelligence Software Maturity Model (MMSIA)

The adoption of ISO/IEC 5338 provides a comprehensive process reference model for AI systems; however, organisations require structured approaches to assess the maturity of these processes and formulate systematic improvements according to their particular business context. To address this need, an Artificial Intelligence Software Maturity Model (titled MMSIA), for which a first approximation of the model has already been made in [25], has been defined. The model aims to serve as a framework for assessing maturity and capability that merges the process structure of ISO/IEC 5338 with the measurement framework of the ISO/IEC 33000 family. The MMSIA model provides a pragmatic approach for organisations, especially those involved in the development of AI systems, to assess and improve their AI lifecycle software processes, both at the project and organisational levels. As mentioned above, this new model is based on two widely used international standards:

- ISO/IEC 5338: new ISO standard that establishes a reference catalogue with all the software processes necessary to carry out the development of an AI product/service.
- ISO/IEC 33000 family of standards: set of international standards that defines a framework for the correct measurement and evaluation of the capabilities of a particular software process and organisational maturity.

In this way, the MMSIA model is defined, which aims to establish a reference model for processes specifically adapted to AI system development activities and to define a set of maturity levels that denote increasingly advanced practices in the implementation and management of these processes. The model seeks to facilitate the quantitative and qualitative evaluation of AI development process capabilities and to support continuous quality improvement.

The process reference model provides a systematic compilation of the essential processes for the development of AI systems, accompanied by best practices that define the characteristics of those processes. In establishing the AI system lifecycle reference model for the MMSIA framework, the processes articulated in ISO/IEC 5338 served as a fundamental reference.

According to ISO/IEC 33004 [9], the defined MMSIA model specifies a domain within the reference model that covers the fundamental processes necessary for the development of AI systems, particularly by AI development SMEs, although it is applicable to organisations of another size. Therefore, although ISO/IEC 5338 defines a total of 33 software processes, the MMSIA model has selected those that cover from project inception to operational deployment and performance monitoring. For this reason, more transversal or specific processes are not included in the domain, such as operation, maintenance, or disposal processes, which have been removed from the scope of the MMSIA model. This selection was made through a process guided by three principles: Relevance (including those processes directly influenced by the quality, robustness, and reliability of

AI systems), Applicability (selecting realistic processes that can be implemented and evaluated in an SME organization), and Completeness (compiling complete coverage of processes involved in the AI lifecycle for the established domain). In addition, this selection process has been validated by several expert researchers and professionals with experience in developing anothers' maturity models based on ISO standards, such as the MMIS model for traditional software development processes.

This resulted in a model that incorporates a total of 24 processes derived from the ISO/IEC 5338 standard. For each process, the following has been defined: a purpose (with the objective of the process within the AI context), a set of expected outcomes (observable results that demonstrate the correct implementation of the process), a set of activities and tasks (specific actions that ensure the achievement of the above outcomes), and a series of work products (tangible artifacts that serve as evidence and are produced by the implementation of the model).

Once the reference process model has been established, it is essential to define the relationship between the defined processes and their intended application context. This relationship clarifies how the processes are integrated with the levels described in the maturity model, addressing several aspects that AI system development organizations must consider, such as project management, organizational management, resource management, data and expertise management, engineering, model development, and training, as well as product and process performance evaluation. Each maturity level represents a step in the incremental institutionalization of the organization's capability to develop AI systems.

Five maturity levels are defined, each introducing new processes to be implemented within the organization. The following Table 3 illustrates the classification of the reference model processes and their alignment with the respective maturity levels.

Defining maturity using these levels ensures that the proposed improvements are sustainable and consistent with both business objectives and regulatory requirements.

Once the processes necessary for the development of AI systems have been outlined using a reference model covering various levels of maturity, the MMSIA model introduces a measurement and evaluation framework aligned with ISO/IEC 33000 standards. A critical component of evaluating organizational processes in accordance with the ISO/IEC 33000 family is measuring the capability level of each process. Assessing the capability of a software process involves determining the degree of implementation of a process within an organization. Each process is assessed across 5 capability levels, and to assess the capability of a process, a series of process attributes (PAs) are defined, which serve as elements for assessing specific aspects of a process's capabilities and competencies. These attributes are universal and applicable to all processes, including management practices and generic work products. They work as indicators of the performance capability of the process, enabling the individual measurements needed to determine the level of achievement of each attribute and, consequently,

Table 3. MMSIA Maturity Levels with defined processes. Source: Adapted [25].

Maturity Level	Defined Processes
Level 1: Basic	Project Planning Process, Implementation Process and AI Data Engineering Process
Level 2: Managed	Supply Process, Life Cycle Model Management Process, Quality Assurance Process, Project Assessment and Control Process, Measurement Process, Configuration Management Process, Stakeholder Needs and Requirements Definition Process and Knowledge Acquisition Process
Level 3: Established	Infrastructure Management Process, Human Resources Management Process, Decision Management Process, Risk Management Process, Architecture Definition Process, Integration Process, Verification Process, Validation Process, System Requirements Definition Process and Continuous Validation Process
Level 4: Predictable	Portfolio Management Process
Level 5: Innovative	Knowledge Management Process and Business Analysis Process

the capability level of the process being assessed. In this way, the assessment of the capability level of a specific process can be performed based on the results identified during the assessment and gathering of evidence for each attribute of the process being assessed. The following Table 4 describes the capability levels along with the corresponding process attributes, as defined in ISO/IEC 33020 [11].

Thus, the degree of implementation of a process attribute or result is quantified using an ordinal scale, as well as defining a nomenclature for its qualification. Table 5 specifies this scale.

In order to obtain the final implementation level of a process attribute, and after determining the different levels of achievement in the process attribute results, an average of the values obtained in the table above is calculated, and an implementation level for the process attribute is calculated according to the criteria in the following Table 6.

To determine the capability level of each process, an aggregation method is used that conforms to the following criterion: a process has a capability level X if all process attributes at the previous levels are rated as "Fully implemented" (F) and the process attributes at capability level X are rated at least as "Largely implemented" (L).

Once the capacity levels of an organization's processes have been determined, an organizational maturity assessment is carried out. The purpose of this assessment is to determine the level to which an organization executes the processes essential to achieving its business objectives in an AI development environment. By using the process profiles established for each of the maturity levels mentioned

Table 4. Capability levels and process attributes. Source: Adapted [25].

Capability Level	Key PA	Process Attribute (PA)
Level 0. Incomplete Process	–	–
Level 1. Performed Process	PA 1.1	Process performance
Level 2. Managed Process	PA 2.1	Performance management
	PA 2.2	Document information management
Level 3. Established Process	PA 3.1	Process definition and improvement
	PA 3.2	Process deployment
	PA 3.3	Process assurance
Level 4. Predictable Process	PA 4.1	Quantitative process analysis
	PA 4.2	Quantitative process control
Level 5. Innovating Process	PA 5.1	Process innovation
	PA 5.2	Implementation of process innovation

Table 5. Qualification nomenclature for outcomes process attributes.

Key	Rating	Definition
N	Not achieved	There is little or no evidence of achievement of the defined outcome in the evaluated process.
P	Partially achieved	There is some evidence of focusing and achieving the defined outcome in the process being evaluated. Some aspects of the achievement of the process attribute may be unpredictable.
L	Largely achieved	There is evidence of a systematic approach and significant achievement of the defined outcome in the evaluated process. There may exist some deficiencies related to this process attribute in the evaluated process.
F	Fully achieved	There is evidence of a comprehensive and systematic approach and full achievement of the defined outcome in the evaluated process. There are no significant weaknesses related to this process attribute in the evaluated process.

above, it is possible to illustrate organizational behaviors and facilitate continuous and gradual process improvement. However, in order to accurately define an organization's maturity level, it is essential to establish a correlation between process capability levels and organizational maturity levels. Consequently, Fig. 2 illustrates the relationships between capability levels and their corresponding maturity levels within the MMSIA model.

After establishing the different processes, attributes, and characteristics of the MMSIA model, a four-stage assessment process has been defined, which aims to provide a systematic assessment involving an evaluator profile and another

Table 6. Process attribute qualification method.

Key	Rating	Definition
N	Not implemented	The degree of implementation of the outcomes of the process is from 0% to 15%.
P	Partially implemented	The degree of implementation of the outcomes of the process is from 16% to 50%.
L	Largely implemented	The degree of implementation of the outcomes of the process is from 51% to 85%.
F	Fully implemented	The degree of implementation of the process outcomes is from 86% to 100%.

more experienced evaluator who acts as the lead assessor, the latter being responsible for reviewing the assessments carried out [24]. Therefore, the assessment of process attributes involves the evaluator's judgment of the degree to which the artefacts of the process attribute and the defined results are fulfilled, based on the evidence and conclusions identified during the evaluation. These four stages are:

1. Initial stage, which aims to establish the scope of the evaluation, identify the stakeholders, and obtain a set of documents on the development process to serve as input for the evaluation process.
2. Review stage, which begins with a documentary review of the relevant elements associated with the development of the AI systems to be evaluated, as well as conducting various structured interviews with the stakeholders involved in the development of these systems. These interviews consist of a series of questions addressed to those involved about artefacts, results, or activities carried out during the AI system development lifecycle, which have been derived from the characteristics described in the process reference model. The questions are classified into different sections of the AI system development lifecycle, such as requirements, project management, architecture and implementation, measurement and quality, validation and verification, or a section on essential features of AI system development such as data/expert knowledge acquisition and preprocessing.
3. Analysis stage: throughout the interviews, participants will provide evidence and proof that will enable the evaluator to formulate observations and findings on the degree of implementation of the processes involved in the development lifecycle within the project or organization. These observations will be analysed and classified with the aim of determining the degrees of implementation of the process attributes for each process evaluated, using for this purpose their comparative results with the process outcomes (PA 1.1) and the associated management practices (PA 2.1, PA 2.2, PA 3.1, PA 3.2, PA 3.3, PA 4.1, PA 4.2, PA 5.1 and PA 5.2).

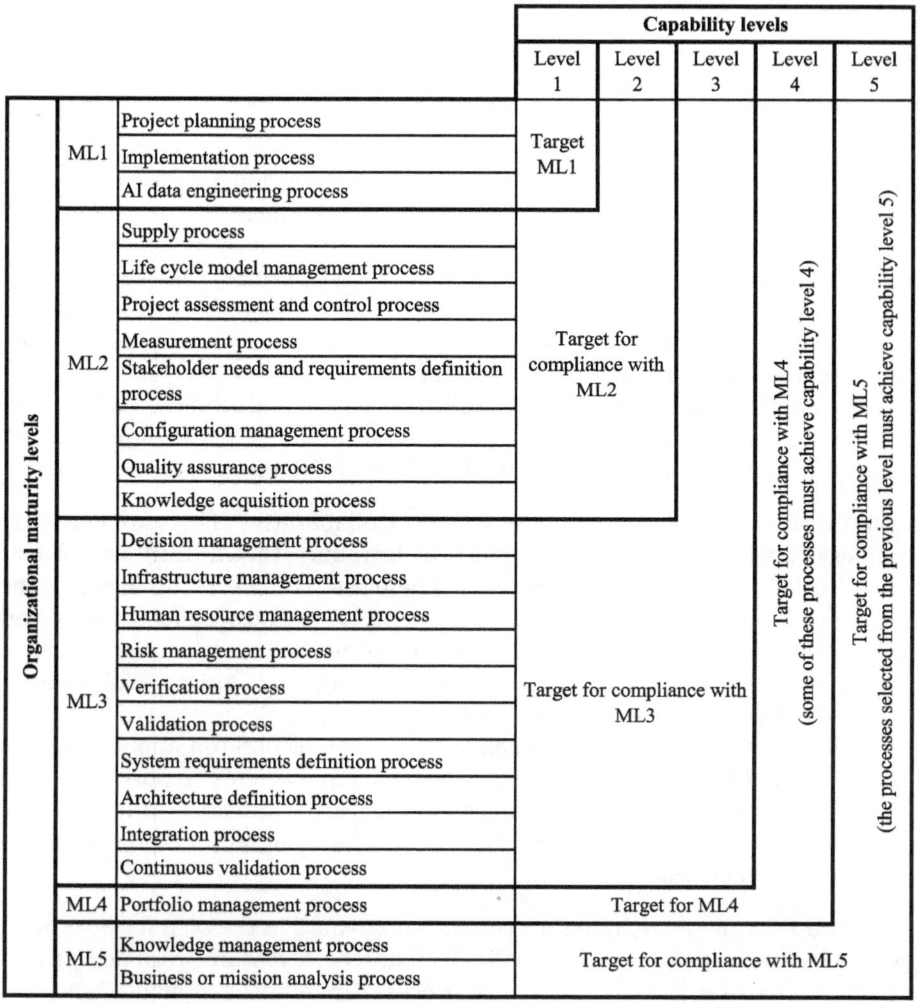

Fig. 2. Correlation between maturity levels and capability levels. Source: [25]

4. Calculation stage: using the levels of implementation of the different process attributes, the capacity levels of all the processes involved are calculated and an organizational maturity level is derived. Finally, based on the gaps identified, a series of specific improvement measures has been proposed.

5 Conclusions and Future Works

AI has become a fundamental element of digital transformation, facilitating new forms of automation, decision-making, and innovation in various sectors. However, the quality and reliability of AI systems depend not only on functional performance but also on the robustness of the processes used in their design, implementation, validation, and management. The lack of standardized assessment tools for these processes has historically limited the organization's ability to ensure reliable and reproducible AI results.

This paper addresses this gap by introducing an Artificial Intelligence Software Maturity Model, or MMSIA, a structured model designed for the assessment and improvement of processes in the AI development lifecycle. Based on the international standards ISO/IEC 5338 (AI system lifecycle processes) and the ISO/IEC 33000 family (process capability and maturity assessment), the MMSIA model offers a systematic, evidence-based approach to assessing the effectiveness of AI-related processes in terms of their definition, implementation, and continuous improvement within organizations.

Although the MMSIA establishes a solid conceptual and methodological baseline, it is necessary to continue advancing research and developing improvements to make it a more robust model. Thus, the following improvements are proposed:

1. Empirical validation through case studies: Collaborative efforts are currently underway with AI-focused companies to introduce the MMSIA model into real-world development environments. These case studies aim to evaluate the applicability of the model, gather evidence on its diagnostic effectiveness, and refine the associated process indicators. In addition, extending validation to other sectors, such as healthcare, manufacturing, and finance, will improve the overall generalization of the model.
2. Development of a digital assessment tool: A web or desktop application will be developed to automate process assessment, manage test repositories, and visualize results through comprehensive dashboards. This tool will facilitate longitudinal tracking of process capabilities, enabling automatic capture of data-driven metrics.

The MMSIA model represents a significant advance in the systematic evaluation of AI software processes. It provides a comprehensive framework designed to help organizations achieve high levels of process capability, compliance, and reliability. By prioritizing both technical rigor and ethical governance, the MMSIA model encourages the development of AI systems that are transparent, trustworthy, and aligned with international standards and social values.

As the field of artificial intelligence continues to advance at a rapid pace, process maturity models such as the MMSIA will be critical in bridging the gap between technological innovation and responsible implementation. This approach will ensure that advances in artificial intelligence are not only efficient and competitive, but also sustainable and reliable.

Acknowledgments. This research has been supported by the ANDANTE Project (Ref. SBPLY/24/180225/000039) funded with the support of the UE through the FEDER and the JCCM, and the "Agencia de Investigación e Innovación de CLM"; SINERGIA (2025-GRIN-38310), financial support for the execution of applied research projects, within the framework of the UCLM Own Research Plan, 85% co-funded by the European Regional Development Fund (FEDER); and RiskIA Project (Ref.

3930718/2025) funded with the support of the UE through the FEDER and the JCCM, and the "Programa de apoyo a la innovación: Innova-Adelante".

References

1. Arinez, J.F., Chang, Q., Gao, R.X., Xu, C., Zhang, J.: Artificial intelligence in advanced manufacturing: current status and future outlook. J. Manuf. Sci. Eng. **142**(11), 110804 (2020)
2. Chakraborty, S., Sarangi, T., Ghosh, S., Misra, B., Dey, N.: Responsible ai adoption in healthcare: opportunities and challenges. In: 2024 10th International Conference on Advanced Computing and Communication Systems (ICACCS), vol. 1, pp. 1198–1205. IEEE (2024)
3. CMMI Institute: CMMI V3.0 (2023). https://cmmiinstitute.com/products/cmmi/content-release
4. European Commission: Laying Down Harmonised Rules On Artificial Intelligence (Artificial Intelligence Act) and Amending Certain Union Legislative Acts. Proposal for a regulation of the European parliament and of the council, April 2021
5. Fornasiero, R., Kiebler, L., Falsafi, M., Sardesai, S.: Proposing a maturity model for assessing artificial intelligence and big data in the process industry. Int. J. Prod. Res. **63**(4), 1235–1255 (2025)
6. Government of Canada: Artificial Intelligence and Data Act. Bill C-27 (2022)
7. Holmes, W., Tuomi, I.: State of the art and practice in ai in education. Eur. J. Educ. **57**(4), 542–570 (2022)
8. ISO: ISO/IEC 33000 Family (2015). https://committee.iso.org/sites/jtc1sc7/home/projects/flagship-standards/isoiec-33000-family.html
9. ISO: ISO/IEC 33004:2015 Information technology — Process assessment — Requirements for process reference, process assessment and maturity models (2015). https://www.iso.org/standard/54178.html
10. ISO: ISO/IEC/IEEE 12207:2017 Systems and software engineering — Software life cycle processes (2017). https://www.iso.org/standard/63712.html
11. ISO: ISO/IEC 33020:2019 Information technology — Process assessment — Process measurement framework for assessment of process capability (2019). https://www.iso.org/standard/78526.html
12. ISO: ISO/IEC 22989:2022 Information technology — Artificial intelligence — Artificial intelligence concepts and terminology (2022). https://www.iso.org/standard/74296.html
13. ISO: ISO/IEC 23053:2022 Framework for Artificial Intelligence (AI) Systems Using Machine Learning (ML) (2022). https://www.iso.org/standard/74438.html
14. ISO: ISO/IEC 25010:2023 Systems and software engineering — Systems and software Quality Requirements and Evaluation (SQuaRE) — Product quality model (2023). https://www.iso.org/standard/78176.html
15. ISO: ISO/IEC 25059:2023 Software engineering — Systems and software Quality Requirements and Evaluation (SQuaRE) — Quality model for AI systems (2023). https://www.iso.org/standard/80655.html
16. ISO: ISO/IEC 5338:2023 Information technology — Artificial intelligence — AI system life cycle processes (2023). https://www.iso.org/standard/81118.html
17. ISO: ISO/IEC/IEEE 15288:2023 Systems and software engineering — System life cycle processes (2023). https://www.iso.org/standard/81702.html

18. Kitsios, F., Kamariotou, M.: Artificial intelligence and business strategy towards digital transformation: a research agenda. Sustainability **13**(4), 2025 (2021)
19. Makridakis, S.: The forthcoming Artificial Intelligence (AI) revolution: its impact on society and firms. Futures **90**, 46–60 (2017). https://doi.org/10.1016/j.futures.2017.03.006
20. Oviedo, J., Rodriguez, M., Piattini, M.: An environment for the assessment of the functional suitability of AI systems. In: Bertolino, A., Pascoal Faria, J., Lago, P., Semini, L. (eds.) Quality of Information and Communications Technology, QUATIC 2024. Communications in Computer and Information Science, vol. 2178. Springer, Cham (2024). https://doi.org/10.1007/978-3-031-70245-7_2
21. Rodriguez, M., Verdugo, J., Pino, F., Delgado, B., Piattini, M.: Software development process assessment with MMIS v.2, an ISO/IEC 33000-based model. IT Prof. **23**, 17–23 (2021)
22. Sonntag, M., Mehmann, S., Mehmann, J., Teuteberg, F.: Development and evaluation of a maturity model for ai deployment capability of manufacturing companies. Inf. Syst. Manag. **42**(1), 37–67 (2024)
23. United Kingdom Government: A pro-innovation approach to AI regulation. UK's White Paper (2023)
24. Unterkalmsteiner, M., Gorschek, T., Islam, A.M., Cheng, C.K., Permadi, R.B., Feldt, R.: Evaluation and measurement of software process improvement-a systematic literature review. IEEE Trans. Softw. Eng. **38**(2), 398–424 (2011)
25. Villalta, R.M., Lara, J.V., Monje, M.R., Velthuis, M.P.: MMSIA: towards ai systems maturity assessment. In: International Conference on Software Technologies, ICSOFT 2025 (2025)

A Systematic Literature Review of Approaches to Maturity Model Implementation in Public Bodies Using Agile Initiatives

Alfredo Gabriel de Sousa Oliveira and Sandro Ronaldo Bezerra Oliveira(✉)

Graduate Program in Computer Science (PPGCC), Institute of Exact and Natural Sciences (ICEN), Federal University of Pará (UFPA), Belém, PA, Brazil
alfredo.oliveira@icen.ufpa.br, srbo@ufpa.br

Abstract. For public bodies, implementing maturity models is vital for enhancing competitiveness and service quality. Adopting flexible and adaptable processes enables organizations to better meet the demands of a dynamic society. However, adopting agile methodologies requires careful planning. The variety of agile methodologies (e.g. Scrum, SAFe and Kanban) can be confusing, making it challenging to select the most appropriate approach. Poorly planned implementation can lead to process overload, team resistance and, ultimately, failure to achieve the desired outcome. To mitigate these challenges, public bodies should invest in a gradual, personalized implementation process and process models adopted by other organizations. When choosing an agile methodology, factors such as team size, project complexity, organizational culture, and strategic objectives must be considered. Additionally, strong support from senior management and engagement from all employees are crucial. A gradual, personalized approach increases the likelihood of successfully implementing a maturity model using agile methodologies. This work presents an extended Systematic Literature Review (SLR) aimed at identifying effective approaches to implementing maturity models in public bodies. The SLR analyzed 13 primary studies, revealing practices, recommendations, standards, implementation strategies, benefits, challenges, and considerations in these processes. The shared characteristics of the implementation processes reported in different bodies suggest that these findings could form the basis for other public bodies to adopt similar methodologies. This work makes a valuable contribution by consolidating recommendations that can streamline the implementation of maturity models, enabling managers and stakeholders to develop clearer implementation plans and ensure a smoother process.

Keywords: Maturity Model · Public Body · Agile Methodology · Systematic Literature Review

1 Introduction

The landscape of software development is in a state of perpetual flux, primarily due to the increasing complexity of technology. This dynamism is the main driver behind the continuous evolution of maturity models. The rapid pace of technological obsolescence,

M. Mecella et al. (Eds.): ICSOFT 2025, CCIS 3144, pp. 105–133, 2027.
https://doi.org/10.1007/978-3-032-37353-3_5

coupled with the constant emergence of new tools and approaches, means that activities, methodologies, and processes must constantly adapt. This relentless pursuit of adaptation is essential for organizations to remain competitive and relevant in an ever-changing market.

In this context, adopting update models in the software development process, particularly within public bodies, is promising, as the ultimate goal is to deliver solutions to the general population more quickly and effectively, thereby improving the provision of public services. However, implementing such models in public sector entities is far from straightforward. Such implementations often involve navigating a complex web of relationships and challenges, including stringent legal restrictions, bureaucratic inertia leading to slowness in executing activities, and strong, often rigid, hierarchical structures within these organizations [1]. These factors collectively create a challenging environment for the successful integration of maturity models.

The historical evolution of software development methodologies has been driven by the constant pursuit of alternatives to traditional approaches. Conventional approaches are often characterized by excessive bureaucracy, which can stifle innovation and efficiency [2]. In response to these limitations, software engineering researchers began exploring strategies to make their processes more flexible and dynamic. The growing relevance of this topic is evident in the nearly 400% increase in research interest over 20 years, as shown by Google Trends (see Fig. 1), whose research was carried out in a Brazilian context. This substantial increase highlights the importance and timeliness of the debate on improving software development practices, ultimately leading to the widespread adoption of more agile approaches [3, 4].

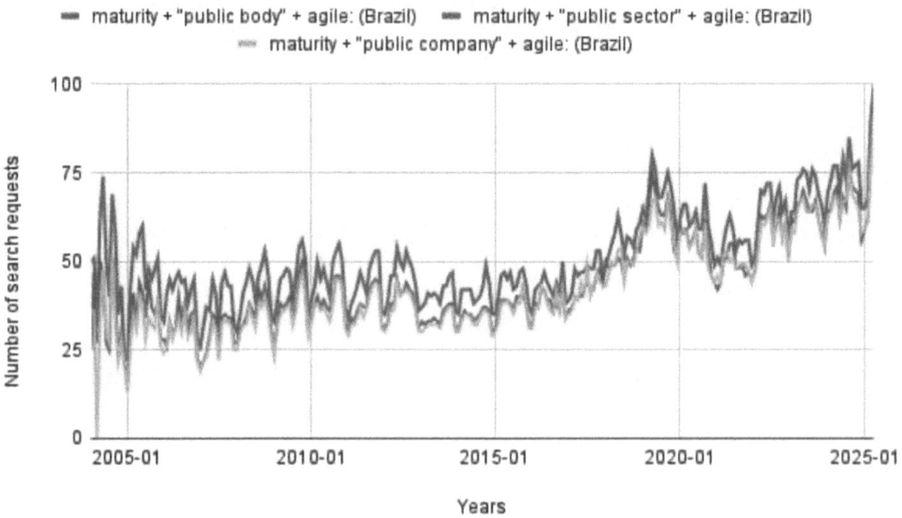

Fig. 1. Research on the topic in Google Trends.

Given this developmental trajectory, agile methodologies have emerged as prominent contenders, characterized by their inherent flexibility and adaptability. They overcome many limitations of traditional approaches by promoting better collaboration and the continuous, incremental delivery of functionalities. They also cultivate a robust ability to respond quickly and effectively to changes. The increasing demand for greater efficiency and higher quality in processes has been a significant catalyst for the widespread adoption of maturity models across various sectors, particularly in software development [5].

Building upon this context, the present work introduces a systematic literature review (SLR). This SLR was conducted with the primary objective of identifying the specific methodologies adopted for successfully implementing maturity models through integrating agile initiatives within public bodies [6]. A rigorous selection process was employed to identify 13 primary studies. These studies serve two purposes [6]: first, they present the maturity models successfully adopted by other public entities to information technology (IT) managers in public bodies, offering valuable insights and benchmarks; secondly, the SLR aims to provide concrete recommendations for activities that can be adopted effectively in the context of implementing maturity models. This includes outlining beneficial agile practices, detailing their associated benefits and impacts on organizational performance, and critically identifying difficulties and areas for improvement that could hinder the implementation of these models.

The findings of this SLR provide a comprehensive overview of the scenarios in which various public bodies have successfully implemented maturity models. The overarching goal in presenting these results is to actively encourage and facilitate the adoption of maturity models by other public sector organizations, thereby improving software development practices and enhancing public service delivery. This work builds upon [6], expanding the analysis and discussions presented in the original paper with a more extensive literature review and detailing the research methods, approaches, and challenges involved in implementing maturity models with agile initiatives in public agencies.

This work is therefore structured as follows. Following this introduction, Sect. 2 provides the fundamental concepts and definitions relevant to the topic. Section 3 describes the research methodology, while Sect. 4 details the results. Section 5 presents a discussion of these main findings. Section 6 addresses potential threats to the validity of this work and Sect. 7 reviews related research. Finally, Sect. 8 concludes the work by summarizing the main findings.

2 Background

This section describes the theoretical foundation for understanding this work.

2.1 Systematic Literature Review

Systematic reviews are a well-established research method in software engineering [7] that employ explicit and systematic approaches to gather and synthesize findings from studies addressing specific research questions [8]. These secondary studies synthesize primary studies to provide high-quality, evidence-based summaries that offer insights into effectiveness in real-world conditions, and reveal correlations between exposures and outcomes. The rigorous methodology inherent in systematic reviews ensures that data is collected impartially, thereby minimizing bias and increasing the reliability of the conclusions [9].

Beyond their analytical capabilities, systematic reviews are crucial for formulating actionable recommendations based on their findings, as well as for prioritizing future research efforts [9, 10]. They guide the development of new technologies, the improvement of existing processes, and the identification of knowledge gaps requiring further investigation, serving as a compass for researchers and practitioners. By consolidating a body of evidence, systematic reviews empower informed decision-making and drive the continuous advancement of the field of software engineering.

A systematic review that is methodologically sound is characterized by transparency, replicability, and adherence to clear eligibility criteria [11]. Transparency ensures that all steps of the process, from formulating the research question to synthesizing the results, are clearly and accessibly documented, enabling other researchers to understand and evaluate the validity of the study. Replicability means that, under the same conditions and using the same methods, an independent study should reach similar conclusions, thereby reinforcing the robustness of the findings. Adherence to rigorous eligibility criteria ensures that only relevant, high-quality studies are included, preventing contamination from research with methodological flaws or misalignment with the review's objectives.

However, although valuable, systematic reviews are often resource- and time-intensive, often requiring a team of reviewers to work over a long period to complete the process [12]. The complexity of searching and evaluating a vast range of literature, the need for multiple reviewers to ensure consistency and resolve disagreements contribute to the time-consuming and labour-intensive nature of these reviews. Careful planning, adequate resource allocation, and effective team collaboration are therefore essential to mitigate these challenges and ensure the successful completion of a systematic review. Despite these difficulties, systematic reviews play an invaluable role in generating reliable knowledge and guiding future research, making them a crucial investment in the software engineering landscape.

2.2 Maturity Models

Maturity models are crucial conceptual frameworks for evaluating an organization's level of development and inherent ability to execute specific processes. These models primarily serve to measure the efficiency and effectiveness of internal processes, offering insight into how organizational practices are implemented, managed, and controlled [13]. They are more than mere diagnostic tools; they serve as strategic roadmaps for continuous improvement. Process maturity is intrinsically linked to the adoption of practices that result in greater control, more predictable established goals, optimized costs, and a substantial increase in overall organizational performance [14]. Consequently, organizations seeking operational excellence often turn to these models to identify their strengths and weaknesses, and to chart a clear development path.

The maturity of a process is characterized by incremental stages, each requiring the implementation of increasingly sophisticated organizational practices [15]. This sequential and incremental approach ensures continuous development of organizational efficiency and promotes constant, sustained improvement [16]. Each stage represents a higher level of formalization, control, and optimization, where uncertainties are minimized and predictability is maximized. Therefore, measuring process maturity is not merely a formality, but an essential step in understanding the dynamics of process management and verifying the effective achievement of desired results. According to Gudelj et al. [17], assessing maturity enables the identification of operational gaps and opportunities for enhancement, allowing for a thorough analysis of business process implementation. This analysis enables organizations to allocate resources more efficiently, prioritize improvement initiatives, and monitor progress over time.

In addition to assessing maturity, analyzing process effectiveness is equally fundamental [18]. Process effectiveness can be defined as the extent to which planned tasks are executed in accordance with predefined requirements within an established timeframe and the extent to which these requirements are met according to previously agreed criteria [19]. While maturity focuses on 'how' processes are executed (i.e. the quality and degree of formalization), effectiveness focuses on 'what' is achieved (i.e. whether the expected results are delivered according to specifications). This duality between maturity and effectiveness is vital for a holistic view of organizational performance, as a process can be mature (well documented and controlled) yet ineffective (failing to achieve the desired objectives), or vice versa.

Against this backdrop, the importance of reference models becomes apparent. Models such as CMMI (Capability Maturity Model Integration) and MPS.BR (Brazilian Software Process Improvement) provide well-defined criteria for assessing a company's maturity. CMMI, for example, establishes an evolutionary journey across five maturity levels: Level 1 (Initial), where processes are unpredictable and reactive; Level 2 (Managed), where practices are planned and controlled at project level; Level 3 (Defined), where processes are standardized across the organization; Level 4 (Quantitatively Managed), where statistical data is used to control performance; and Level 5 (Optimizing), which is focused on continuous, proactive improvement [20].

Meanwhile, MPS.BR, adapted to the Brazilian context, offers a more granular progression with seven levels (from G to A) that map the same journey. It begins with Levels G (Partially Managed) and F (Managed), which correspond to CMMI Level 2. It then progresses through Levels E, D, and C (Defined), which are equivalent to CMMI Level 3. It culminates in Levels B (Quantitatively Managed) and A (In Optimization), which are analogous to CMMI Levels 4 and 5, respectively [21].

Adopting these models validates and solidifies the idea that mature processes are connected to operational effectiveness. By integrating these models, organizations can identify weaknesses in their processes and implement gradual, systematic improvements, consequently significantly enhancing their operational effectiveness. This creates a virtuous cycle of continuous improvement, where the maturity achieved at each stage contributes directly to optimizing results, increasing customer satisfaction, reducing risk, and consolidating a culture of excellence and innovation. Implementing these models is a continuous journey of adaptation and refinement, driving organizations to achieve ever-higher levels of performance.

2.3 Agile Methodology

For a long time, software development was closely associated with traditional methodologies, characterized by their sequential, rigid, and highly predictive nature. Approaches such as the Waterfall Model prioritized extensive documentation throughout the project life cycle, from conception to implementation. This required detailed and meticulous planning before any code could be written. The main focus was on final product delivery, and changes to requirements throughout the project's life cycle were seen as problematic and costly. However, this rigidity often resulted in delays, customer dissatisfaction, and products that did not fully meet their constantly evolving needs [3].

However, the rapid evolution of technology, the growing complexity of systems and the demand for solutions that are faster and more flexible and that align with customer expectations have spurred a revolution in software development: the emergence of agile methodologies [3]. In an era of constant uncertainty and change, traditional approaches began to show their limitations, paving the way for a new paradigm.

Published in 2001 by a group of seventeen software developers, the Agile Manifesto [3] represented a significant milestone in the transformation of project management and software development. It established a set of four fundamental values and twelve principles that contrasted directly with traditional approaches. The Agile values prioritize individuals and interactions over processes and tools (recognizing that human collaboration is more important than any formality); working software over comprehensive documentation (the value lies in a functioning product, not paperwork); customer collaboration over contract negotiation (customers should be active partners in the process); and responding to change over following a plan (adaptability is crucial in a dynamic environment) [3]. Although these values emerged in the context of software development, they transcend this sphere and are applicable in various other areas and industries. They promote greater flexibility and adaptability, as well as an uncompromising focus on customers and value delivery.

Several agile methodologies have been developed in line with the principles of the Agile Manifesto, offering specific frameworks and practices for project management [22]. The most prominent of these are defined below.

Scrum [23] is perhaps the most popular and widely adopted methodology. It divides projects into short, iterative cycles called 'sprints', typically lasting from one to four weeks. During each sprint, cross-functional teams aim to deliver a usable software increment. Scrum is characterized by well-defined roles (Product Owner, Scrum Master, and Development Team), regular events (Daily Meetings, Sprint Planning, Sprint Review, and Sprint Retrospective) and work products (Product Backlog, Sprint Backlog, and Increment), which together promote transparency, inspection, and adaptation. This approach enables teams to deliver value to customers incrementally and iteratively while receiving continuous feedback and adjusting their approach as necessary.

Unlike Scrum, Kanban does not impose a fixed development cycle, instead emphasizing continuous workflow and process visualization. It is based on a visual board (the Kanban board), on which tasks are represented by cards that move through the various stages of the workflow. The fundamental principles of Kanban include visualizing the workflow, limiting work in progress (WIP), managing and measuring the flow, making process policies explicit, and encouraging collaborative improvement. By optimizing the flow and identifying bottlenecks, Kanban enables teams to respond swiftly to changes and ensure continuous value delivery [23].

XP (eXtreme Programming) methodology focuses on practices to improve code quality and responsiveness to change. It promotes constant communication and active customer participation in the development process through practices such as pair programming, test-driven development (TDD), continuous integration, refactoring, and frequent, small-scale releases. The aim is to produce high-quality, easy-to-maintain and adaptable software, while keeping the customer involved in every step of the process [23].

Organizations that adopt agile methodologies reap a wide range of benefits. These include greater customer satisfaction, since continuous collaboration, and incremental delivery ensure the final product aligns with expectations; reduced costs, as early problem detection and adaptability minimize waste; improved product and service quality, driven by practices such as continuous feedback and automated testing; and increased team productivity, as they become more engaged, autonomous, and focused on delivering value. By prioritizing collaboration, adaptability, and continuous value delivery, agile methodologies optimize the development process and enable organizations to become more resilient, innovative, and consequently more competitive in an increasingly dynamic, volatile, and demanding global market. Agility is a mindset that empowers companies to thrive in environments of constant transformation, not just a methodology.

3 Research Methodology

As previously mentioned, this work builds upon the research of Oliveira and Oliveira [6]. Consequently, the same research methodology adopted in [6] has been employed here. Therefore, this study aims to identify the strategies and approaches used to implement maturity models adopting agile initiates in public bodies, as reported in the relevant literature. It is hypothesized that there are recurring characteristics in the practices, stages, and attention points of projects to implement maturity models in public bodies, which should be taken into consideration during implementation.

The Goal-Question-Metric (GQM) approach, developed by Basili [24], was used to formalize this study's research objective. Thus, this study seeks to:

- Analyze: primary studies using a systematic literature review (SLR),
- In order to: identify the methodologies and strategies used in implementing maturity models reported in the literature,
- Regarding: the reduction of delivery time for software products and the evolution of software development processes,
- From the point of view of: public service collaborators and users,
- In context: of public bodies.

Thus, we propose the following research questions (RQ):

- RQ1: How can maturity models be implemented in public bodies using agile methods?
- RQ2: What models and standards were used?
- RQ3: What agile methods and practices were adopted?
- RQ4: What were the benefits and impacts of implementing the models and standards?

- RQ5: What difficulties were encountered when implementing these models?
- RQ6: What are the points for improvement/attention when implementing the methodology?

To achieve the objective of this study, a systematic literature review (SLR) was conducted. An SLR is a secondary study approach that aims to systematically identify, analyze, and interpret relevant documents from primary studies in order to provide evidence relating to the established research questions [11].

We conducted the SLR between May and October 2024. The study was organized into four steps, adapted from [11, 25], as follows:

- Step 1 – Definition of research questions. In this step, six research questions were defined based on the study's objective,
- Step 2 – Search. Based on the research questions, a replicable process was defined for searching selected scientific databases,
- Step 3 – Study selection. In this step, a replicable process was defined and applied to select only the relevant studies according to the objective of this work,
- Step 4 – Study classification and data extraction. In this step, based on the research questions, we defined a strategy to: (i) map relevant data from primary studies, and (ii) present the work's results.

The work was planned and executed by two researchers: a Master's student in Computer Science and a professor/researcher with a PhD in Software Engineering.

The search was carried out automatically using a string comprising a set of keywords and their respective synonyms. These keywords were defined based on the research questions using the PICOC (Population, Intervention, Comparison, Outcomes, and Context) structure suggested in reference [11].

However, the aim of this study is merely to identify approaches related to the implementation of maturity models in public bodies, as reported in the literature, with no intention of comparing them. Therefore, the 'Comparison' criterion was discarded. Furthermore, as the 'intervention' criterion addresses the actions to be carried out, including keywords for it was unnecessary. Thus, the string was formulated with terms related to (i) population, (ii) outcomes, and (iii) context:

- Population: Public bodies,
- Outcome: Maturity model and practices applied by agile methods
- Context: Software development.

The search string used was: *("cmmi" OR "spi" OR "iso" OR "model" or "standard" or "norm") AND "agile" AND ("method*" OR "practice" OR "technique" OR "principle") AND ("bod*" OR "agency" OR "administration" OR "sector") AND ("public" OR "government").*

This search string was applied to the following databases: IEEE Xplore Digital Library, ACM DL, Scopus, and Web of Science.

This phase of the research involved applying inclusion (IC) and exclusion (EC) criteria to identify works that specifically addressed our research questions. The IC and EC are detailed below:

- IC - (IC1) Studies with public bodies that can present an implementation case of the proposed approach (use of maturity models and agile methods), as well as an evaluation of the implementation,
- EC - (EC1) Studies from before the Agile Manifesto (2001 onwards); (EC2) Studies not written in English or Portuguese; (EC3) Duplicate studies; (EC4) Studies not available for open download or via the institutional IP of the researchers; (EC5) Studies not in the form of full papers/articles.

We also included Portuguese language studies because we need to analyze studies published in Brazilian conferences. Even if these studies are written in Portuguese, they are indexed in repositories such as ACM and IEEE (used to conduct the SLR), which report on the application of maturity models in public bodies.

Each study underwent a four-step selection process: (i) Two researchers conducted a pre-selection by reading the titles and abstracts of all the studies and applying the exclusion criteria; (ii) The researchers discussed any discrepancies in applying the exclusion criteria to reach a consensus; (iii) The researchers read the titles and abstracts, and the full texts of the studies selected in the first step, if necessary, to apply the inclusion criteria; and (iv) The researchers discussed any discrepancies in applying the inclusion criteria to reach a consensus. This process resulted in thirteen primary studies (PS), which are listed in Table 1.

The Parsifal database management tool was used in the review methodology to assist with the preliminary selection and application of the inclusion and exclusion criteria. The selected data were then organized and tabulated in Google Sheets for quantitative analysis. The results were displayed in tables and charts, enabling quantitative analysis of the research data.

4 Data Summary and Extraction

This section presents the results of the SLR. An overview is provided in Subsect. 4.1. Subsections 4.2 to 4.7 detail the results for RQs 1 to 6, respectively. These subsections reference and identify primary studies by codes, which, along with the tables used to summarize the extracted data, are available at Table 1.

4.1 Bibliometric Results

The SLR search was limited to studies published between 2001 and 2024. For this study, we analyzed studies based on different inclusion and exclusion criteria. The results provide insight into the distribution and concentration of these components in relation to each criterion.

The results showed that 42 studies were excluded based on EC3, accounting for 57% of the 74 studies excluded in the post-selection stage. This suggests a high rate of duplicate studies within the context of the study. Conversely, EC1 and EC5 did not result in the removal of any of the identified studies; EC2 removed only one study. EC4 resulted in the removal of 25 studies due to the impossibility of analyzing them, and finally, after applying IC1, only 13 studies remained. Table 2 therefore presents the condensed results of applying the criteria in the selection phase.

Table 1. Selected Studies.

Identifier	Title
PS1	Business process management effectiveness and maturity through lean management practices: the Brazilian federal police experience
PS2	Development of a hybrid agile management model in local self-government units
PS3	ER2C SDMLC: enterprise release risk-centric systems development and maintenance life cycle
PS4	From a Scrum Reference Ontology to the Integration of Applications for Data-Driven Software Development
PS5	Scrum@PA: Tailoring an Agile Methodology to the Digital Transformation in the Public Sector
PS6	Towards improving agility in public administration
PS7	Lean enterprise architecture method for value chain based development in public sector
PS8	Towards a unified semantic-driven methodology framework for eGovernment systems development
PS9	Agile Implementation and Expansive Learning: Identifying Contradictions and Their Resolution Using an Activity Theory Perspective
PS10	IAMPS: an process to support the MPS. BR implementation together with agile methods
PS11	Contracting agile developments for mission critical systems in the public sector
PS12	Exploring the Landscape of e-Government Maturity Models: Insights from Systematic Mapping Study and Comparative Analysis
PS13	Towards a Process Model for Agile Transformation in E-government Projects

Table 2. Results of the Selection Phases [6].

Databases	Studies	Pre-Selection	Post-Selection
IEEE	7	2	0
Scopus	110	22	5
Web of Science	83	12	6
ACM	515	52	2
Total	715	88	13

Figure 2 highlights the scarcity of studies on the topic due to its inherent complexity and the regulations governing these bodies, which are often statutory. The ingrained bureaucratic culture of these bodies also hinders the implementation of agile methodologies. However, we saw an increase in publications in 2020, possibly due to the significant changes caused by the 2020–22 pandemic in the functioning of public bodies and the resulting need for a new organizational paradigm.

In 2021, the production of studies decreased. Nevertheless, it is important to note that the topic remained the subject of research in subsequent years, highlighting its ongoing relevance to the academic and professional communities. This temporal analysis emphasizes the growing need to understand the crucial role of software engineering in public bodies and to find ways to improve the software development process and consequently improve the delivery of solutions for the benefit of the population.

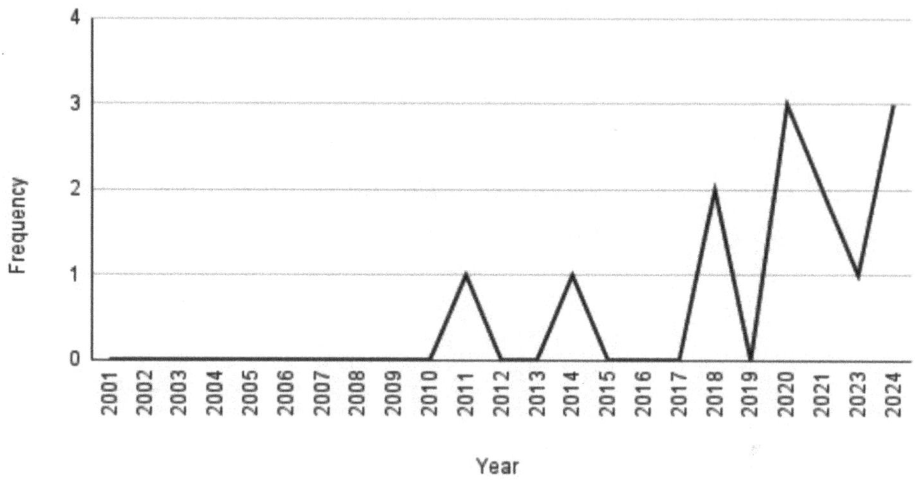

Fig. 2. Distribution of studies per year [6].

Figure 3 shows the results of a country-specific data analysis. In Latin America, only Brazil contributed to research in this area, publishing three studies representing 16.7% of the total scientific output during the analyzed period. In other countries, academic output was mostly limited to a single study, except for Germany, Italy, and Spain, which each published two studies. These findings highlight the greater level of concern among public bodies, particularly in Brazil, regarding the issue in question.

Figure 4 shows that 69.2% of studies are published in journals, compared to 30.8% in conferences. However, it is important to emphasize that the choice of publication vehicle does not appear to be related to geographic region, as both formats are present on all continents. This distribution suggests that the decision to publish in journals and/or conferences may be more closely linked to factors specific to each piece of research, such as the target audience and the stage at which the work is in development.

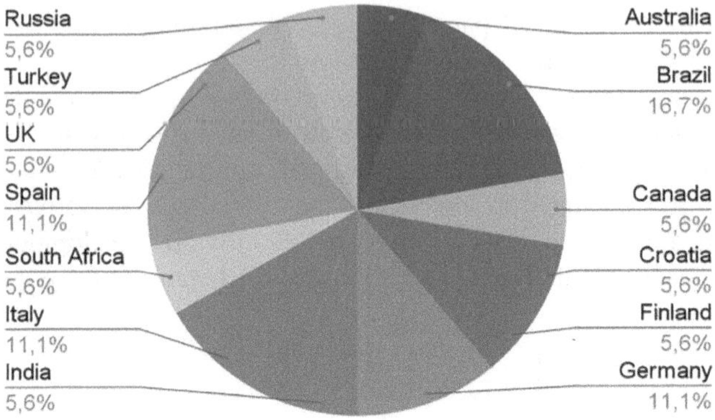

Fig. 3. Distribution of studies per country [6].

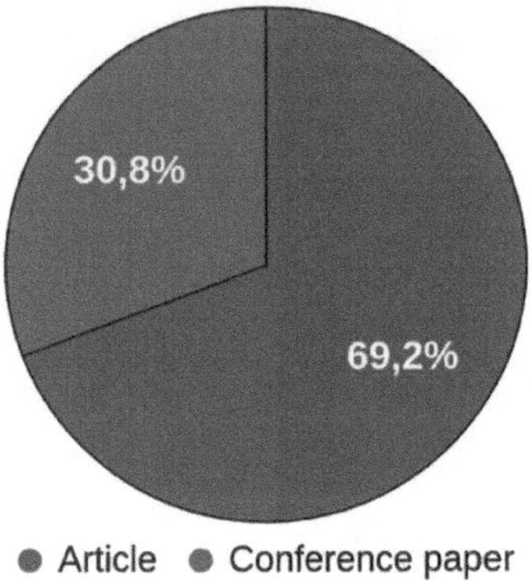

Fig. 4. Distribution by publication vehicle [6].

4.2 RQ1: How Can Maturity Models Be Implemented in Public Bodies Using Agile Methods?

An analysis of various studies has provided valuable insights into the implementation of maturity models in the public sector, shedding light on the inherent challenges and complexities involved. Notably, only a limited number of studies (PS1, PS2, PS3, PS5, PS7, and PS10) provided a clear sequence of steps essential for successfully adopting these models. This suggests a potential gap in the existing literature regarding guidelines for implementing maturity models in public bodies.

To further elucidate these findings, Table 3 provides a comprehensive overview of the identified recommendations, their corresponding citations, and their frequency of occurrence. This table serves as a crucial reference point, offering a quantitative understanding of the emphasis placed on different recommendations across the various studies. The occurrence percentages underscore the prevalence of certain strategies and implicitly indicate areas where additional research and practical guidance would be most beneficial for public sector entities seeking to enhance their organizational maturity.

Table 3. Recommendations for activities to assist in the implementation of maturity models.

Activities	Studies	Percentage
Define roles, authority and interrelationships based on Agile principles	PS2, PS5, PS10	23.08%
Definition of the communication model	PS2, PS5, PS10	23.08%
Iterative implementation of the model	PS2, PS7, PS10	23.08%
Service value	PS1, PS5	15.38%
Leadership support	PS1, PS5	15.38%
Define the basic organizational structure	PS2, PS10	15.38%
Define the necessary skills	PS2, PS5	15.38%
Definition of risks	PS3, PS10	15.38%
System view	PS1	7.69%
Long term thinking	PS1	7.69%
Waste disposal	PS1	7.69%
Continuous improvement	PS1	7.69%
Defining the probability of each risk occurring	PS3	7.69%
Ensure stakeholders receive adequate training	PS5	7.69%
Set goals	PS10	7.69%
Establish deployment group	PS10	7.69%
Know the current development process	PS10	7.69%
Propose Changes to Organizational Improvement Implementation Objectives (if applicable)	PS10	7.69%
Validate results of each iteration	PS10	7.69%
Monitor process improvement	PS10	7.69%
Publish Results	PS10	7.69%

It is important to note that the analyzed studies highlight a clear focus on the organizational structure of public institutions as a prerequisite for the introduction and implementation of maturity models. Failing to recognize this can severely compromise the effectiveness of any transformation initiative. Existing structures, which are often characterized by bureaucratic rigidity and systemic complexity, pose a significant challenge to the successful adoption and implementation of these models.

Studies PS2, PS5, and PS10 all emphasize the critical importance of meticulously preparing the organizational foundation for change. This process begins with securing the support of leadership. In this context, leadership is not merely a passive endorser, but the primary catalyst and facilitator for any paradigm shift. Once this support is in place, the organization can move on to defining and establishing a basic organizational structure that is flexible and conducive to agility. This new structure must be designed to optimize workflows and collaboration. At the same time, it is essential to form a dedicated deployment group composed of individuals with the authority to lead and manage the entire implementation effort.

Within this renewed organizational structure, clearly defining roles, assigning authority, and establishing interrelationships are all crucial aspects aligned with Agile principles. This goes beyond merely creating a list of responsibilities; it involves a deliberate attempt to clarify decision-making power at all levels and, more importantly, to encourage collaborative and synergistic relationships between different teams and departments. Once roles have been clearly defined, the organization must identify and define the necessary competencies and skills for these new positions and revised processes. This step naturally precedes the imperative need to ensure that all relevant stakeholders receive adequate and comprehensive training, equipping them with the necessary knowledge, tools, and mindset to thrive in the transformed environment.

Finally, creating and implementing a robust and transparent communication model is essential to ensure strategic alignment and visibility throughout the organization. This involves carefully selecting appropriate communication channels for different types of interaction that respect the new organizational structure. Clear and efficient pathways must be created for communicating progress, strategic objectives, and achieved results to all stakeholders to ensure everyone is informed and engaged.

The authors of studies PS2, PS7, and PS10 emphatically advocate an iterative implementation of the maturity model. This flexible approach allows for continuous adaptation and gradual learning, optimizing the process over time. The process should begin with a thorough effort to understand the organization's current development process, as this is vital for establishing an accurate baseline. From this baseline, clear, specific, and measurable goals must be set with an unwavering focus on delivering tangible service value to end users or citizens.

A central and indispensable component of this planning is the precise definition of potential risks and the assessment of the probability of each occurring. This strategic foresight enables the team to adopt a proactive stance rather than a reactive one, thereby mitigating potential negative impacts. As implementation progresses, each iterative cycle provides a valuable opportunity to propose and incorporate changes to organizational improvement implementation objectives based on new learning and insights gained. At the end of each iteration, it is crucial to rigorously validate the results to ensure they are perfectly aligned with the pre-established goals.

The entire transformation and implementation process must be guided by a philosophy of continuous improvement that goes beyond the mere execution of tasks. This mindset requires a systemic and holistic view to understand how changes in one area can affect the organization as a whole. It also requires long-term thinking to ensure that the implemented improvements are sustainable and generate lasting value. A key practice in fostering this culture is actively eliminating waste by systematically identifying and removing inefficiencies in workflows and processes. By consistently using metrics and performance indicators to monitor process improvement, and publishing the results transparently and accessibly, the organization creates a virtuous feedback loop. This cycle drives the continuous maturation of the model and catalyses sustainable organizational success.

4.3 RQ2: What Models and Standards Were Used?

After analyzing the selected studies, it was found that only PS10, of the 13 reviewed studies, followed the guidelines of the MPS.BR standardizing body and proposed a process to implement the Brazilian Software Process Improvement model (MPS.BR). To this end, PS10 integrated the development practices encouraged by agile methods, which are also suitable for projects in micro and small enterprises (MSEs). This proposal combines agile practices with the organized structure of process standardization offered by the MPS.BR Model for Software Development (MR-MPS-SW), seeking to align flexibility and formality in software development. This process is called 'Support for the Implementation of MPS – IAMPS'.

PS1 opted to apply the Lean Management methodology. First presented by Toyota, this methodology is an organizational philosophy with 5 phases: identifying value from the customer's perspective; mapping the workflow for value delivery; defining a fluid, uninterrupted workflow; developing a system to identify whether a given task is necessary for value delivery; and finally, continuous process improvement.

Similarly, PS2 proposed its own model, the Hybrid Agile Model. Derived from the Agile Manifesto, this model aims to structure existing organizational units according to human resource development and existing organizational culture in the most flexible way possible. It presents the roles and responsibilities of each member in order to complete activities in the most effective and reliable way possible while tolerating organizational changes.

PS3 presented the ER2C SDMLC model, which is compatible with the ISO 15288:2015 standard. This life cycle model is based on legal recommendations made to an Australian government body. It was developed to address continuous development systems and focuses on managing risks in product deliveries. Different levels of rigour are applied according to the project stage.

PS5 presented a variation of the Scrum model called Scrum@Scale, which focuses more on the data destination. To this end, new roles have been created to address this responsibility, while existing roles, such as the Scrum Team, have been tasked with considering population needs.

PS7 adopted Lean Enterprise Architecture (LEAD), a mandatory organizational model for local government which was adapted due to its complexity and associated costs. LEAD can be adapted to suit companies of different sizes and combines an operational model based on the value chain with agile Enterprise Architecture (EA) practices. The focus is on achieving strategic alignment between IT and business by linking EA directly to business demands and adding value for customers.

Finally, PS9 outlined the implementation of the Structured Agile Framework (SAFe), which is a set of organizational standards and workflows designed to facilitate the application of agile practices on a large scale within companies. SAFe offers a structured body of knowledge providing detailed guidance on roles and responsibilities, work planning and management, and the values that must be upheld throughout the process.

The variety of approaches highlights the methodological diversity adopted by public bodies and companies, who adapt their choices according to organizational context, applicable standards, and available resources. This flexibility in selecting and adapting models aims to overcome the specific challenges of each organization, ensuring greater efficiency and adherence to institutional needs.

4.4 RQ3: What Agile Methods and Practices Were Adopted?

Research question 3 focuses on identifying and analyzing the agile methods and practices adopted and implemented when establishing a maturity model within public sector organizations. To address this question comprehensively, Table 4 has been meticulously compiled. This table serves as a central reference point, detailing the various agile methods and practices that were explicitly mentioned or observed throughout the investigation. Furthermore, it quantifies their prevalence by presenting their percentage occurrence, offering valuable insight into the most commonly utilized approaches in this context. This detailed breakdown enables a thorough understanding of the practical application of agile methodologies in the public sector's pursuit of enhanced organizational maturity.

Table 4. Identified methods and practices present in the implemented models.

Methods and Practices	Studies	Percentage
Daily	PS2, PS3, PS5, PS7, PS9, PS10	46.15%
Planning	PS2, PS3, PS5, PS7, PS9, PS10	46.15%
Retrospective	PS2, PS3, PS5, PS7, PS9, PS10	46.15%
Backlog	PS2, PS3, PS5, PS7, PS9, PS10	46.15%
Iterative value delivery	PS2, PS3, PS5, PS7, PS9, PS10	46.15%
Requirements Engineering	PS2, PS3, PS5, PS7, PS9, PS10	46.15%
Metrics Collection	PS3, PS4, PS5, PS6, PS7, PS10	46.15%
Risk Analysis	PS2, PS3, PS5, PS9, PS10	38.46%
Interaction between participants	PS2, PS3, PS5, PS7, PS9	38.46%

Based on our analysis of the collected works (see Table 4), we identified a set of common practices in agile projects. Taking a closer look at these practices reveals how they are interconnected to create an adaptive, value-focused work environment.

Daily meeting is a quick, time-boxed synchronization ceremony (usually 15 min), during which the team aligns. It is more than just a status report; its goal is to foster transparency and self-organization. Each team member shares what they did the previous day to meet the iteration goal, what they will do today and, crucially, any impediments blocking their progress. This allows problems to be identified and resolved almost immediately.

Sprint planning held at the beginning of each cycle (sprint), defines the work to be performed. The team selects a set of items from the backlog and creates a detailed action plan to turn them into an increment of value. The meeting seeks to answer two essential questions: 'What' can be delivered in this iteration? And 'how' will the chosen work be done? The result is the Sprint Backlog, representing the team's commitment for that cycle.

Retrospective, as a pillar of continuous improvement, takes place at the end of each iteration. This structured meeting enables the team to review its work processes, discuss successes and areas for improvement, and agree on practical actions to be implemented in the next cycle. The focus is always on improving processes and collaboration to ensure that the team learns and evolves with each cycle.

Backlog is the single source of truth for all work to be carried out on a project. It is an ordered and prioritized list of all the necessary features, requirements, improvements, and fixes. It is actively managed, with items being added, removed, and re-prioritized as understanding of the product and customer needs evolves. This ensures that the team is always working on the items that offer the greatest value.

Iterative value delivery, rather than delivering everything at the end of the project in one large batch, agile development involves delivering small functional parts (increments) in short cycles (iterations). This approach enables the customer to receive value early and continuously. More importantly, it enables constant feedback to be collected, reducing the risk of building a product that is misaligned with expectations and allowing for agile course corrections.

Requirements engineering, in an agile context, is an ongoing process rather than an initial phase. Requirements are gathered and refined throughout the entire project, often using techniques such as 'user stories', which maintain focus on the end user's perspective and needs. This ensures constant alignment and enables the product to adapt to new developments.

Metrics collection, agile teams monitor their performance through metrics to make data-driven decisions. Indicators such as velocity (volume of work delivered per iteration), burndown/burnup charts (progress against time) and cycle time (time taken to complete a task) help the team understand its capacity, increase its predictability, and identify bottlenecks in the workflow.

Risk analysis is an integral part of the agile process. Short iterations, constant feedback, and daily transparency are powerful mitigation mechanisms in themselves. Rather than creating a large initial risk plan, uncertainties are identified and addressed continuously as they emerge as impediments in daily meetings, enabling a rapid and adaptive response.

Interaction between participants, in line with the Agile Manifesto's core principle of prioritizing individuals and interactions over processes and tools, collaborative communication forms the basis of the entire ecosystem. Prioritizing direct and constant dialogue among all those involved (developers, clients and users) accelerates decision-making, promotes a shared understanding, and strengthens collective responsibility for the project's success.

Upon analyzing the methods and practices used, it is noticeable that there is a convergence around the principles of the Agile Manifesto. However, it is important to emphasize that each public body makes specific adaptations to meet its particular needs and the context in which it operates.

4.5 RQ4: What Were the Benefits and Impacts of Implementing the Models and Standards?

Research question 4 aimed to identify the benefits and impact of implementing maturity models in public sector organizations. A comprehensive analysis was conducted to address this, and the findings are summarized in Table 5. This table details the various benefits identified in the literature and cross-references each benefit with the specific studies that reported it. Furthermore, it provides the percentage occurrence of each benefit, indicating its prevalence across the surveyed research. This approach provides a clear, quantitative understanding of the most frequently cited benefits of implementing maturity models in public bodies, offering valuable insights into their practical impact.

Table 5. Benefits and impacts of implementing maturity models.

Benefits and Impacts	Studies	Percentage
Stakeholder engagement	PS2, PS3, PS5, PS10	30.77%
Strategic alignment	PS2, PS3, PS5, PS10	30.77%
Definition of risk profiles	PS2, PS3, PS5, PS10	30.77%
Increased capacity and maturity	PS1, PS2, PS3, PS10	30.77%
Process optimization	PS1, PS10	15.38%
Identification of deviations	PS4, PS5	15.38%
Matrix organization	PS2	7.69%
Different levels of rigor in each iteration	PS3	7.69%
Better data management	PS5	7.69%
Easy implementation	PS7	7.69%
Reduction in the rework rate	PS10	7.69%

As reported in PS2, PS3, PS5 and PS10, engaging with stakeholders is an essential pillar for the success of any endeavour, whether a project, product, or organizational strategy. Involving these parties from the outset allows organizations to reap the benefits of their participation. These include the active collaboration of stakeholders and transparent communication about work stages and objectives. This fosters a strong sense of cohesion and belonging throughout the initiative's lifec ycle. This synergy results in greater engagement, a better understanding of expectations, and, consequently, the development of more aligned and sustainable solutions.

Strategic alignment, as detailed in PS2, PS3, PS5, and PS10, plays a crucial role in translating business values and objectives into achievable goals through the implementation of maturity models. This practice ensures that agile projects remain perfectly aligned with the organization's long-term vision, optimizes resource allocation, and maximizes the impact of initiatives. By ensuring that every action contributes to the organization's overall strategic objectives, it avoids deviations, enhances its return on investment, and strengthens its competitive position in the market.

Defining risk profiles (PS2, PS3, PS5, and PS10) is a critical step in identifying, classifying, and evaluating potential deviations and their respective impact on a company's operations. Systematically mapping these risks enables the creation of a robust and effective management plan, providing enhanced control over processes, promoting resource optimization, and enabling more assertive and informed decision-making. This proactive approach contributes significantly to risk mitigation and crisis prevention, while also driving continuous improvement of organizational processes. Applying different levels of rigour to the process (PS3) in accordance with the severity of the risks involved ensures that management efforts are proportional and effective, protecting the organization against uncertainties and unforeseen events.

Increasing an institution's capability and maturity is an evolutionary and continuous process. As the studies (PS1, PS2, PS3, and PS10) demonstrate, implementing maturity models provides a structured framework that consolidates the experiences and skills acquired over time. This systematic approach is instrumental in identifying gaps (PS4 and PS5), optimizing processes continuously (PS1 and PS10), and promoting sustainable organizational growth, notably by significantly reducing rework rates (PS10). Adopting these models enables institutions to build a solid foundation for operational excellence, innovation and adaptability, ensuring they are prepared for future challenges and can consistently deliver value to their stakeholders.

In summary, implementing maturity models in public bodies generates a wide range of benefits and positive impacts. These outcomes are intrinsically linked to the evolutionary process of the work, acting as a catalyst for the transformation of these bodies. This modernization of public management contributes to the optimization of resources and improvement of services, resulting in more efficient, effective, and transparent services for society. The application of these models strengthens governance, improves the quality of outputs, and fosters a culture of continuous improvement, which is essential for development and citizen satisfaction.

4.6 RQ5: What Difficulties Were Encountered in Implementing These Models?

The aim of research question 5 was to identify the most common challenges faced when implementing maturity models in public sector organizations. Table 6 provides a comprehensive illustration of the primary obstacles, which are intricately linked to the inherent bureaucratic nature of public bodies. These bureaucratic hurdles can manifest in various ways, from communication-related complexities such as convoluted approval processes or fragmented information flow, to more substantial external pressures. These external pressures often stem from the broader governmental or political landscape and include rigid legal frameworks, shifting policy priorities and a general resistance to change deeply embedded within public administrative culture. Consequently, successful implementation requires addressing not only internal organizational inefficiencies, but also navigating and mitigating these significant external influences that can impede progress.

Table 6. Difficulties reported in implementation.

Difficulties	Studies	Percentage
Adjustment of the functional organizational structure to a more flexible structure	PS2, PS7	15.38%
Promoting cross-functional communication	PS2, PS13	15.38%
Legal constraints	PS7, PS13	15.38%
Lack of funding	PS2	7.69%
Rigid hierarchical structure	PS13	7.69%
Organization of roles within the work framework	PS2	7.69%
The issue of individual responsibility	PS2	7.69%
Evaluation of project progress and success	PS2	7.69%
Alignment of Agile practice with LSGU regulations	PS2	7.69%
Lack of Procurement Sector	PS2	7.69%
Correct definition of the level of rigor of an iteration	PS3	7.69%

Studies PS2 and PS7 both highlight the rigidity of organizational structures as a key obstacle to successfully implementing maturity models. In many public institutions, traditional hierarchies and rigid departmentalization create information silos and hinder cross-sectoral collaboration. To mitigate this, it is crucial to promote organizational restructuring that prioritizes flexibility, integration, and alignment with shared strategic goals. This may involve creating cross-functional teams, revising workflows, and adopting more agile approaches to allow faster adaptation to changes and societal demands. The culture of bureaucracy, which is often deeply ingrained after decades of practice, must gradually be replaced by a culture of innovation and adaptability.

Studies PS2 and PS13 corroborate the problem of structural rigidity by highlighting the difficulty of inter-functional communication as a significant obstacle. Without effective communication channels or a culture of information sharing, collaboration is compromised and the achievement of organizational goals is hindered. To overcome this, it is crucial to foster integration between the various areas by encouraging the exchange of knowledge, discussion of ideas, and teamwork. Implementing collaborative platforms, promoting interdepartmental meetings, and establishing joint goals can contribute to more fluid communication and building a more cohesive work environment.

Studies PS7 and PS13 demonstrate that legal restrictions pose a significant obstacle to the implementation of maturity models within public bodies. The obligation to adhere to rigid and occasionally inefficient processes, such as TOGAF and other frameworks, restricts the flexibility and capacity for innovation of organizations. While legal compliance is important, it is crucial to strike a balance that enables the adoption of more modern, adaptable approaches without compromising transparency, and accountability. This may require critically analyzing existing regulations, proposing legislative adjustments and flexibly interpreting norms to accommodate innovation within legal limits. Exploring governance models that allow for controlled experimentation and continuous learning is a promising approach.

Study PS2 highlights the lack of funding as a significant challenge for public institutions. Insufficient financial resources for executing projects and acquiring modern technologies compromises these institutions' ability to meet societal demands fully. Scarcity of resources not only limits the implementation of maturity models, but also the expansion of essential services and the continuous improvement of operations. To address this issue, it is essential to seek alternative funding sources, optimize the allocation of existing resources, and demonstrate the return on investment of maturity projects in order to justify larger budget allocations. Developing long-term investment plans and pursuing strategic partnerships can also be viable solutions.

Study PS13 supplements the discussion on organizational rigidity, emphasizing the rigid hierarchical structure as a substantial impediment to employee involvement in decision-making processes. Centralization of power and limited autonomy at lower levels hinder fluid communication, inhibit the exchange of ideas, and restrict the organization's ability to innovate and adapt to change. To overcome this, a culture must be promoted that values the active participation of employees at all levels, encouraging them to propose solutions, discuss problems, and contribute to continuous improvement. Implementing feedback mechanisms, creating multidisciplinary working groups, and delegating responsibilities can foster a more participatory and engaging environment.

The difficulty in defining roles and responsibilities, as discussed in PS2, is closely linked to organizational culture. In many cases, civil servants' resistance to taking on new responsibilities or adapting to new work models reflects a culture that values comfort zones and discourages proactivity. Implementing maturity models requires profound cultural change, encouraging collaboration, autonomy, responsibility, and results-driven thinking. To promote this transformation, investment is needed in training and development programs, awareness campaigns and an environment that values continuous learning and experimentation. Leadership must act as a catalyst for this change by exemplifying the desired values.

Finally, Study PS2 highlights the difficulty that public institutions face in evaluating the progress and success of their projects. The absence of clear metrics and indicators, coupled with an ineffective monitoring system, makes it challenging to measure results, pinpoint areas for improvement, and justify investments. To address this issue, it is essential to develop and implement a robust monitoring and evaluation system. This should include defining relevant performance indicators, regularly collecting data, and analyzing the results. Using Business Intelligence (BI) tools and training employees in data analysis can contribute to more accurate evaluations and evidence-based decision-making. Transparency in disclosing results, including both successes and challenges, is also fundamental to building trust and legitimizing efforts to improve maturity.

In summary, implementing maturity models in public bodies is a challenging yet essential process for modernizing and improving the efficiency of public administration. Overcoming the obstacles identified in the studies requires a comprehensive strategic vision integrating structural, cultural, technological, and procedural changes, with continuous improvement and value delivery to society always at the forefront.

4.7 RQ6: What Are the Points for Improvement/attention in Implementing the Methodology?

When implementing maturity models, it is crucial to identify areas for improvement and collect data from previous experiences to ensure the success of the initiative. Analyzing reports from other studies enables the creation of a more effective action plan, overcoming common challenges and optimizing results. Table 7 summarizes the main points identified for attention in the PS2, PS5, and PS9 studies. It presents the points for improvement/attention, the studies that cite them, and the percentage of occurrence, in order to support other bodies seeking to implement maturity models.

Table 7. Points for improvement and attention reported.

Points of Improvement/Attention	Studies	Percentage
Constant Training	PS2, PS5, PS9	23.08%
Communication Plan	PS2, PS5	15.38%
Formation of Cross-Functional Teams	PS5	7.69%
Adoption by all interested parties	PS9	7.69%

The continuous training of employees is a fundamental and indispensable pillar for the successful implementation of maturity models within public bodies. It is a recurring theme cited as a priority in 23% of the works identified in specialized literature (PS2, PS5, and PS9). This finding highlights the strategic importance of investing in the development and enhancement of civil servants' skills. By promoting in-depth, systematic learning about all stages of a maturity model, from conception and planning to execution and evaluation, governmental institutions can ensure that proposed changes are fully understood and applied effectively and consistently in day-to-day organizational activities. This process of knowledge internalization is crucial for maturity methodologies to be organically integrated into organizational culture, transforming them into an intrinsic part of an institution's modus operandi. Consequently, maturity models cease to be perceived as mere obstacles or management impositions, and are recognized and valued as genuine, powerful tools for continuously improving processes, and driving the efficiency and quality of public services.

Alongside training, developing an effective and comprehensive communication plan is a valuable strategic tool for successfully implementing maturity models in public bodies (PS2, PS5). When well-planned and executed, communication has the power to unite and engage everyone involved. This strategic plan ensures that all phases of the implementation process are communicated impeccably—with clarity, objectivity and complete transparency—to all stakeholders, without exception. This includes everyone from senior management, who define guidelines and strategies, to front-line employees, who execute daily tasks and act as agents of change. The primary objective is to ensure that each participating individual understands the 'why' as well as the 'what' of the adopted practices and tools—that is, the underlying purpose and the greater goal of improving the public body's productivity and value delivery. This shared understanding fosters alignment, minimizes resistance, and builds an environment of collaboration and co-responsibility.

Additionally, the formation and operation of multifunctional teams (PS5) is one of the essential pillars for successfully implementing maturity models. By bringing together professionals with diverse knowledge, experience, and perspectives from different areas, departments and hierarchical levels, these teams can provide a holistic, integrated view of organizational processes. This diversity of viewpoints is a potent catalyst for innovation and allows areas for improvement to be identified that might go unnoticed in a departmental approach. Furthermore, multifunctional teams facilitate the development of more comprehensive, robust, and effective solutions by considering multiple angles and impacts. Complementing this strategy, the active and continuous involvement of all stakeholders (PS9) from the outset is crucial for the success and sustainability of the changes. When invited to participate and contribute from the outset, those involved develop a strong sense of belonging and consequently a deeper commitment to the proposed changes. This early and constant engagement strengthens the legitimacy of the initiatives and significantly increases the chances that the results will be lasting and effectively incorporated into the public body's routine and culture.

5 Analysis of Results

This section summarizes our key findings and impressions of the results presented in Sect. 4.

Thus, with the aim of identifying the challenges and strategies involved in implementing maturity models in public bodies, our detailed investigation revealed that, while the inherent bureaucracy of the public sector presents a central obstacle, the feasibility of implementing these models is supported by a flexible approach guided by adaptable recommendations and a continuous commitment to process improvement. Analysis of the various studies consulted converges on the conclusion that bureaucracy rooted in the organizational structure of public bodies is the main factor hindering the implementation of maturity models. The most frequently cited difficulties, present in 15.38% of the studies (PS2, PS7, and PS13), are:

- Adjustment of the organizational structure: The rigidity of hierarchical structures and departmentalization makes it difficult to adapt to new methodologies and reallocate resources and responsibilities,
- Legal constraints: Public sector-specific legislation, while essential for transparency and legality, often imposes barriers to more agile and innovative processes,
- Difficulty of inter-functional communication: A culture of information silos between different departments and hierarchical levels impedes the efficient flow of data and the collaboration necessary for implementing maturity models.

These issues are intrinsic to public service and are deeply ingrained in an organizational culture that has historically prioritized stability and compliance over agility and innovation.

Despite the challenges presented, the cataloged studies offer valuable recommendations for overcoming these problems. The most frequently cited strategies, present in 23.08% of the works, are as follows:

- Clear definition of roles, authority, and interrelationships based on agile principles: Adopting agile principles that focus on collaboration, self-organization, and adaptability allows for a more fluid redefinition of responsibilities and a more efficient workflow,
- Definition of an effective communication model: Creating clear and open communication channels that promote the exchange of information among all stakeholders is fundamental to breaking down silos and fostering collaboration,
- Iterative implementation of the model: The iterative approach involves implementation in short cycles with constant feedback, allowing for continuous adjustments and improvements while minimizing risks and facilitating adaptation to specific contexts.

It is noteworthy that the studies do not rigidly prescribe documents or ceremonies. Instead, they emphasize the importance of reporting the context and objectives of each recommendation, providing a flexible guide. The diversity of models and standards adopted demonstrates this flexibility, as they are adjusted to the reality of each body. For instance, study PS10 outlines a process to facilitate the implementation of MR-MPS-SW in Brazil, whereas PS7 illustrates the implementation of LEAD, a mandatory model in Finland. This variety reinforces the idea that successful implementation relies on adaptable activity recommendations rather than rigid obligations.

In terms of practices, there is strong alignment with the principles of the Agile Manifesto. Examples of these practices include daily meetings (Daily Scrums), collaborative planning, retrospectives for continuous learning, maintaining a task backlog, and iterative value delivery. These practices are present in 46.15% of the identified studies. This high prevalence highlights the importance and added value of these practices in the implementation of maturity models in public bodies.

Implementing these models and practices generates significant benefits for public bodies. The most frequently cited practices, present in 30.77% of the studies, were:

- Stakeholder engagement: Proximity to stakeholders allows for a better understanding of the population's needs, which contributes to reducing rework and increasing citizen satisfaction,
- Strategic alignment: Implementing maturity models aligns activities with the organization's strategic objectives, thereby enhancing the delivery of value to society,
- Definition of risk profiles: Identifying and managing risks more effectively enables public bodies to anticipate problems and implement mitigating measures more efficiently.

Beyond the initial implementation difficulties, the analysis highlights the importance of focusing on the continuity and sustainability of the maturity model. Attention must be given to the continuous training of employees (cited in 23.08% of the studies, e.g. PS2, PS5, PS9) and the creation of an effective communication plan (mentioned in 15.38% of the studies, e.g. PS2, PS5). These elements are crucial for:

- Internalizing the new practices in the organizational culture: Continuous training and communication ensure that the new methodologies become an integral part of the organization's daily operations,

- Ensuring long-term success: Maintaining engagement and continuously adapting the model to new circumstances is essential to ensuring the long-term success of the organization.

In summary, implementing maturity models using agile initiatives in public bodies is a challenging but viable process. Success fundamentally depends on the ability to customize the process by adapting best practices and recommendations to the particular reality of each organization, regardless of any preexisting legal or cultural restrictions.

The innovative nature of this work lies in consolidating findings on a topic with scarce literature, thereby filling a significant knowledge gap. By offering a comprehensive and practical overview, this study can guide other public entities in modernizing their processes, optimizing the delivery of value to society, and promoting a culture of continuous improvement and adaptability. Therefore, flexibility and resilience are the pillars of transforming bureaucracy into fertile ground for innovation and efficiency in public service.

6 Threats to Validity

This section addresses potential threats to the validity of the study and outlines the measures implemented to mitigate them, in line with the suggested framework.

6.1 Construct Validity

To test the effectiveness of the search string and ensure that the systematic literature review (SLR) provided relevant studies, four studies that met the search criteria were manually selected. The search string was then run against the databases and returned the same four studies, confirming its effectiveness.

6.2 Internal Validity

To ensure impartiality and accuracy during the extraction process, studies were assessed and ranked through discussions and consensus in weekly meetings. We recognize that subjective judgement can introduce bias into some studies, and we sought to mitigate this through our collaborative and judicious approach to study selection.

6.3 External Validity

It is possible that the SLR does not provide all the relevant studies on the strategies and approaches applied when implementing agile maturity models in public bodies. To mitigate this risk, we identified and relied on analogous studies, thus avoiding starting the search from scratch.

6.4 Conclusion Validity

To ensure the validity of our conclusions, Sect. 4 presents tables that illustrate the results obtained directly from the data. The observations, approaches and concerns that emerge from these results are discussed to ensure a high degree of traceability between the data and the conclusions. The study's corpus is available to other researchers, and the SLR process was overseen by a professor with a PhD and extensive experience in conducting similar studies, with a proven track record of publications in software engineering.

7 Related Works

Okan [26] conducted a systematic literature mapping study (SLM) to identify and compare maturity models proposed between 2010 and 2022. To this end, the authors selected and evaluated 17 studies. The main reports refer to the evaluation of maturity models implemented by public bodies, which the authors argue are more robust because they consider the application context.

It is noted from the related work that there is some distinction in relation to this study, as it focused on identifying the approaches adopted in the implementation of maturity models in public bodies.

8 Conclusion

This systematic literature review, conducted between May and October 2024, meticulously investigated existing approaches to implementing maturity models using agile initiatives within public bodies. A comprehensive search was conducted across four leading academic repositories: the ACM Digital Library, IEEE Xplore, Scopus, and Web of Science. From an initial pool of 715 identified works, a rigorous selection process yielded 13 highly relevant studies. These studies covered the substantial period from 2001 to 2024, offering a comprehensive historical overview of the development and application of agile maturity models in the public sector.

Analyzing the selected literature revealed a wealth of recommendations that are crucial for successfully implementing agile methodologies. These recommendations covered various critical areas, such as defining roles and responsibilities within agile teams, clarifying the relationships between different organizational units involved in agile adoption, and establishing effective communication models to promote transparency and collaboration. Together, these insights provide a framework to help managers, consultants, and key stakeholders in public bodies develop strategic implementation plans, set clear goals and objectives for their agile initiatives, and use existing experiences and best practices to overcome potential challenges.

Some contributions to society and academia that can be highlighted from this work include:

- Dissemination of implementation cases: The review consolidates and disseminates real-world examples of the implementation of the maturity model using agile initiatives within public bodies, offering invaluable practical insights and lessons learned,

- Presentation of common practices and recommendations: It systematically presents common practices and actionable recommendations for effectively adopting and scaling agile methodologies in the public sector, serving as a practical guide for practitioners,
- Showcasing benefits and impacts: The work highlights the tangible benefits and positive impacts of implementing maturity models, including improved project success rates, enhanced stakeholder satisfaction, and increased organizational efficiency,
- Highlighting potential difficulties: It candidly addresses potential difficulties and obstacles that may arise during implementation, enabling organizations to anticipate and mitigate risks proactively,
- Identifying critical points for effective implementation: The review pinpoints critical success factors and key considerations for achieving effective and sustainable agile maturity in public sector organizations,
- Contributing to resource waste reduction: By promoting efficient and effective agile adoption, the research ultimately helps to reduce resource waste, optimize public expenditure, and maximize value delivered to citizens.

Ultimately, this research serves as a comprehensive and authoritative guide, empowering public bodies to adopt agile methodologies with confidence and effectiveness. In doing so, it enables them to deliver enhanced value to the populations they serve, fostering greater responsiveness, transparency, and efficiency in public services.

Despite its valuable contributions, the study acknowledges certain limitations. A significant challenge was the scarcity of reports on the implementation of maturity models using agile initiatives within public bodies in the existing academic literature. This highlights a gap in current research and documentation practices. Furthermore, some potentially relevant studies could not be included in the review due to limitations in accessing their full content, highlighting challenges related to open access and data availability.

Regarding future work, the results of this review can inform a more in-depth investigation into problems related to the implementation of maturity models by public bodies. This could include a deeper investigation into the specific factors that contribute to failed adoption attempts, providing crucial insights to prevent similar outcomes in the future. Additionally, analyzing and adapting the best practices identified in this systematic review based on case studies and empirical research involving public agencies that have successfully adopted maturity models and agile practices could facilitate broader and more effective adoption across the public sector.

References

1. Looks, H.: A reference framework for agile transformation in public administration. In: CAiSE (Doctoral Consortium), pp. 62–68 (2022). ISSN 1613–0073
2. Nuottila, J., Aaltonen, K., Kujala, J.: Challenges of adopting agile methods in a public organization. Int. J. Inf. Syst. Proj. Manag. **4**(3), 65–85 (2016)
3. Vacari, I.: Um estudo empírico sobre a adoção de métodos ágeis para desenvolvimento de software em organizações públicas. Dissertação (Mestrado) – Faculdade de Informática, Pontifícia Universidade Católica do Rio Grande do Sul, PUCRS, Porto Alegre, RS, Brazil (2015)

4. Almeida, F.: Challenges in migration from waterfall to agile environments. World J. Comput. Appl. Technol. (CEASE PUBLICATION) **5**(3), 39–49 (2017)
5. Gonçalves, M. B., Paiva, D., Cagnin, M. I.: IAMPS: an process to support the MPS.BR implementation together with agile methods. In: 2014 XL Latin American Computing Conference, Uruguay (2014)
6. Oliveira, A.G.S., Oliveira, S.R.B.: Approaches adopted in the implementation of maturity models using agile initiatives in public bodies: a systematic literature review. In: 20th International Conference on Software Technologies - ICSOFT, ISBN 978–989–758–757–3, ISSN 2184–2833, SciTePress, pp. 120–131 (2025)
7. Budgen, D., Brereton, P., Drummond, S., Williams, N.: Reporting systematic reviews: some lessons from a tertiary study. Inf. Softw. Technol. **95**, 62–74 (2018)
8. Page, M.J., McKenzie, J.E., Bossuyt, P.M., et al.: The PRISMA 2020 statement: an updated guideline for reporting systematic reviews. BMJ **372**(71) (2021)
9. Sargeant, J.M., Reynolds, K., Winder, C.B., O'Connor, A.M.: Completeness of reporting of systematic reviews in the animal health literature: a meta-research study. Prev. Vet. Med. **195**, 105472 (2021)
10. Page M.J., Moher, D., Bossuyt, P.M., et al.: PRISMA 2020 explanation and elaboration: updated guidance and exemplars for reporting systematic reviews. BMJ **372**(160) (2021)
11. Kitchenham, B., Charters, S.: Guidelines for performing systematic literature reviews in software engineering. EBSE Technical Report, University of Durham (2007)
12. Belur, J., Tompson, L., Thornton, A., Simon, M.: Interrater reliability in systematic review methodology: exploring variation in coder decision-making. Sociological Methods Res. **50**(2), 837–865 (2018)
13. Carr, C.N., Carr, R.F., Do Nascimento, C.M., Mendes, G.A., Da Silva, I.H.M., Magalhães, A.F.B., Santos, A.J. de S.: Uma Análise Comparativa entre os Modelos de Maturidade de Processos de Software MPS-BR e CMMI: Descobrindo as Diferenças e Semelhanças. Revista Contemporânea **3**(6) 4959–4986 (2023)
14. Lockamy, A. III., McCormack, K.: The development of a supply chain management process maturity model using the concepts of business process orientation. Supply Chain Manage. Int. J. **9**(4), 272–278 (2004)
15. Škrinjar, R., Bosilj-Vukšić, V., Indihar-Štemberger, M.: The impact of business process orientation on financial and non-financial performance. Bus. Process. Manag. J. **14**(5), 738–754 (2008)
16. Vlahovic, N., Milanovic, L., Skrinjar, R.: Turning points in business process orientation maturity model: an east european survey. WSEAS Trans. Bus. Econ. **7**(1), 22–32 (2010)
17. Gudelj, M., Delic, M., Kuzmanovic, B., Tesic, Z., Tasic, N.: Business process management model as an approach to process orientation. Int. J. Simul. Model **20**(2), 255–266 (2021)
18. Dumas, M., La Rosa, M., Mendling, J., Reijers, H.A.: Fundamentals of Business Process Management, 2nd edn. Springer, , Heidelberg (2018)
19. Seyyedamiri, N., Tajrobehkar, L.: Social content marketing, social media and product development process effectiveness in high-tech companies. IJOEM **16**(1), 75–91 (2019)
20. Faria, K. S. O.: Uma análise sobre a aplicabilidade de modelos de maturidade em empresas de desenvolvimento de Software no Brasil. Rima - Universidade Federal Rural do Rio de Janeiro (2024)
21. Softex: Guia Geral MPS de Software. Brazil (2024)
22. de Oliveira, R.A., Zych, D.R., Oliveira, J.D., Michaloski, A.O.: Desafios no uso de metodologias ágeis de gestão de projetos em órgãos públicos: um estudo de caso da Receita Estadual do Paraná. Revista de Gestão e Projetos **11**(2), 12–36 (2020)
23. Lemma, M. G., Garcia, N., Kifle, M.: Systematic Literature Review Report on the Challenges of Agile Scrum. Preprints.org (2025)

24. Basili, V.R.: Software modeling and measurement: the Goal/Question/Metric paradigm. Technical Report, University of Maryland at College Park, United States (1992)
25. Petersen, K., Vakkalanka, S., Kuzniarz, L.: Guidelines for conducting systematic mapping studies in software engineering: an update. Inf. Softw. Technol. **64**, 1–18 (2015)
26. Okan, A.A.: Exploring the landscape of e-Government maturity models: insights from systematic mapping study and comparative analysis. Digital Government: Res. Practice **5**(2), 1–26 (2024)

Software Systems and Applications

Developing and Configuring Artificial-Intelligence Systems in Manufacturing: Adoption Insights from a Practitioner Survey

Richard May[1(✉)], Leonard Cassel[2], Hashir Hussain[1], Muhammad Talha Siddiqui[1], Tobias Niemand[3], Paul Scholz[4], and Thomas Leich[1]

[1] Harz University of Applied Sciences, Wernigerode, Germany
{rmay,u38568,u38641,tleich}@hs-harz.de
[2] Fraunhofer Institute for Production Technology IPT, Aachen, Germany
leonard.cassel@ipt.fraunhofer.de
[3] Siemens Mobility GmbH, Brunswick, Germany
tobias.niemand@siemens.com
[4] Hilti AG, Thüringen, Austria
paul.scholz@hilti.com

Abstract. Artificial-Intelligence (AI) systems are increasingly regarded as key enablers of smart manufacturing, offering benefits such as reduced downtime, improved efficiency, or enhanced quality. Yet, the adoption of scientific approaches in practice remains limited due to persistent challenges in appropriate transfer, implementation, deployment, and configuration. In this article, we report on a survey with 26 AI-system practitioners from the manufacturing domain, focusing on their opinions and experience regarding three pillars: development, configuration, and perceived value. Our results show that development is primarily hindered by data quality and integration barriers, while configuration problems, such as version conflicts or unintended feature interactions, occur frequently and lead to business-critical impacts, including downtime and vulnerabilities. Nevertheless, practitioners perceive clear value in AI systems, especially in predictive maintenance, although broader applications, such as real-time optimization or advanced quality control, remain underexploited. Overall, the study provides valuable insights into how AI systems are currently adopted in manufacturing practice. The findings highlight the need for configurable, reusable, and scalable solutions, as well as systematic data management and configuration practices to facilitate sustainable adoption in manufacturing settings.

Keywords: Artificial Intelligence · Manufacturing · Production · Value · Adoption · Configuration · Challenges · Survey

M. Mecella et al. (Eds.): ICSOFT 2025, CCIS 3144, pp. 137–164, 2027.
https://doi.org/10.1007/978-3-032-37353-3_6

1 Introduction

In recent years, Artificial Intelligence (AI) has gained increasing relevance in manufacturing, supporting the transition from traditional to data-driven processes based on advanced machine learning (ML) capabilities. The concept of smart manufacturing exploits the large volumes of data generated by machines and their components, which are typically embedded in complex cyber-physical systems [70]. Leveraging their data enables a broad range of applications, such as recommender systems, computer vision, or robotics [55], offering measurable benefits including improved efficiency, shorter production times, or cost savings [38,44]. With rising data volumes and growing processing capabilities, AI applications are becoming increasingly complex, often connected in systemic contexts that form entire AI systems, i.e., connecting multiple software and hardware layers while covering data acquisition, processing, and decision-making [5]. Not surprisingly, AI systems as a specific type of cyber-physical systems are therefore inherently complex. In recent years, however, an additional layer of complexity has emerged through their configurability, i.e., AI systems are typically high-configurable systems [43]. While configurability enables AI systems to be adapted to diverse industrial use cases and stakeholder demands (e.g., the strategic triangle [54]), it simultaneously creates new challenges for their effective adoption and operation [26,68].

A variety of AI systems for manufacturing has already been proposed in research, for example, in predictive maintenance and condition monitoring [28,50,51]. Yet, only a limited number of these solutions are transferred into industrial practice [39,56], as many research prototypes lack the required maturity, standardization, or economic justification to overcome the so-called *valley-of-death* between scientific innovation and industrial adoption [9]. Thus, only a few companies have successfully adopted AI systems to gain competitive advantages [21]. This disconnect between research progress and industrial adoption has already motivated studies on adoption processes and best practices [44].

What remains largely underexplored, in contrast to the research perspective, is the perspective of practitioners, i.e., those directly involved in the development, integration, and daily operation of AI systems. Moreover, while existing studies provide conceptual views on technical potentials and adoption, empirical insights from practice are rare. In particular, little is known about how practitioners adopt AI systems in heterogeneous environments, configure them to specific requirements, or perceive their added value. This lack of knowledge is largely explained by the novelty of such systems and their comparatively slow integration into industrial practice [28,56].

In previous work [32], we reported results on adoption challenges and perceived value based on a survey with 26 experts on AI systems in manufacturing. In this extended article, we present the full scope of the survey and provide a more comprehensive analysis that connects these earlier findings with additional insights into configuration and practitioners' experiences in dealing with it. Accordingly, our study not only revisits adoption and added value but also integrates them with configuration aspects in the context of the application of

AI systems. In this way, we aim to identify the key insights into ✿ development, ☰ configuration, and 📈 personal experiences related to the added value of AI systems. To the best of our knowledge, this is the first work that systematically combines the perspectives of AI-system practitioners on adoption, configuration, and added value from a software-oriented perspective. Overall, our contributions are as follows:

- ✿ **Development:** We highlight the main challenges practitioners face when adopting AI systems in manufacturing and discuss the strategies they use to address them.
- ☰ **Configuration:** We examine how practitioners deal with configuration issues related to AI systems as well as their handling strategies.
- 📈 **Experiences:** We describe how practitioners perceive the implementation incentives and added value of AI systems in manufacturing practice.
- **Repository:** We provide a publicly available repository, including the questionnaire and all participant responses to enable replication and further analysis.[1]

Overall, our study provides a comprehensive understanding of what challenges practitioners face in AI-system development and configuration, why they implemented them, and how they perceive their added value for smart manufacturing. In this way, we aim to support both researchers and practitioners in improving development, deployment, and (successful) long-term adoption. Some insights may also extend beyond the manufacturing domain, highlighting their relevance in other cyber-physical contexts. Note that our findings have not yet been validated, which, however, is already planned in the context future follow-up studies.

The remainder of this paper is structured as follows: Sect. 2 introduces essential background on smart manufacturing and AI systems. Next, Sect. 3 outlines our research objective, questions, and study design. In Sect. 4 we systematically present the survey results. After that, Sect. 5 discusses these results structured according to our research questions. Then, we consider potential threats to validity in Sect. 6. In Sect. 7 we describe related work and describes how our work contributes to the research landscape. Finally, in Sect. 8 we conclude the article, including directions for future research.

2 Background

Next, we give background information on the two main fields of this study: smart manufacturing and AI systems. In particular, the theoretical framework brings together smart manufacturing as the main application area and AI systems as the technological foundation.

[1] https://doi.org/10.5281/zenodo.17235195.

2.1 Smart Manufacturing

Smart manufacturing describes the integration of digital technologies and data-driven processes into industrial cyber-physical systems. In this paradigm, components, machines, and systems are interconnected through Internet-of-Things-enabled sensors, advanced analytics, or robotic automation, enabling real-time monitoring or even predictive decision-making. In particular, smart manufacturing aims to increase flexibility, efficiency, and product quality while maintaining responsiveness to dynamic environments [16,22].

The foundations of the transformation from traditional to smart manufacturing are rooted in production management, which traditionally focuses on the planning, design, control, and monitoring of manufacturing systems to achieve the strategic triangle of cost efficiency, quality, and delivery performance [54]. However, these goals are interdependent. For example, efforts to lower costs can inadvertently compromise quality or timeliness [4]. Smart manufacturing addresses such tensions through adaptive processes and by incorporating lean principles, where continuous improvement and waste reduction enhance organizational performance [14,53]. Configurability plays an increasing role here, as the modification of systems, their components and parameters, or whole workflows enables adaptation to stakeholder requirements (e.g., industry standards, use cases) but simultaneously adds complexity to system management [64,65].

At the center of smart manufacturing is the use of data as a strategic resource. High-quality data forms the foundation for deriving information and actionable insights, and therefore determines the success of ML and other advanced approaches (e.g., deep learning). Quality requirements extend across dimensions such as accuracy, completeness, consistency, relevance, interpretability, and accessibility [56,66]. Failure to meet these criteria undermines the reliability of decisions and predictions, highlighting the importance of systematic data (pre)processing [41].

2.2 Artificial-Intelligence Systems

AI systems, a specific type of cyber-physical systems, are typically designed to perform tasks that traditionally require human intelligence by leveraging computational techniques to process large amounts of data and recognize patterns [33,57]. Introduced conceptually by John McCarthy in 1956, AI has since become a core element of modern manufacturing and an essential response to the growing complexity and variability of manufacturing data [35,49]. By automating analysis and decision-making, AI systems relieve human operators from tasks that are increasingly infeasible to perform manually [60].

At their core, AI systems are built on ML, which generates models from data rather than explicit programming [47]. Through iterative training, these models refine their internal parameters and improve predictive accuracy over time [8]. Advanced approaches such as deep learning, inspired by neural architectures, extend these capabilities to high-dimensional and unstructured data [35,56]. AI systems are typically characterized by their learning strategies (i.e., supervised, unsupervised, reinforcement, or hybrid), the tasks they address (e.g., classification, regression, prediction), and the operations they employ (e.g., neural networks, decision trees) [11,19,28,37]. The growing variability of strategies and applications expands the potential of AI systems, but also increases the number of configuration decisions, thereby raising system complexity [2,32].

Practical applications in manufacturing are diverse, ranging from predictive maintenance and condition monitoring to process optimization and quality assurance [52]. Their success, however, depends critically on the quality and representativeness of training data. Issues, such as imbalanced datasets, sensor drift, or changing operating conditions, can compromise performance if not addressed with appropriate preprocessing and validation strategies [67]. Moreover, insufficiently configured models, applications, or whole systems may not only reduce effectiveness but can also introduce safety or security vulnerabilities, emphasizing the importance of considering configuration alongside adoption and value in the context of AI systems [27,32].

3 Survey Methodology

In this section, we present an overview of our methodological approach. We outline the main objective and research questions, followed by the survey design (i.e., questionnaire and participants) and its conduct. Figure 1 provides a corresponding methodological overview.

3.1 Objective and Research Questions

In this study, our objective is to gain a comprehensive understanding of experiences practitioners made in the context of AI systems adoption in manufacturing practice. To structure our study, we formulated three guiding Research Questions (RQ):

RQ1_1 **Which challenges do practitioners face in AI-system development, and how are they addressed?**
Here, our focus is on identifying relevant trends in the challenges associated with development. In addition, we examine how practitioners currently to manage these issues and which open problems remain to be addressed in the future.

RQ1_2 **Which challenges do practitioners face in AI-system configuration, and how are they addressed?**
This question targets the challenges that arise from AI system configuration. We investigate how practitioners perceive and handle such issues in practice, which approaches have proven effective, and where existing solutions show limitations.

RQ1_3 **To what extent do AI system implementations currently add value in manufacturing practice according to practitioners' perceptions?**

Finally, we consider the broader experiences practitioners have gained with AI systems in real-world settings. In particular, this includes their perceptions of added value, benefits, and limitations, as well as how such experiences influence expectations related to implementation incentives.

3.2 Survey Design

Next, we describe the design of our survey. More specifically, we first outline the characteristics of the participant sample, followed by a description of the questionnaire and its structure.

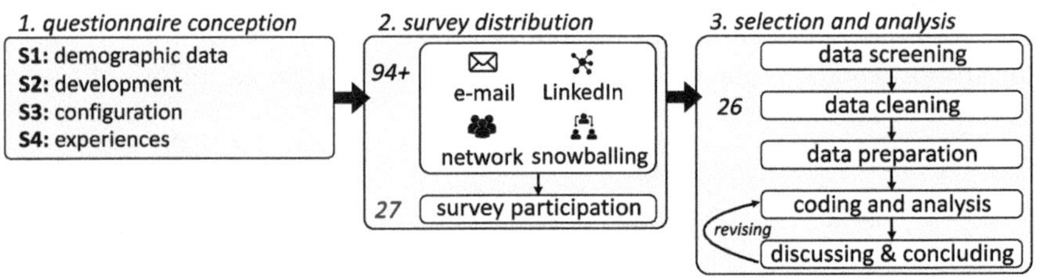

Fig. 1. Overview of the survey methodology, including amount of practitioners involved (numbers).

Sample. Our study exclusively targeted practitioners who actively work in the field of AI systems and are involved in the design and deployment of such systems. This group included, for instance, programmers and data scientists who possess substantial experience with applying AI systems in real-world settings. To ensure that the collected data could provide meaningful answers to our research questions, we deliberately restricted the focus to practitioners from the manufacturing industry. By restricting the sample to this specific niche field, we aimed to capture insights that are both relevant and directly aligned with our research objectives and questions. No further inclusion or exclusion criteria were defined.

Participants were recruited through four distribution channels: (1) the professional network of the authors, (2) a manually created mailing list of AI-system practitioners, (3) the LinkedIn network of the first author (RM), and (4) a distribution of the questionnaire by the participants themselves (i.e., snowballing). As all invitations were directed at individuals working predominantly in European country, the external validity of our findings is necessarily constrained (i.e., limited generalizability). Furthermore, we cannot exclude personal connections between some participants and the authors, as several recruitment channels relied on professional networks. Such limitations may have introduced a certain degree of selection bias.

Questionnaire. Our survey was designed in accordance with established guidelines and quality criteria for conducting surveys with (online) questionnaires in software-engineering research [36]. The development process of the questionnaire followed a collaborative approach. The third author (HH) and the fourth author (MTS) prepared the initial draft in English language, which was substantially revised and extended by the first author (RM) after several discussions with the second (LC), third (HH), and fourth author (MTS). This iterative refinement ensured that the questionnaire adequately reflected the objectives of our study and addressed the formulated research questions in a focused manner. The final version of the survey contained an introduction text, including a basic consent form for participants, and a total of 19 questions structured into four thematic sections (cf. Figure 1). The estimated time required to complete the questionnaire was approximately 10–15 min, balancing comprehensiveness with common issues related to the feasibility for busy practitioners. To further improve clarity and consistency, the remaining authors acted as reviewers and provided targeted feedback in a dedicated evaluation round prior to distribution.

The survey was implemented using the Microsoft Forms platform, which enabled straightforward distribution and collection of responses as Excel spreadsheet. Particular attention was paid to ethical and legal considerations. Consequently, all responses were anonymized (i.e., no conclusions about participants or organizations could be drawn) and securely stored on a German server, thereby ensuring compliance with the privacy and data protection laws of the European Union. In this way, both confidentiality and integrity of the collected data were guaranteed.

Section 1 (demographics): The first section gathered background information related to the participants to better contextualize later responses and to capture the diversity of roles and backgrounds represented in the sample. We asked for their years of professional experience in the field (Q_1, single choice), the main industries of their companies (Q_2, multiple choice), and their current area of employment within the company (Q_3, multiple choice). For Q_2 and Q_3, participants were offered an *other* option (free text) to cover additional cases. All three questions also included the option *prefer not to say*, allowing respondents to refrain from sharing personal or organizational details.

Section 2 (⚙ development): The second section addressed information related to the development (e.g., hurdles, strategies) of AI systems in manufacturing practice. First, participants were asked whether AI systems were already part of the daily business practice in their companies (Q_4, 5-level Likert scale on agreement). Then, we explored in which development phases the greatest difficulties occur (Q_5, multiple choice), the specific challenges that practitioners considered most relevant (Q_6, free text), and the strategies applied to overcome them (Q_7, free text). Note that this section in particular refers to $\mathbf{RQ_1}$.

Section 3 (configuration): In the third section, we asked for experiences made in the context of configuration issues of AI systems, in particular to understand the relevance and impact of configuration issues in practice. The first questions of this section referred to the awareness of AI system configurability and related issues in industry (Q_8, 5-level Likert scale on agreement). After that, we asked for common configuration issues practitioners face in industrial settings (Q_9, multiple choice). Next, we aimed to find out whether configuration issues arise more within AI systems themselves or in combination with other systems (Q_{10}, single choice) and how often configuration issues actually occur (Q_{11}, 5-level Likert scale on frequency). Then, we asked for the impact of such issues on AI systems' performance and reliability (Q_{12}, multiple choice), whether there are certain AI system working areas which are more prevalent for configuration issues (Q_{13}, free text), and how configurations issues in AI systems may differ from those in tradition software systems (Q_{14}, free text). Finally, we referred to strategies to overcome these issues (Q_{15}, multiple choice). In general, we provided fixed answers for all multiple-choice questions as well as an *other* option (free text). Note that this section is in particular related to $\mathbf{RQ_2}$.

Section 4 (experiences): The final section focuses on practitioners' own experiences with AI systems, in particular aimed to provide an understanding not only for technical aspects but also the incentives, added value, and practical outcomes that drive AI system adoption in manufacturing. To avoid overly broad answers, participants were instructed to refer to a single AI system: the one implemented most frequently in their company and the one with which they were personally most familiar. We first asked them to specify the use case of this system (Q_{16}, single choice) and the learning strategy applied (Q_{17}, single choice). Both questions also included an *other* option (free text) to ensure completeness. To assess the perceived added value, participants were then asked to describe the reasons for implementing the system (Q_{18}, free text) and to evaluate whether the implementation was considered worthwhile from an economic point of view (Q_{19}, 5-level Likert scale on agreement). Note that this section is aimed to answer $\mathbf{RQ_3}$.

3.3 Conduct

The distribution of the survey started on May 22, 2024, and was carried out by the first author (RM) through the predefined channels. In this process, 89 practitioners were contacted directly by e-mail, while another five participants were recruited through LinkedIn by means of a post in the first author's (RM) personal network. In addition, further practitioners were reached via the professional network of the authors as well as through snowballing, leading to an unrestricted number of iterations. Overall, the exact number of individuals reached through these channels remains unknown.

All responses were collected centrally in a shared Microsoft Forms project. The platform enabled systematic storage and later export of the complete dataset as an Excel spreadsheet. In an initial quality screening step, the first author (RM) screened and cleaned all entries. This process led to the exclusion of one response that primarily consisted of empty fields. After a short exchange with the third author (HH) and fourth author (MTS), the dataset was prepared for coding and analysis, including 26 participants.

The analysis itself was conducted primarily by the third author (HH) and fourth author (MTS). For all closed questions with predefined categories, descriptive evaluation was applied. In contrast, the free-text responses (e.g., Q_6, Q_7) were examined using qualitative methods, namely open coding and card sorting [73]. In this phase, the third author (HH) and fourth author (MTS) independently identified recurring themes and assigned them to suitable categories. These provisional categories were then reviewed and discussed in two iterative rounds together with the first author (RM) and second authors (LC) until a consensus was reached. This procedure ensured that the qualitative data was systematically interpreted and that the categories reflected the perspectives of all involved researchers. This overall methodological process is illustrated in Fig. 1.

4 Results

After describing the methodological approach of our survey study, we focus on the results in the following section. Note that this section is structured according to the questionnaire sections. The associated research questions are then answered in Sect. 5 based on the discussion of the following results.

Table 1. Summary of participant demographics (n=26) acc. May et al. [32]

question	answers	responses	
Q_1: years of experience	0 to 2	2	8 %
	3 to 5	7	27 %
	6 to 10	7	27 %
	11+	10	38 %
Q_2: main industry	manufacturing	20	42 %
	IT	14	29 %
	research	10	21 %
	logistics	3	6 %
	prefer not to say	1	2 %
Q_3: employment area	research and development	23	89 %
	operations	11	42 %
	quality	3	12 %
	management	2	8 %
	other	2	8 %

4.1 Demographics

First, the results related to the participants' demographics are reported (cf. Table 1). With respect to professional experience in developing AI systems within the manufacturing domain (Q_1), 65% of the respondents indicated a total of at least six years. Within this group, 38% reported more than eleven years of experience, while 27% stated between six and ten years. The remaining participants reported shorter durations of experience, with 27% indicating three to five years and 8% specifying a maximum of two years.

The companies' main industries (Q_2) cover several different sectors. A total of 42% of the participants are employed in manufacturing, 29% in information technology, and 21% in research. A smaller proportion of 6% reported working in logistics. In addition, one participant selected the option *prefer not to say*. Information on the respondents' employment areas (Q_3) shows that the largest share, 89%, referred to research and development. A further 42% reported working in operations. Other areas were mentioned less frequently, including quality (12%), management (8%), and risk analysis (4%). As multiple answers were possible for this question, the percentages may overlap.

4.2 Development

Second, the results related to development are reported (cf. Table 2). In terms of the implementation status of AI systems (Q_4), 69% of the practitioners agreed or strongly agreed that such systems are already in use within their companies and form part of day-to-day business practice. In contrast, 27% neither agreed nor disagreed, while 4% expressed disagreement. With regard to the development phases (Q_5), data preparation was most frequently identified as the most challenging task, with 73% of the respondents selecting this option. Deployment, operation, and change management were each mentioned by 65% of the participants, while testing was chosen by 37%. Design was considered challenging by 27%, and implementation by 23%.

Concerning typical challenges (Q_6), the most common references were to data quality and to the customization or configuration of AI systems, each indicated by 46% of the respondents. Further issues included system adaptability and stakeholder expectations, both mentioned by 23%. Data handling was reported by 19%, and system efficiency by 15%. Less frequently cited were challenges related to change management and to system scalability, each selected by 12% of the participants.

The strategies reported for handling these challenges (Q_7) cover a wide range of measures. Ensuring high data quality was emphasized by 46% of the respondents, while 42% highlighted the importance of testing and validation of either data quality or system functions. The use of AI system templates for designing new solutions was mentioned by 27%, and 23% referred to efforts to safeguard data processing quality. Requirements-engineering measures were selected by 12%, stakeholder communication aimed at reducing change management issues by 19%, and iterative feature integration by 12%. Finally, 12% of the participants stated that systematic handling of common challenges is hardly feasible and that practical experience remains the decisive factor.

4.3 Configuration

Third, we report the results related to configuration (cf. Table 3). For awareness on AI system configurability and related issues in industry (Q_8), half of

Table 2. Summary of participant responses on development (n=26) acc. May et al. [32].

question	answers	responses	
Q_4: implementation status	agree	13	50 %
	neither agree nor disagree	7	27 %
	strongly agree	5	19 %
	disagree	1	4 %
Q_5: challenging development phases	data preparation	19	73 %
	deployment	17	65 %
	operation	17	65 %
	change management	17	65 %
	testing	10	37 %
	design	7	27 %
	implementation	6	23 %
Q_6: common challenges	data quality	12	46 %
	customization/configuration	12	46 %
	system adaptability	6	23 %
	stakeholder expectations	6	23 %
	data handling	5	19 %
	system efficiency	4	15 %
	change management	3	12 %
	system scalability	3	12 %
Q_7: handling strategies	ensuring data quality	12	46 %
	testing or validation	11	42 %
	AI system templates	7	27 %
	protecting data processing	6	23 %
	stakeholder communication	5	19 %
	requirements engineering	3	12 %
	iterative feature integration	3	12 %
	hardly feasible/practical experience	3	12 %

the respondents neither agreed nor disagreed (50%). A further 31% (strongly) agreed, and 19% disagreed. Regarding common configuration issues (Q_{10}), version issues (e.g., updates) were reported by 81% of the respondents, dependency issues by 77%, and both scalability limitations and feature interactions by 62%. Incorrect parameter settings were indicated by 46%, hardware-software mismatch and programming errors each by 31%, while 8% mentioned other issues, such as security limitations in the target infrastructure (e.g., blocked interfaces, missing internet connection).

Concerning the origin of issues (Q_{11}), 92% stated that these occurred in combination with other systems, while 8% located them within AI systems. In

Table 3. Summary of participant responses on configuration (n=26).

question	answers	responses	
Q_8: awareness	neither agree nor disagree	13	50 %
	agree	6	23 %
	disagree	5	19 %
	strongly agree	2	8 %
Q_{10}: common issues	version issues	21	81 %
	dependency issues	20	77 %
	scalability limitations	16	62 %
	feature interactions	16	62 %
	incorrect parameter settings	12	46 %
	hardware-software mismatch	8	31 %
	programming errors	8	31 %
	others	2	8 %
Q_{11}: origin	in combination with other systems	24	92 %
	within AI systems	2	8 %
Q_{12}: frequency	frequently	12	46 %
	sometimes	8	31 %
	very frequently	5	19 %
	rarely	2	4 %
Q_{13}: impact	increased downtime	21	81 %
	scalability issues	17	65 %
	system vulnerabilities	15	58 %
	inconsistent outputs	15	58 %
	computational inefficiency	8	31 %
	reduced accuracy	7	27 %
Q_{14}: working area specificity	unknown	10	39 %
	all working areas	7	27 %
	working areas with real-time data	4	15 %
	feature-rich working areas	4	15 %
Q_{15}: differences to traditional systems	higher complexity	10	25 %
	continuously usable real-time data	8	20 %
	more complex versioning	5	13 %
	greater data dependencies	5	13 %
	more (hyper)parameters	4	10 %
	lack of standards	3	8 %
	more complex requirements	3	8 %
	more difficult error detection	2	5 %
Q_{15}: handling strategies	regular testing	22	85 %
	continuous monitoring	21	81 %
	implementing configuration management tools	5	13 %
	reducing system variability	4	10 %
	other	3	8 %

terms of configuration issue frequency (Q_{12}), 46% reported issues occurring frequently, 31% sometimes, 19% very frequently, and 4% rarely. Regarding the typical impact of configuration issues, in particular on the performance and reliability of AI systems (Q_{13}), increased downtime was reported by 81% of the respondents, scalability issues by 65%, and both system vulnerabilities and inconsistent outputs by 58%. Computational inefficiency was reported by 31%, and reduced accuracy by 27%. With respect to working area where configuration issues are more prevalent in AI systems (Q_{14}), 62% of the respondents stated that they do not know if there are specific working areas. However, 27% explicitly mentioned that there are no working areas where such issues are more prevalent. 15% mentioned working areas with real-time data (e.g., maintenance or monitoring AI systems), another 15% referred to feature-rich working areas with many feature interactions (e.g., mismatches between learning and security features).

When asked about differences to traditional systems (Q_{15}), higher complexity (i.e., number of features, their dependencies, and interactions) was named by 25% of the respondents, continuously usable real-time data by 20%, more complex versioning and greater data dependencies each by 13%, and more (hyper)parameters by 10%. Lack of (harmonized) standards and more complex requirements were mentioned by 8% each, while more difficult error detection was selected by 5%. Finally, strategies to overcome configuration issues (Q_{15}) mainly included regular testing (85%) and continuous monitoring (81%). Moreover, participants reported the use of configuration management tools (13%), reducing system variability (10%), and other measures, such as hyper-parameter optimization (8%).

4.4 Experiences

Fourth, the results concerning the participants' experiences are reported (cf. Table 4). In terms of use cases (Q_{16}), half of the responses referred to the prediction of machine or component failures (50%). Further frequent indications were the prediction of quality parameters (15%) as well as the assistance of scheduling or planning tasks and the control of manufacturing parameters, each mentioned by 8%. In addition, five further use cases were each cited once, including, among others, fraud and solvency risk management.

With regard to the learning strategies applied (Q_{17}), the majority of AI systems were reported to rely on supervised learning (77%). Unsupervised learning and semi-supervised learning were each mentioned by 4% of the participants. Moreover, 12% stated that they did not know which learning strategy had been implemented. For the incentives to implement AI systems (Q_{18}), five categories were predefined. The reduction of effort and system downtime was selected by 46%, improvements in system efficiency by 42%, and the optimization of process quality by 31%. Cost savings were reported by 23% and enhanced decision making by 19%.

Concerning the worthiness of AI system implementations in manufacturing practice (Q_{19}), 73% of the respondents agreed or strongly agreed with this state-

Table 4. Summary of participant responses on experiences (n=26) acc. May et al. [32].

question	answers	responses	
Q_{16}: use case	*prediction*		
	failures	13	50 %
	quality parameters	4	15 %
	assistance		
	parameter control	2	8 %
	scheduling/planning	2	8 %
	other	5	19 %
Q_{17}: learning strategy	supervised	20	77 %
	not known	3	12 %
	semi-supervised	1	4 %
	unsupervised	1	4 %
	other	1	4 %
Q_{18}: added value	effort/downtime	12	46 %
	system efficiency	11	42 %
	quality	8	31 %
	costs	6	23 %
	decision making	5	19 %
Q_{19}: worthiness	agree	15	58 %
	neither agree nor disagree	7	27 %
	strongly agree	4	15 %

ment. The remaining 27% neither agreed nor disagreed, while no participant expressed disagreement. Focusing specifically on responses related to the prediction of machine or component failures, such solutions were reported to rely predominantly on supervised learning (85%). They were most frequently implemented with the aim of reducing efforts and downtime (54%), followed by cost savings (39%) and increasing system efficiency (31%). In this subset, 61% agreed or strongly agreed that the implementation was worthwhile, whereas 39% neither agreed nor disagreed.

5 Practitioner Insights

In the following section, we discuss the results and put them into context (i.e., insights) regarding development (RQ_1), configuration (RQ_2), and added value (RQ_3). Overall, we provide 12 insights, derived from the practitioners responses. Note, in particular in the context of development as well as configuration, some insights depend on each other since configuration is a fundamental part during the development of AI systems. In addition, certain insights may be applicable beyond the manufacturing context, i.e., expanding their value to other cyber-physical domains, such as healthcare.

5.1 RQ_1: ✿ Development

First, we present the insights related to development of AI systems, including implications and trends, surrounding the challenges practitioners face in AI-system development and how they handle them.

$Insight_1$: Data Readiness. The strong focus on data preparation as the most challenging development phase (73%) clearly points to a systemic issue of data readiness in industrial AI system projects. This finding is in line with earlier observations that fragmented legacy systems and the absence of harmonized data formats continue to hinder smooth integration of AI solutions in manufacturing environments [34]. As long as data remains heterogeneous, incomplete, or inconsistent, even advanced AI methods cannot deliver reliable results, reflecting the well-known *garbage-in garbage-out* principle [17].

We argue that the implication for practice is that companies must prioritize foundational investments in data management infrastructures, ensuring that data pipelines are stable, secure, and verifiable before pursuing more sophisticated AI system deployments. Such investments may include harmonized interfaces, standardized data schemas, and robust governance processes for ensuring data quality over time. In addition, automated and strictly verified tools for pre-processing, cleaning, and enrichment of datasets are likely to become increasingly important to address this bottleneck [20], at best, as early as possible during the development life cycle. As one participant emphasized:

> *"[...] consider infrastructure requirements early in the system design process [...] apply techniques for data augmentation/synthesis to enrich datasets" (P14)*

Beyond this, approaches such as digital twins or ontology-based modeling can provide an additional pathway for improving data readiness: by structuring, visualizing, and combining data with expert and user knowledge, these technologies can pre-process large parts of the data, generate meaningful labels, and thereby improve subsequent AI predictions [15,58].

$Insight_2$: Post-Development Issues and Change Management. Deployment, operation, and change management were each reported as challenging phases by 65% of the respondents, indicating persistent difficulties once AI systems leave the development stage (cf. Figure 2). Such issues typically arise when new workflows must be introduced, when systems are deployed across heterogeneous environments, or when data sources change over time [61]. They are further intensified by staff resistance to change and the complexity of embedding AI solutions into existing manufacturing routines [3]. In addition, practitioners

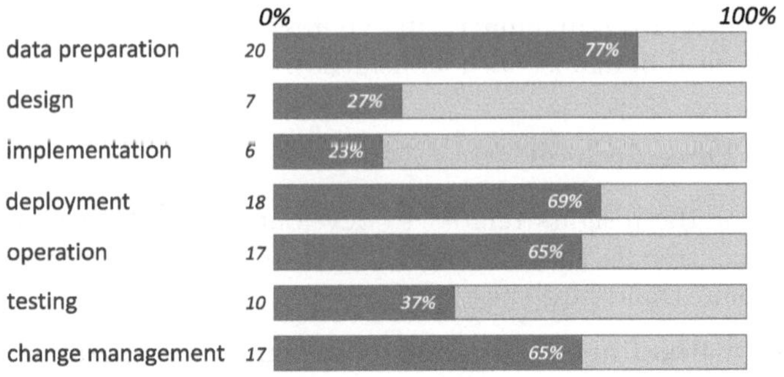

Fig. 2. Perceived challenges across different AI-system-development phases (Q_5) oriented towards May et al. [32]. Bars indicate the percentage and number of practitioners who selected each phase (multiple answers possible).

highlighted that variability in target environments and the coexistence of older and newer technologies can further complicate deployment. Managing such variability requires organizational flexibility and adaptive workflows, as deployment failures or misconfigurations may otherwise cause downtime or disruptions.

To address these problems, practitioners point to the need for robust change-management strategies and the design of user-centric systems that facilitate smoother adoption. Clear stakeholder communication, iterative rollouts, and early involvement of employees can help overcome barriers and ensure alignment with organizational practices [61]. In addition, compliance with IT requirements and the establishment of governance structures are crucial to guarantee sustainable deployment and operation, particularly in multi-site manufacturing settings.

Insight$_3$: Experience Dependency and Stakeholder Integration. Several practitioners pointed out that managing development challenges is often dependent on individual experience rather than standardized procedures, indicating a lack of formalized frameworks or best practices (or their adoption) for AI systems. As one participant noted:

> *"[...] experience is important and [you need] a bit of luck" (P10)*

This reliance on personal expertise emphasizes the need for stronger mechanisms of knowledge formalization and sharing [24]. Actively involving manufacturing employees as stakeholders can play a decisive role in this process, as their domain expertise helps identify practical requirements and supports effective collaboration with AI-system developers. By qualifying and incentivizing employees, organizations can reduce concerns about automation, avoid costly recruitment, and secure long-term knowledge retention [13]. Such empowerment enables employees not only to co-design solutions but also to support AI-system deployment and data preparation, ensuring that systems remain aligned with production realities. While these issues are most visible during deployment, operation, and change management, they actually affect all phases of development. Thus, early and continuous stakeholder communication, complemented by systematic user feedback, is crucial to adapt AI systems to real-world settings [61].

Insight$_4$: Governance and Organizational Adaptation. Beyond the more technical issues, AI-system projects also face pure organizational challenges during development. Decisions about which features to prioritize, how to scope a Minimum Viable Product (MVP), or whether to adopt standardized templates directly affect both stakeholder satisfaction and long-term adoption success. Some practitioners warned that templates may limit customer satisfaction by restricting available features:

> *"[...] however, you restrict the number of possible features which are potentially interesting for customers [leading to a] problem of customer satisfaction" (P7)*

Others emphasized that limiting features can also be a strength, helping to align solutions more closely with stakeholder needs and reducing unnecessary complexity:

> *"limiting [...] function[s] as much as possible to fit the need of the stakeholders" (P15)*

These perspectives illustrate that development must balance stakeholder alignment, governance, and long-term adaptability [59] – which, however, is a huge challenge itself. Potential solutions might include agile requirements engineering strategies [63] adapted to the specific manufacturing settings or company workflows.

RQ$_1$: ⚠ Development

The main challenges in AI-system development are referred to data readiness, post-development integration, and resistance to organizational change. Projects often depend heavily on individual expertise rather than standardized frameworks, which hinders reproducibility and scalability. To address these, companies rely on pragmatic solutions such as iterative rollouts, stakeholder involvement, and governance mechanisms, though many issues remain only partially addressed. Overall, these findings highlight that sustainable deployment requires not just technical integration but also robust organizational strategies and harmonized knowledge sharing.

5.2 RQ_2: Configuration

Second, we focus on insights related to the configuration of AI systems, covering awareness, the growing complexity of configuration, the frequency and impact of issues, and the diversity of underlying drivers.

$Insight_5$: Awareness. Although configuration issues can critically affect availability and reliability, awareness of their relevance remains limited. Half of the practitioners expressed no clear opinion (50%), while almost one fifth explicitly disagreed (19%) that configurability represents a significant challenge (Q_8). We argue that this ambivalence might suggest that configuration is often perceived as a purely technical matter rather than a strategic concern in system design and operation. As a result, systematic investments in configuration management and monitoring infrastructures are frequently postponed, increasing the likelihood of recurring failures and inconsistent performance [72]. In fact, this problem is of central importance not only in manufacturing but also in other cyber-physical domains (e.g., healthcare [18]), which further highlights the relevance of this gap and also motivates to explore the potential of successful solutions from other domains for manufacturing.

$Insight_6$: Configuration Complexity. According to our participants, configuration in AI systems is substantially more complex (i.e., more features, interactions, dependencies) than in traditional software (Q_{15}).

> *"[AI systems] are usually more complex, [they] rely more on real time data and their usage, versioning is typically neglected (which is really pain!)" (P25)*

Typical issues are related to versioning (81%, cf. P25), dependency problems (77%), and unintended feature interactions (62%) (Q_{10}). Such issues were rarely described as isolated but instead as emerging in combination with other systems (92%, Q_{11}), which underlines their systemic nature in interconnected cyber-physical environments. We argue that due to the increasing complexity of AI systems, (unwanted) feature interactions and (cross)dependency issues may grow in criticality, leading to highly critical issues the more systems, applications, models or data streams are connected. In such scenarios, even minor changes, such as a library update or a mismatch between sensor firmware and middleware, can propagate across dependencies and trigger emergent errors [71].

This situation is similar to the well-known *dependency hell* in software engineering. Thus, such issues are already known from traditional systems [30] but based on the survey results we believe that they could become even more frequent and interactive in the context of AI systems, for example, due to AI's dependence on highly-variable real-time data and models. In the context of manufacturing, which heavily builds on safety-critical cyber-physical systems [42], the issues might create even more potential risks that need to be investigated in the future.

Insight$_7$: Fequency and Critical Impact. Configuration issues do not represent isolated exceptions but rather recurrent phenomena in practice. Nearly two thirds of practitioners reported encountering them frequently or very frequently (64%, Q_{12}). Correlation analysis suggests a trend that higher awareness of configurability is linked to lower reported frequency of configuration issues. This pattern is also reflected in the distribution of responses (cf. Figure 3, not statistically significant), where participants with low awareness more often reported very frequent issues, whereas higher awareness correlates with less extreme frequencies.

However, the consequences extend well beyond technical inconvenience, with downtime, scalability limitations, inconsistent outputs, and security vulnerabilities repeatedly described as direct outcomes (Q_{13}). These impacts demonstrate that misconfigurations undermine not only technical performance but also economic viability and cyber resilience [12,27], making configuration issues to business-critical risk factors. In particular, security concerns can be highly critical: once misconfigurations open attack vectors, adversaries can exploit them to compromise data integrity and physical processes of both data model and cyber-physical system (i.e., AI systems) [1,25]. This situation, in turn, might threaten safety of the systems [29].

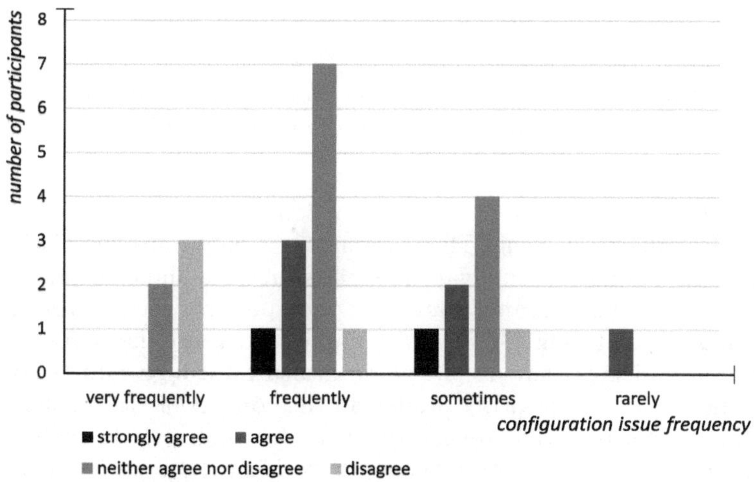

Fig. 3. Distribution of reported configuration issue frequencies across different levels of practitioners' awareness regarding configuration issues.

Insight$_8$: Configuration Issue Drivers. Configuration issues do not stem from a single source but arise from a broad spectrum of technical and organizational factors. While many practitioners were unable to specify particular areas, some emphasized contexts with real-time data, whereas others pointed to feature-rich domains with complex feature interactions (e.g., predictive maintenance). This finding indicates that data variability, feature interactions and dependencies, as well as real-time constraints are central drivers of configuration risks [32,69], as stated by one participant:

> *"Configuration issues are more common in the areas of real-time quality control and predictive maintenance due to high data variability and stringent performance requirements." (P08)*

Beyond such domain-specific challenges, AI systems differ from traditional systems by requiring continuous tuning of hyperparameters, coordination of interdependent models, and the maintenance of heterogeneous datasets. Some practitioners also highlighted that these challenges are amplified by the absence of adopting standards and by the difficulty of detecting errors at data or model level:

> *"[There is] missing experience in using standards in the field of [AI systems]" (P10)*

> *"Models and data [lead to] additional complexity. But errors are not as easy to detect. Tests for data and model[s] are more complex." (P21)*

Overall, these perspectives show that configuration drivers are multifaceted and often mutually reinforcing. They originate not only from technical variability but also from organizational gaps in standardization and error management. Interestingly, some participants state that they perform regular testing (85%) and continuous monitoring (81%), which suggests reactive measures. Nevertheless, our data indicates that despite these measures, a high number of configuration issues still seem to arise. Studies in the context of traditional software systems [31] have shown that testing typically does not include explicit testing of all possible configurations of a system. Surprisingly, only a few participants (10%) state that they consciously restrict the number of features (cf. Insight_4). Our implication is that configuration issues are difficult to anticipate and resolve without holistic approaches. For research, this underlines the need for secure configurability-aware frameworks that conceptualize configuration as a multi-level phenomenon, rather than treating it as a collection of isolated technical flaws.

RQ$_2$: Configuration

Configuration
challenges in AI systems arise from version and (cross)dependency issues, feature interactions, and organizational gaps in standardization. They occur regularly and can lead to downtime, inconsistent outputs, and vulnerabilities, making them business-critical. Compared to traditional systems, AI systems are more difficult to configure due to higher variability, real-time constraints, and complex interdependencies. Practitioners mostly rely on reactive strategies (e.g., testing and monitoring), highlighting the need for more preventive and security-aware approaches.

5.3 RQ$_3$: Added Value

Insight$_9$: Added Value and Optimization. The perceived added value of AI-system implementations in manufacturing is predominantly positive. Practitioners emphasized improvements in operational efficiency, reduced downtime, and process optimization as the most important benefits. The dominant application is predictive maintenance (50%), where the prediction of machine or component failures minimizes unplanned downtime and secures production continuity [28]. Other applications, such as quality parameter prediction, scheduling assistance, and manufacturing parameter control, were mentioned less frequently, yet they directly influence decision making, production planning, and quality assurance. For instance, AI-supported scheduling and process control can optimize machine utilization, sequencing, and material disposition, thereby transforming production management [59]. We argue that extending AI use cases beyond predictive maintenance, particularly into advanced quality control and real-time process optimization, offers significant potential to increase the value of AI across a wider range of manufacturing functions.

Insight$_{10}$: Learning Strategy Dependence. Most reported AI systems rely on supervised learning (77%), indicating a strong preference for structured and well-defined learning approaches in manufacturing settings [28,56]. In contrast, unsupervised and semi-supervised learning were mentioned only rarely, even though these strategies could help detect hidden patterns and optimize processes with less reliance on labeled data [46]. This reliance on supervised learning shows a certain conservatism in industrial practice, but also highlights underutilized potential. So, encouraging broader experimentation with diverse learning strategies could increase adaptability and unlock value in more complex or data-scarce manufacturing scenarios.

Insight$_{11}$: Incentives for Adoption. The leading incentives for adopting AI systems include reducing effort and downtime (46%), improving system efficiency (42%), and optimizing quality (31%). These drivers are closely aligned with core manufacturing objectives of productivity and cost reduction, which form part of the established strategic triangle [54]. Importantly, practitioners often described these incentives as interdependent, since improvements in quality also reduce downtime, and efficiency gains contribute to cost savings. This interrelation was summarized by one participant:

> *"Improved accuracy in predicting quality parameters and machine failures, resulting in reduced downtime and maintenance costs, optimized manufacturing processes and improved decision-making capabilities" (P9)*

Such statements illustrate that incentives are rarely isolated but reinforce each other in practice, strengthening the business case for adoption.

Insight$_{12}$: Acceptance. Despite the overall positive perception, acceptance of AI systems is not universal. A considerable share of respondents (23%) neither agreed nor disagreed that implementations are worthwhile, suggesting difficulties in demonstrating clear benefits. This hesitation may result from fluctuating implementation success, contextual differences across companies, or the absence of standardized benchmarks for measuring value. In practice, starting with an MVP that demonstrates tangible benefits may help build confidence and foster further adoption [59]. Overall, while predictive maintenance and efficiency improvements are widely acknowledged as valuable [50], broader use cases remain underutilized. Future adoption will likely depend on reducing technical and organizational barriers, diversifying use cases, and improving scalability, configurability, and reusability of AI solutions. Techniques such as product-line engineering [45,64] may offer a pathway to systematic reuse and adaptability. In addition, clearer cost–benefit analyses and success metrics could support practitioners who remain uncertain, while structured trade-off assessments may improve decision-making in the adoption process.

RQ$_3$: Added Value

AI systems are generally perceived as valuable, primarily through benefits such as reduced downtime, improved efficiency, and optimized quality. Predictive maintenance dominates current applications, while broader use cases, such as quality prediction, scheduling, or process control, remain underutilized. Despite positive perceptions, uncertainty persists as some practitioners struggle to see clear returns, partly due to inconsistent outcomes and missing benchmarks. To strengthen adoption, future work must diversify applications, ensure scalability and reusability, and provide clearer cost–benefit evidence.

6 Threats to Validity

Like any study, our work faces several threats to validity. We discuss them along the dimensions of internal (i.e., causal inference), construct (i.e., measurement of variables), external (i.e., generalizability), and conclusion validity (i.e., strength of inferences).

Internal Validity. Researcher bias in interpreting free-text responses may distort results. To address this issue, multiple authors were involved in coding and iteratively aligned categories. Selection bias is another concern, as participants were mainly recruited via professional networks. We mitigated this by snowball sampling. Response bias may also occur, with participants providing socially desirable answers, particularly regarding economic benefits. Here, anonymization and *prefer not to say* options were provided to reduce this risk. Finally, the small sample size may limit robustness, but recurring patterns across responses increase our confidence.

Construct Validity. Survey concepts such as *use cases*, *learning strategies*, or *configuration issues* might have been interpreted differently by respondents. We relied on established terminology and tested the questionnaire internally to reduce confusion. Closed questions (e.g., Likert scales) were complemented by open-ended ones to capture nuances. Inconsistent responses and outliers were screened, with one incomplete response excluded. Nevertheless, more subtle perspectives of practitioners may have been overlooked by us.

External Validity. The generalizability of our findings is limited by the small sample size (n=26), a return rate below 30%, and the focus on European practitioners. Self-selection bias may also have influenced participation. Despite this, 65% of respondents had more than six years of professional experience, and the sample included diverse roles and industries, enhancing credibility. Validation against related studies is still pending and is already planned for follow-up research.

Conclusion Validity. We argue that the significance of our conclusions is limited by the exploratory design. Descriptive statistics and qualitative coding do not allow causal claims, and the small sample reduces statistical significance. As the study captures a single point in time, evolving practices may not be fully represented. To mitigate these risks, we report percentages only when they add interpretive value and contextualize quotes carefully to avoid overgeneralization. Thus, our results should be seen as indicative insights that lay the groundwork for validation and verification.

7 Related Work

AI systems in manufacturing have been widely discussed in literature. For example, Nelson et al. [40] systematically reviewed industrial applications, highlighting societal implications such as workforce impact and security concerns. Kovalenko et al. [20] emphasized the role of robust data infrastructures and human–AI collaboration for successful integration, while Espina-Romero et al. [10] provided a bibliometric analysis of challenges and opportunities. Configurability has also been addressed conceptually, for example, Todescato et al. [62] focused on sustainable manufacturing enabled by configurability, and Rehman et al. [48] proposed a framework for self-configuration in AI-driven manufacturing systems.

Currently, insights from practitioners remain limited. Culot et al. [6] conducted a Delphi study with 76 participants from research and practice to identify key expectations and barriers of Industry 4.0, with AI systems highlighted as a core pillar. Demlehner et al. [7] used a Delphi study with 39 practitioners from automotive manufacturing to determine high-value AI system use cases. Kutz et al. [23], based on ten semi-structured interviews, reported success factors and barriers of AI system adoption, particularly regarding data quality, operational processes, and stakeholder engagement. These studies highlight the relevance of practice-oriented insights but remain limited in scope, either focusing on specific sectors or emphasizing individual aspects of adoption.

In our previous work [32], we reported initial survey findings based on the same data basis, focusing, however, mainly on adoption challenges and value perception without taking into account configuration aspects. This article substantially extends all related work including the initial study by considering and further discussing (1) development challenges and handling strategies in industrial practice, (2) configuration issues and related handling strategies, and (3) the perceived added value of AI systems from software-oriented perspective. Thus, our study complements prior literature with a broader understanding of AI-system adoption in manufacturing.

8 Conclusion

In this survey study, we explored the perspectives of 26 manufacturing practitioners on the development (RQ_1), configuration (RQ_2), and added value (RQ_3) of AI systems, leading to 12 relevant insights. Overall, our results highlight three core findings. First, development is constrained by the following main issues: data readiness remains the main bottleneck, and integration into heterogeneous environments causes persistent challenges. Reliance on individual expertise rather than standardized frameworks limits reproducibility and scalability. Second, configuration has emerged as a business-critical risk, which is currently insufficiently addressed by reactive measures. Version conflicts, dependency chains, and feature interactions at system boundaries can lead to downtime, inconsistent outputs, and vulnerabilities. Third, AI systems offer clear added value in predictive maintenance through efficiency gains and downtime reduction. Yet, broader applications, such as process optimization and quality control remain, underutilized, while uncertainty about return-on-investment and missing benchmarks slow adoption and scaling.

Future research and development should focus on addressing the challenges identified in this study. Still, we strongly recommend prioritizing configurable, reusable, and scalable AI-system solutions, however, considering holistic, configuration-aware data-management and AI-system-development practices will be key for manufacturing companies. Establishing clearer success metrics and cost–benefit benchmarks will also be essential to increase confidence in AI-system investments. We believe that by tackling these challenges, the adoption of AI systems in manufacturing can be considerably facilitated in the future.

References

1. Alharthi, N.W., Brandão, M.: Physical and digital adversarial attacks on grasp quality networks. In: International Conference on Robotics and Automation (ICRA), pp. 1907–1902. IEEE (2024)
2. Ali, Y.A., Awwad, E.M., Al-Razgan, M., Maarouf, A.: Hyperparameter search for machine learning algorithms for optimizing the computational complexity. Processes **11**(2), 349 (2023)
3. Arias-Pérez, J., Vélez-Jaramillo, J.: Ignoring the three-way interaction of digital orientation, not-invented-here syndrome and employee's artificial intelligence awareness in digital innovation performance: A recipe for failure. Technol. Forecast. Soc. Chang. **174**, 121305 (2022)
4. Bolstorff, P., Rosenbaum, R.: Supply chain excellence: A handbook for dramatic improvement using the SCOR model. J. Supply Chain Manag. **39**(4), 38 (2007)
5. Chryssolouris, G., Alexopoulos, K., Arkouli, Z.: Artificial intelligence in manufacturing systems. In: A Perspective on Artificial Intelligence in Manufacturing, pp. 79–135 (2023) Springer
6. Culot, G., Orzes, G., Sartor, M., Nassimbeni, G.: The future of manufacturing: A delphi-based scenario analysis on industry 4.0. Technological forecasting and social change, vol. 157, p. 120092. (2020)
7. Demlehner, Q., Schoemer, D., Laumer, S.: How can artificial intelligence enhance car manufacturing? a Delphi study-based identification and assessment of general use cases. Int. J. Inf. Manage. **58**, 102317 (2021)
8. El Naqa, I., Murphy, M.: What is machine learning? In: Machine Learning in Radiation Oncology, pp. 3–11 (2015)
9. Ellwood, P., Williams, C., Egan, J.: Crossing the valley of death: Five underlying innovation processes. Technovation **109**, 102162 (2022)
10. Espina-Romero, L., Gutiérrez Hurtado, H., Ríos Parra, D., Vilchez Pirela, R.A., Talavera-Aguirre, R., Ochoa-Díaz, A.: Challenges and opportunities in the implementation of ai in manufacturing: a bibliometric analysis. Sci **6**(4), 60 (2024)
11. Ge, Z., Song, Z., Ding, S.X., Huang, B.: Data mining and analytics in the process industry: the role of machine learning. IEEE Access **5**, 20590–20616 (2017)
12. Hasan, S.M., Shahid, A.R., Imteaj, A.: Evaluating sustainability and social costs of adversarial training in machine learning. IEEE Consumer Electron. Mag. (2024)
13. Jaiswal, A., Arun, C.J., Varma, A.: Rebooting employees: Upskilling for artificial intelligence in multinational corporations. In: Artificial Intelligence and International HRM, pp. 114–143., Routledge (2023)
14. Jeziorek, O.: Lean production. Lean Production, pp. 3–27 (1994)
15. Kabashkin, I.: Ontology-driven digital twin framework for aviation maintenance and operations. Mathematics **13**(17), 2817 (2025)
16. Kang, H.S., et al.: Smart manufacturing: past research, present findings, and future directions. Int. J. Precision Eng. Manufact.-Green Technol. **3**, 111–128 (2016)
17. Kilkenny, M.F., Robinson, K.M.: Data quality: "garbage in–garbage out" (2018)
18. Kim, M.O., Coiera, E., Magrabi, F.: Problems with health information technology and their effects on care delivery and patient outcomes: a systematic review. J. Am. Med. Inform. Assoc. **24**(2), 246–250 (2017)
19. Kotsiantis, S.B., Zaharakis, I., Pintelas, P., et al.: Supervised machine learning: a review of classification techniques. Emerg. Artif. Intell. Appl. Comput. Eng. **160**(1), 3–24 (2007)

20. Kovalenko, I., Barton, K., Moyne, J., Tilbury, D.M.: Opportunities and challenges to integrate artificial intelligence into manufacturing systems: thoughts from a panel discussion [opinion]. Robot. Autom. Mag. **30**(2), 109–112 (2023)
21. Kovič, K., Tominc, P., Prester, J., Palčič, I.: Artificial intelligence software adoption in manufacturing companies. Appl. Sci. **14**(16), 6959 (2024)
22. Kusiak, A.: Smart manufacturing. Int. J. Prod. Res. **56**, 508–517 (2018)
23. Kutz, J., Neuhüttler, J., Spilski, J., Lachmann, T.: Implementation of AI technologies in manufacturing-success factors and challenges. In: International Conference on Applied Human Factors and Ergonomics (AHFE), pp. 24–28 (2022)
24. Lepore, D., Dubbini, S., Micozzi, A., Spigarelli, F.: Knowledge sharing opportunities for industry 4.0 firms. J. Knowl. Econ. **13**(1), 501–520 (2022)
25. Li, Y., Cheng, M., Hsieh, C.J., Lee, T.C.M.: A review of adversarial attack and defense for classification methods. Am. Stat. **76**(4), 329–345 (2022)
26. Martínez-Fernández, S.: Software engineering for ai-based systems: a survey. Trans. Softw. Eng. Methodol. **31**(2), 1–59 (2022)
27. May, R., Krüger, J., Leich, T.: Sok: How artificial-intelligence incidents can jeopardize safety and security. In: International Conference on Availability, Reliability and Security (ARES), pp. 1–12. ACM (2024)
28. May, R., Niemand, T., Scholz, P., Leich, T.: Design patterns for monitoring and prediction machine learning systems: Systematic literature review and cluster analysis. In: International Conference of Software Technologies (ICSOFT), pp. 209–216. SciTePress (2023)
29. May, R.: A systematic mapping study on security in configurable safety-critical systems based on product-line concepts. In: International Conference of Software Technologies (ICSOFT), pp. 217–224. SciTePress (2023)
30. May, R., et al.: Vulnerably (mis)configured? Exploring 10 years of developers' Q&As on Stack Overflow. pp. 112–122. ACM (2024)
31. May, R., Biermann, C., Krüger, J., Leich, T.: Asking security practitioners: Did you find the vulnerable (mis)configuration? In: Working Conference on Variability Modelling of Software-Intensive Systems (VaMoS), pp. 30–39. ACM (2025)
32. May, R., Cassel, L., Hussain, H., Siddiqui, M.T., Niemand, T., Scholz, P., Leich, T.: Adopting artificial-intelligence systems in manufacturing: A practitioner survey on challenges and added value. In: International Conference of Software Technologies (ICSOFT), pp. 87–98. SciTePress (2025)
33. Mehak, R., Ashima, M., Kiran, R.: Artificial intelligence. Int. J. Adv. Res. Sci., Commun. Technol. **3**(7), 20–30 (2023)
34. Meyer, O., Rauhoeft, G., Schel, D., Stock, D.: Industrial internet of things: covering standardization gaps for the next generation of reconfigurable production systems. In: International Conference on Industrial Informatics (INDIN), pp. 1039–1044. IEEE (2018)
35. Mijwil, M.M., Abttan, R.A.: Artificial intelligence: a survey on evolution and future trends. Asian J. Appl. Sci. **9**(2), (2021)
36. Molléri, J.S., Petersen, K., Mendes, E.: Survey guidelines in software engineering: an annotated review. In: International Symposium on Empirical Software Engineering and Measurement (ESEM), pp. 1–6 (2016)
37. Monostori, L.: Ai and machine learning techniques for managing complexity, changes and uncertainties in manufacturing. Eng. Appl. Artif. Intell. **16**(4), 277–291 (2003)
38. Monostori, L., et al.: Cyber-physical systems in manufacturing. Cirp Annals **65**(2), 621–641 (2016)

39. Naz, F., Kumar, A., Agrawal, R., Garza-Reyes, J.A., Majumdar, A., Chokshi, H.: Artificial intelligence as an enabler of quick and effective production repurposing: an exploratory review and future research propositions. Product. Plann. Control **35**(16), 2154–2177 (2024)
40. Nelson, J.P., Biddle, J.B., Shapira, P.: Applications and societal implications of artificial intelligence in manufacturing: a systematic review. arXiv preprint arXiv:2308.02025 (2023)
41. Peixoto, T., Oliveira, B., Oliveira, Ó., Fillipe, R.: Data quality assessment in smart manufacturing: a review. Systems **13**(4), 243 (2025)
42. Pereira, A., Thomas, C.: Challenges of machine learning applied to safety-critical cyber-physical systems. Mach. Learn. Knowl. Extract. **2**(4), 579–602 (2020)
43. Pereira, J.A., Acher, M., Martin, H., Jézéquel, J.M., Botterweck, G., Ventresque, A.: Learning software configuration spaces: a systematic literature review. J. Syst. Softw. **182**, 111044 (2021)
44. Plathottam, S.J., Rzonca, A., Lakhnori, R., Iloeje, C.O.: A review of artificial intelligence applications in manufacturing operations. J. Adv. Manufact. Process. **5**(3), e10159 (2023)
45. Pohl, K.: Software product line engineering: Foundations, principles, and techniques, Springer (2005)
46. Qi, G.J., Luo, J.: Small data challenges in big data era: a survey of recent progress on unsupervised and semi-supervised methods. IEEE Trans. Pattern Anal. Mach. Intell. **44**(4), 2168–2187 (2022)
47. Rebala, G., Ravi, A., Churiwala, S.: An introduction to machine learning, Springer (2019)
48. Rehman, H.U., Chaplin, J.C., Zarzycki, L., Ratchev, S.: A framework for self-configuration in manufacturing production systems. In: Doctoral Conference on Computing, Electrical and Industrial Systems, pp. 71–79. Springer (2021)
49. Ridzuan, F., Zainon, W.M.N.W.: A review on data cleansing methods for big data. Procedia Comput. Sci. **161**, 731–738 (2019)
50. Romanssini, M., de Aguirre, P.C.C., Compassi-Severo, L., Girardi, A.G.: A review on vibration monitoring techniques for predictive maintenance of rotating machinery. Eng **4**(3), 1797–1817 (2023)
51. Ross, N.S., Sheeba, P.T., Shibi, C.S., Gupta, M.K., Korkmaz, M.E., Sharma, V.S.: A novel approach of tool condition monitoring in sustainable machining of ni alloy with transfer learning models. J. Intell. Manuf. **35**(2), 757–775 (2024)
52. Rowley, J.: The wisdom hierarchy: Representations of the dikw hierarchy. J. Inf. Sci. **33**(2), 163–180 (2007)
53. Scholz, P.: Applikation maschinell lernender Systeme in der vernetzten adaptiven Produktion. Apprimus Wissenschaftsverlag (2022)
54. Schuh, G., Schmidt, C.: Produktionsmanagement. Springer (2014)
55. Schuh, G., Scholz, P.: Development of a framework for the systematic identification of ai application patterns in the manufacturing industry. In: Portland International Conference on Management of Engineering and Technology (PICMET), pp. 1–8. IEEE (2019)
56. Schuh, G., Scholz, P., Leich, T., May, R.: Identifying and analyzing data model requirements and technology potentials of machine learning systems in the manufacturing industry of the future. In: International Scientific Conference on Information Technology and Management Science (ITMS), pp. 1–10. IEEE (2020)
57. Scotti, V.: Artificial intelligence. IEEE Instrument. Measure. Mag. **23**(3), 27–31 (2019)

58. Shi, J., Pan, Z., Jiang, L., Zhai, X.: An ontology-based methodology to establish city information model of digital twin city by merging BIM, GIS and IoT. Adv. Eng. Inform. **57**, 102114 (2023)
59. Soldatos, J.: Artificial intelligence in manufacturing: enabling intelligent, flexible and cost-effective production through AI, Springer Nature (2024)
60. Soori, M., Jough, F.K.G., Dastres, R., Arezoo, B.: Ai-based decision support systems in industry 4.0, a review. J. Econom. Technol. (2024)
61. Sorensen, D.G.H., Brunoe, T.D., Nielsen, K.: Challenges in production and manufacturing systems platform development for changeable manufacturing. In: International Conference on Advances in Production Management Systems (APMS), pp. 312–319. Springer (2018)
62. Todescato, M.: Sustainable manufacturing through application of reconfigurable and intelligent systems in production processes: a system perspective. Sci. Rep. **13**(1), 22374 (2023)
63. Tomaselli, G.P., Pinto, N.S., Acuña, C.: Requirements management methods and practices for improving the quality of agile software development processes: a review of the literature. Requirements Eng. 1–28 (2025)
64. Uysal, M.P., Mergen, A.E.: Smart manufacturing in intelligent digital mesh: Integration of enterprise architecture and software product line engineering. J. Ind. Inf. Integr. **22**, 100202 (2021)
65. Vierhauser, M., Egyed, A.: Runtime monitoring for systems of system: A closer look on opportunities for manufacturers in the context of industry 4.0. In: Digital Transformation: Core Technologies and Emerging Topics from a Computer Science Perspective, pp. 203–222. Springer (2023)
66. Vogelsang, A., Borg, M.: Requirements engineering for machine learning: Perspectives from data scientists. In: International Requirements Engineering Conference Workshops (REW), pp. 245–251. IEEE (2019)
67. Wang, J., Shu, J., Alam, M.M., Gao, Z., Li, Z., Tong, R.K.Y.: Drift-aware feature learning based on autoencoder preprocessing for soft sensors. Adv. Intell. Syst. **6**(3), 2300486 (2024)
68. Wei, S., Lin, X., Tu, F., Wang, Y., Liu, L., Yin, S.: Reconfigurability, why it matters in ai tasks processing: a survey of reconfigurable AI chips. IEEE Trans. Circuits Syst. I Regul. Pap. **70**(3), 1228–1241 (2022)
69. Windmann, A., Wittenberg, P., Schieseck, M., Niggemann, O.: Artificial intelligence in industry 4.0: A review of integration challenges for industrial systems. arXiv preprint arXiv:2405.18580 (2024)
70. Xiang, W., Yu, K., Han, F., Fang, L., He, D., Han, Q.L.: Advanced manufacturing in industry 5.0: a survey of key enabling technologies and future trends. Trans. Indust. Inform. **20**(2), 1055–1068 (2024)
71. Zhang, L., Hao, S., Ming, M.: A real-time detection method of software configuration errors based on fine-grained configuration item types. Sci. Program. **2022**, 1–13 (2022)
72. Zhang, S., Ernst, M.D.: Proactive detection of inadequate diagnostic messages for software configuration errors. In: International Symposium on Software Testing and Analysis (ISSTA), pp. 12–23 ACM (2015)
73. Zimmermann, T.: Card-sorting: From text to themes. In: Perspectives on Data Science for Software Engineering, pp. 137–141. Elsevier (2016)

Energy-Aware Analysis of MLOps Stages in Heterogeneous Computing

Julio Corona[1,2(✉)], Pedro Rodrigues[1,2], Mário Antunes[1,2], and Rui L. Aguiar[1,2]

[1] Instituto de Telecomunicações, Universidade de Aveiro, Aveiro, Portugal
{jcamejo,mario.antunes,ruilaa}@av.it.pt, pedrofrodrigues4@ua.pt
[2] DETI, Universidade de Aveiro, Aveiro, Portugal

Abstract. As Machine Learning (ML) becomes a cornerstone of modern computing, ensuring the efficient and energy-conscious execution of Machine Learning Operations (MLOps) pipelines is increasingly critical. While prior work has focused primarily on execution time, the growing energy footprint of these pipelines remains a largely overlooked concern. This paper presents an energy-aware analysis of a complete MLOps workflow across heterogeneous Virtual Machine (VM) configurations, jointly evaluating execution time and energy consumption for four distinct stages: Data Cleaning, Preprocessing, Model Tuning, and Evaluation. The results demonstrate that resource allocation must adapt to the computational characteristics of each stage. Lightweight, sequential stages exhibit negligible performance gains but substantial energy waste from CPU over-provisioning (for instance, CPU count shows a strong positive correlation with energy consumption in sequential tasks). In contrast, the compute-intensive Model Tuning stage benefits from parallelization, although the achievable speedup is constrained by resource imbalance. Crucially, adequate memory acts as an efficiency stabilizer by preventing performance degradation caused by disk thrashing. These findings provide practical insights for designing adaptive resource allocation policies, highlighting that optimal efficiency is achieved by aligning computational resources with stage heterogeneity, thereby contributing to greener and more sustainable Artificial Intelligence practices.

Keywords: Machine Learning · MLOps · Heterogeneous Computing · Energy Efficiency

1 Introduction

The rapid proliferation of Machine Learning (ML) applications has intensified the demand for scalable and efficient execution frameworks. Machine Learning Operations (MLOps) has emerged as a central paradigm for managing the lifecycle of ML models, providing a structured approach for data collection, preprocessing, training, evaluation, and deployment [20]. By integrating DevOps practices with ML-specific requirements, MLOps enables automation, reproducibility,

M. Mecella et al. (Eds.): ICSOFT 2025, CCIS 3144, pp. 165–182, 2027.
https://doi.org/10.1007/978-3-032-37353-3_7

and continuous delivery in production environments. Its adoption spans domains such as network management, industrial automation, and healthcare, reflecting the growing need to operationalize ML workflows at scale [13].

A cornerstone of MLOps is the orchestration of ML pipelines, which consist of sequential stages that progressively transform raw data into actionable insights and predictive models. These pipelines are typically executed in heterogeneous computing environments that integrate processors such as Central Processing Unit (CPUs), Graphics Processing Unit (GPUs), and specialized accelerators, including Field-Programmable Gate Array (FPGAs) and Tensor Processing Unit (TPUs) [14]. However, while heterogeneity enables significant performance gains, it also introduces challenges in task scheduling and resource allocation, often resulting in suboptimal utilization, increased operational costs, and a negative environmental impact.

Previous research, including our earlier work [7], examined how variations in Virtual Machine (VM) configurations, defined by Central Processing Unit (CPU) cores and memory, affect execution times in MLOps pipelines. However, computational performance alone provides an incomplete view of system efficiency. Given the increasing focus on sustainability and the advent of Green Artificial Intelligence (AI), complementing time-based metrics with energy consumption analysis has become increasingly essential [1]. ML workloads are often power-intensive and can contribute substantially to the carbon footprint of large-scale deployments. This issue is particularly acute in cloud and edge environments, where providers face pressure to reduce energy costs and comply with carbon-neutrality targets. Regulatory initiatives in Europe and elsewhere are beginning to address the energy footprint of AI, positioning energy-aware MLOps as both a technical challenge and a compliance requirement [15].

This work extends our previous study [7] by jointly analyzing execution time and energy consumption across heterogeneous virtual configurations, thereby expanding the understanding of resource efficiency in MLOps pipelines. The evaluation, performed on datasets from the network and Internet of Things (IoT) domains, examines how different combinations of CPU and memory resources affect each pipeline stage. The results show that lightweight and sequential stages, such as data cleaning and evaluation, gain little from additional resources, which primarily increase energy consumption. In contrast, computationally intensive stages, such as model tuning, benefit from balanced CPU and memory provisioning. These insights highlight the importance of aligning resource allocation with the computational characteristics of each stage to achieve sustainable MLOps operation.

The contributions of this extended work are threefold:

- Introduction of energy consumption profiling across all MLOps pipeline stages, complementing the execution time analysis from the conference version.
- Comprehensive assessment of how heterogeneous CPU–memory configurations affect both execution efficiency and energy demand in real workloads.

- Formulation of practical recommendations for adaptive, energy-aware resource
  scheduling to support sustainable and cost-efficient MLOps deployments in heterogeneous infrastructures.

By extending computational efficiency studies with energy-aware insights, this work bridges performance and sustainability in MLOps, supporting more informed decisions in both academic and industrial deployments.

The remainder of this paper is organized as follows. Section 2 introduces the concepts of MLOps, heterogeneous computing, and energy efficiency in MLOps environments. Section 3 reviews relevant studies addressing the challenges of executing ML pipelines in heterogeneous infrastructures. Section 4 describes the research methodology, including the datasets, pipeline stages, computational infrastructure, and energy measurement setup. Section 5 presents a detailed analysis of the pipeline behavior in different VM configurations, highlighting how resource allocation affects execution time and energy consumption. Finally, Sect. 6 summarizes the main findings and provides directions for future research.

2 Background

To situate the context and emphasize the importance of analyzing the computational demands of different stages of the MLOps pipeline, this section presents an overview of three key areas. The first subsection outlines the principles and practices of MLOps (Subsect. 2.1), followed by the challenges of executing ML workloads in heterogeneous computing environments (Subsect. 2.2). The final subsection addresses the growing importance of energy efficiency in ML and MLOps (Subsect. 2.3), highlighting the need to consider sustainability in addition to runtime performance.

2.1 MLOps

MLOps is an essential set of practices that automates and streamlines the entire ML workflow and deployment lifecycle. As an extension of the DevOps culture applied specifically to data-driven and ML applications, MLOps unifies ML application development (Dev) with system deployment and operations (Ops). By applying relevant DevOps concepts and creating new specialized practices, it effectively automates the continuous workflow of ML systems, leading to substantial organizational benefits, including improved efficiency, increased scalability and reliability, enhanced collaboration between teams, and reduced operational costs.

A key concept in MLOps is the ML pipeline. ML pipelines consist of multiple sequential steps, also known as components, that span the entire lifecycle of a ML model, from initial development to deployment and ongoing maintenance. These steps typically include data collection, data pre-processing, feature engineering, model training, model evaluation, and model deployment. Each step can be complex and time-consuming, requiring specialized tools and expertise to perform effectively. The use of ML pipelines can help automate and streamline these processes, making it easier to produce high-quality ML models in a reproducible and scalable manner.

Figure 1 presents a structural overview of a typical MLOps workflow organization. This illustration clearly identifies the ML pipeline as the core component, emphasizing the critical importance of optimizing its overall execution and performance.

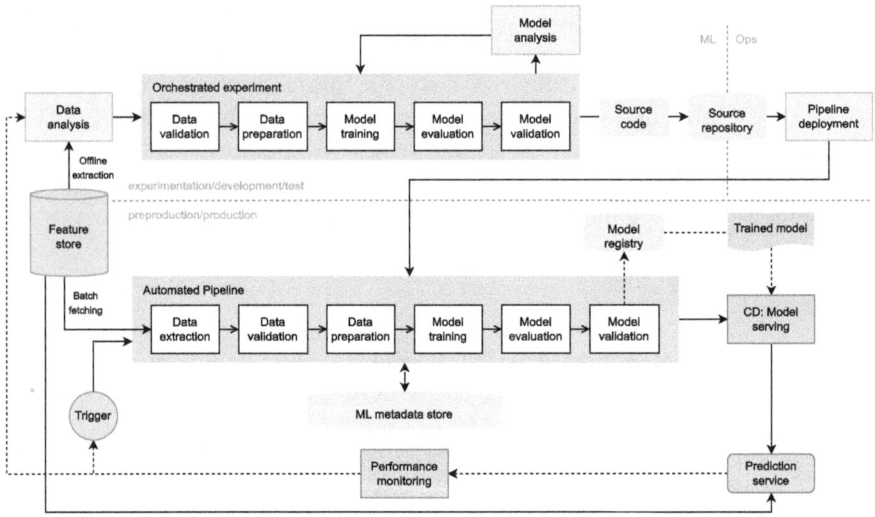

Fig. 1. General overview of a common MLOps workflow. Adapted from [16].

Although MLOps has the potential to enhance the efficiency and effectiveness of ML workflows, it remains an emerging field, and therefore, several challenges need to be addressed. In addition to the traditional challenges associated with adopting new practices and technologies, such as resistance to change, lack of expertise, and organizational silos, one of the key practical challenges that studies of MLOps [12,14,35] have identified is the need for efficient orchestration and scheduling of ML pipelines in heterogeneous computing environments. In this type of environment, where multiple types of hardware are available, the scheduling and orchestration of ML pipelines becomes more complex and challenging. If the components of a pipeline are not correctly placed and scheduled, this can lead to inefficiencies such as under-utilization of resources, wasted computational time, and increased costs. To develop strategies that address these challenges, it is essential first to understand the computational requirements of different stages of the ML pipeline, which is the primary focus of this work.

2.2 Heterogeneous Computing

The convergence of rapidly advancing hardware and the intense computational demands of modern ML workloads has driven the evolution of the computing infrastructure toward heterogeneity. **Heterogeneous computing** refers to systems that integrate multiple types of processing hardware, such as CPUs, GPUs, FPGAs, and TPUs, into a single environment. The core benefit lies in leveraging the unique strengths of each component to maximize overall performance and efficiency. For instance, while GPUs excel at highly parallel processing inherent in deep learning tasks, CPUs are better suited for sequential logic and control tasks. Combining these specialized processors allows a system to surpass the performance achievable with any single type of hardware alone. Figure 2 illustrates a representative example of such a heterogeneous computing cluster.

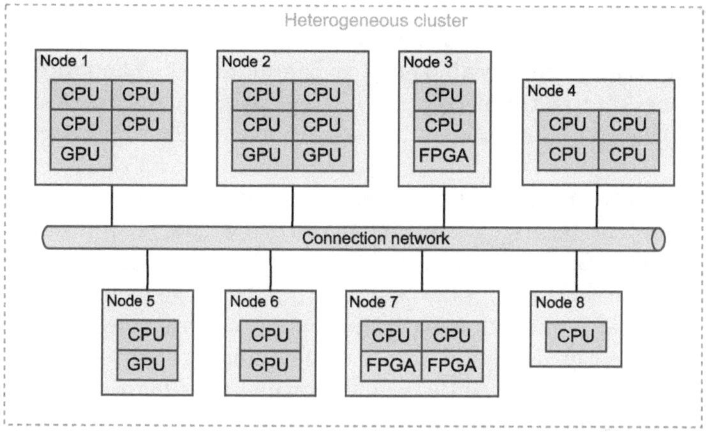

Fig. 2. Simple representation of a heterogeneous cluster. Adapted from [36].

Furthermore, the definition of heterogeneity has expanded to encompass processors based on diverse computer architectures. For example, the Advanced RISC Machine (ARM) architecture has become a viable alternative for specific workloads, offering benefits like higher core density, improved power efficiency, and seamless compatibility with ARM-based mobile ecosystems. Adopting alternative architectures offers innovative solutions for addressing existing and emerging computing tasks.

However, realizing the full potential of heterogeneous environments is critically dependent on effective task placement and orchestration strategies. To fully exploit the diverse resources available, it is essential to develop intelligent scheduling techniques that determine the optimal placement of tasks within a given workload. This is especially vital for ML pipelines, where different stages employ varying algorithms and computational patterns, each benefiting from a distinct type of specialized hardware. By analyzing the computational demands of each pipeline stage and tailoring them to heterogeneous computing environments, strategies can be devised to enhance both the efficiency and the overall effectiveness of ML workflows.

2.3 Energy Efficiency in ML and MLOps

The exponential growth in the size and complexity of modern ML models, particularly deep neural networks, has made power consumption a critical first-class metric, alongside traditional measures such as accuracy and latency. Energy consumption is significant throughout the entire ML lifecycle, affecting training, inference, and execution of automated pipeline stages in MLOps. Addressing this issue is central to the emerging movement of Green AI [1], which promotes sustainable practices in the development and deployment of intelligent systems.

The discussion of sustainability in AI is gaining urgency, as demonstrated by recent works on energy profiling, eco-efficiency, and estimation of the AI carbon footprint [3,31]. High energy consumption directly translates into increased operational costs and considerable environmental impact. Therefore, integrating energy awareness into MLOps practices is essential to ensure that models are not only performant and reliable, but also resource efficient and environmentally responsible.

Although many studies, such as [5,9,27], have focused on optimizing ML workloads solely in terms of runtime performance, far fewer have examined the critical balance between execution time and energy consumption. Our work extends this discussion by emphasizing that, in heterogeneous computing environments, the fastest execution path may not necessarily be the most energy-efficient. Consequently, a holistic MLOps scheduling strategy should incorporate energy consumption models to determine optimal task placement and sequencing, thus balancing performance objectives with sustainability goals. This motivates our quantitative investigation of the relationship between execution time and energy consumption in MLOps stages under diverse resource configurations.

3 Related Work

The challenge of deploying complex ML pipelines across heterogeneous computing environments has spurred important research into intelligent resource scheduling. Le et al. [21] pioneered a solution by introducing AlloX, a framework designed to optimize performance and ensure fairness for ML jobs sharing resources with varying computation rates. AlloX transforms the resource allocation problem into a minimum-cost bipartite matching formulation, enabling it to determine optimal CPU and GPU configurations that outperform existing methods in heterogeneous setups. Complementing this, Chen et al. [4] proposed an improved task scheduling system for Kubernetes-based MLOps frameworks. By framing scheduling as an NP-hard multi-objective knapsack problem, they employed a Genetic Algorithm (GA) to optimize task placement. While not exclusively focused on hardware heterogeneity, the GA's fitness function allows straightforward extension to this domain, demonstrating significant reductions in average execution time compared to the default Kubernetes scheduler.

Focusing specifically on hardware accelerators, several works address scheduling in heterogeneous GPU clusters. Narayanan et al. proposed Gavel [25], a cluster scheduling tool for Deep Neural Network (DNN) training that converts existing scheduling policies to account for heterogeneity and resource allocation. Gavel uses a round-based mechanism to ensure equitable allocation; however, its scope is limited to training jobs and only considers GPU heterogeneity, overlooking other pipeline stages. Similarly, Sia [19] and MixTran [37] concentrate exclusively on optimizing heterogeneous GPU environments. Sia allocates resources to elastic, resource-adaptive jobs by profiling throughput across different batch sizes on each GPU type, achieving significant reductions in average job execution time and makespan. Likewise, MixTran abstracts heterogeneous GPU resources into virtual tickets to ensure fair distribution among users. It then solves a global optimization model to satisfy resource requests and node constraints and, through resource trading, achieves a 30–50% reduction in overall execution time compared to the default Kubernetes scheduler. Despite these advancements, a gap remains in developing holistic scheduling approaches that address the full multi-stage ML pipeline across the broader array of heterogeneous resources (CPUs, GPUs, FPGAs, TPUs) now common in MLOps deployments.

At the same time, the exponential growth in model size and computational requirements has intensified concerns about the energy footprint of ML training and inference. Strubell et al. [30] quantified the financial and environmental costs of training large Natural Language Processing (NLP) models, sparking debate on the sustainability of deep learning research. Henderson et al. [18] proposed systematic reporting of energy and carbon usage, providing tools such as the experiment impact tracker for standardized measurement. These studies highlighted the lack of consistent reporting practices and the need to consider energy-performance trade-offs alongside precision. More recent work broadens the discussion under the umbrella of Green AI, advocating for the inclusion of environmental metrics in AI research and deployment. Mitu and Mitu [22] emphasize AI's carbon footprint across model training, hardware manufacturing, and deployment, proposing mitigation strategies such as renewable-powered data centers and efficient model compression. Chadli et al. [3] provide a systematic mapping of sustainability in MLOps, analyzing environmental costs across pipeline phases, and identifying gaps in industry adoption. Together, these contributions underscore that while energy-efficient algorithms and hardware are advancing, most assessments remain focused on isolated stages, primarily model training, rather than end-to-end MLOps pipelines.

In summary, previous research has predominantly pursued two directions: scheduling and resource allocation frameworks for heterogeneous computing, optimized mainly for performance and fairness, and energy-focused analyses of ML training, often at the level of individual models or isolated pipeline stages. Few works integrate these perspectives to jointly examine execution time and energy consumption throughout the MLOps pipeline operating in heterogeneous infrastructures. This gap motivates the present study, which aims to provide a holistic evaluation of both runtime and energy efficiency in pipeline execution, contributing toward sustainable and cost-effective MLOps practices.

4 Research Methodology

This section outlines the experimental framework adopted in this study. It first introduces the datasets considered, followed by the definition of the analyzed ML pipeline and the computational infrastructure used. Finally, the applied energy measurement strategy is presented, allowing for the joint analysis of execution time and energy efficiency across pipeline stages. For model tuning and evaluation, the datasets are partitioned into training and testing sets, with 20% reserved for testing.

4.1 Datasets

Seven publicly available datasets covering various networks and IoT domains were used to ensure generalizability of the analysis. These datasets were selected for their unique characteristics and suitability for classification tasks. The key attributes and sizes are summarized below.

- **KPI-KQI** [26]: A synthetic dataset with 165 samples and 14 features, capturing Key Performance Indicator (KPIs) and Key Quality Indicator (KQIs) across nine distinct services. The labels correspond to 5G service types.
- **User Network Activities Classification (UNAC)** [28]: Contains 389 samples and 23 features describing network traffic parameters, including protocols, packet sizes, and timestamps. The labels classify user network activities.
- **IoT-APD** [23]: Composed of 10,485 samples with 17 features extracted from IoT simulations, such as source/destination ratios and durations. The labels identify attack types.
- **Network Slicing Recognition (NSR)** [11]: Includes 31,583 samples with 17 features, covering attributes like packet delay and equipment categories. Designed for network slice selection, including failure scenarios.
- **DeepSlice** [34]: Provides 63,167 samples with 10 features describing 5G network slice parameters. The outputs classify different types of network services.
- **NSL-KDD** [32]: An enhanced version of the KDD-CUP dataset with 148,517 samples and 42 attributes (41 describing data characteristics and one attack label). It improves balance and diversity, making it widely used for intrusion detection.
- **IoT-DNL** [29]: A large-scale dataset with 477,426 samples and 13 features derived from wireless IoT environments. It includes frame details and attack labels, supporting anomaly-based Intrusion Detection System (IDS) evaluation.

4.2 Machine Learning Pipeline

The ML pipeline defines the structured workflow for model development, training, and evaluation, transforming raw data into actionable predictions. The execution times for each sequential stage were accurately measured using Python's *exectimeit* library [24]. The pipeline, visually represented in Fig. 3, consists of four distinct stages:

1. **Stage 1 (Data Cleaning):** Initial data quality assurance, including the removal of rows with missing values, duplicates, and irrelevant columns.
2. **Stage 2 (Data Preprocessing):** A multi-step process involving label encoding of categorical variables, removal of low-variance features, Isolation Forest for outlier detection, feature normalization, and finally, Principal Component Analysis (PCA) to reduce dimensionality while retaining 90% of the data's variance.
3. **Stage 3 (Model Tuning):** Hyperparameter optimization is performed for three representative models, namely Logistic Regression (LR), Random Forest (RF), and Multi-Layer Perceptron (MLP), using the genetic algorithm implemented in the *sklearn-genetic-opt* library. Each hyperparameter configuration is evaluated through a 4-fold cross-validation.
4. **Stage 4 (Model Evaluation):** Model performance is assessed using the Matthews Correlation Coefficient (MCC) metric [6], which offers a reliable and balanced assessment, particularly crucial for potential scenarios involving imbalanced datasets.

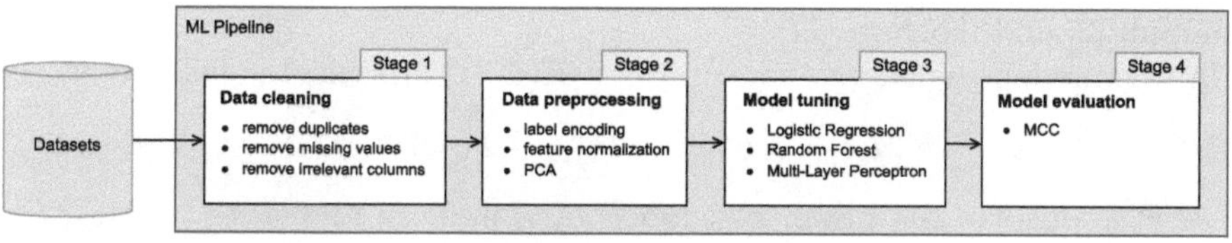

Fig. 3. ML pipeline considered in this work [7].

4.3 Computational Infrastructure

The experiments were conducted on an infrastructure comprising nine identical computing nodes, each hosting a single VM to control and constrain hardware availability. The heterogeneity of our setup is defined solely by the VM's configuration of Virtual Central Processing Unit (vCPU) cores and Random Access Memory (RAM) capacity, as detailed in Table 1.

This intentionally restricted heterogeneous configuration was adopted for two primary reasons: first, it provides a high degree of control over resource combinations, allowing for a precise view of the impact of these two variables; and

Table 1. Virtual Machines Configuration (same as [7]).

VM	vCPU Cores	RAM (GB)
VM 1	1	1
VM 2	1	8
VM 3	1	16
VM 4	4	1
VM 5	4	8
VM 6	4	16
VM 7	8	1
VM 8	8	8
VM 9	8	16

second, it reflects the current availability of computational resources. The varying VM configurations enable a rigorous evaluation of ML stage feasibility and performance under diverse resource constraints, offering valuable insight into resource optimization for varied task requirements.

4.4 Energy Measurement Setup

To complement execution time with energy-aware analysis, energy consumption was estimated using a simulation-based methodology. This approach, initially described in [10] and widely adopted in cloud and IoT studies [8,33], applies the linear energy consumption model used in established simulators such as CloudSim [2] and iFogSim [17].

In this model, the energy consumption $E(u, t)$ (in joules) is defined as:

$$E(u,t) = \left[P_{\text{idle}} + (P_{\text{max}} - P_{\text{idle}})u\right] \cdot t,$$

where P_{idle} denotes the power consumed by a node in idle state (watts), P_{max} represents the power consumed at full utilization (watts), u corresponds to CPU utilization (ranging from 0 to 1), and t is the execution time of the task (seconds).

In this study, the procedure was carried out in three steps. First, the computational capacity of the VMs was benchmarked using the 7-Zip compression test to determine the MIPS performance of the host hardware. Second, CPU utilization and execution time were monitored for each pipeline stage. Finally, these values were applied to the linear model to calculate the estimated energy consumption. While the linear power model provides a consistent energy estimation, it does not account for non-linear effects of memory or I/O subsystems, which may slightly affect absolute energy values.

5 Analysis and Discussion

The following analysis examines how the pipeline stages behave under different VM configurations and evaluates the impact of variations in CPU and RAM allocations on execution time and energy consumption. The goal is to characterize the trade-offs between computational capacity, runtime efficiency, and energy demand across heterogeneous environments.

Figure 4 presents the relationship between execution time and energy consumption for the four pipeline stages. Each data point represents the mean value for a given VM configuration, obtained by averaging the results across all evaluated datasets.

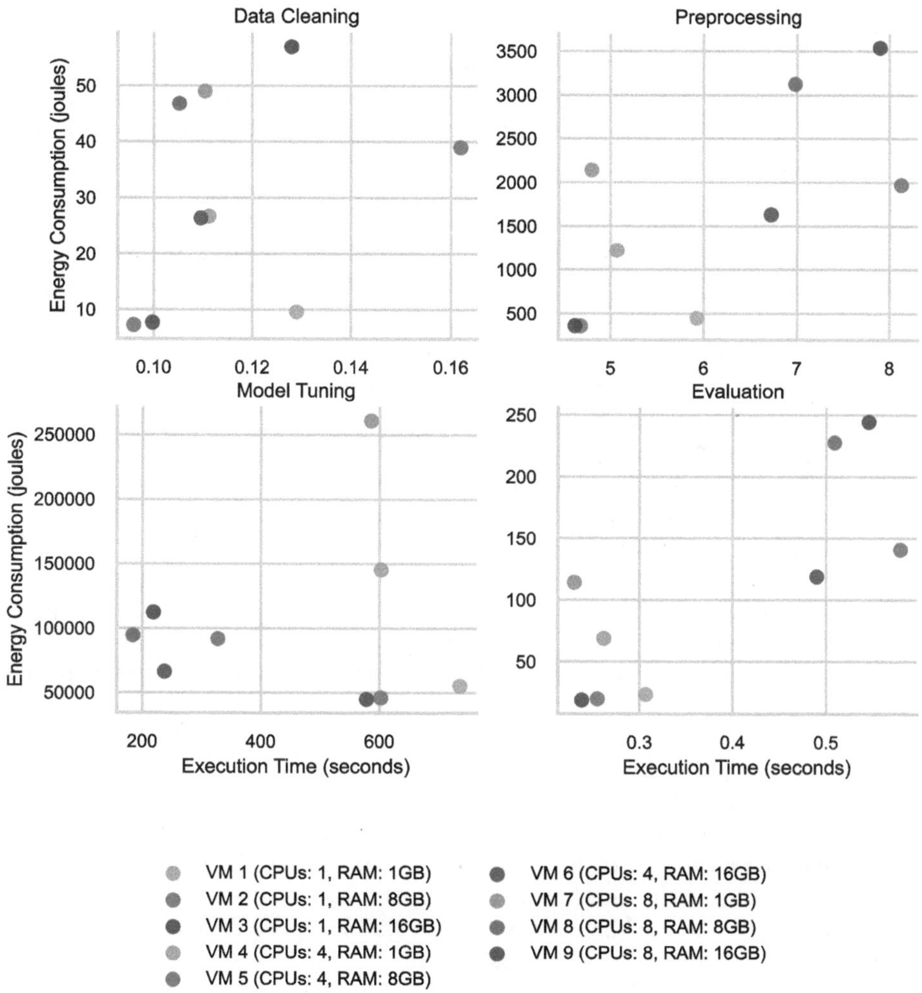

Fig. 4. Execution time versus energy consumption across pipeline stages.

Stage 1, focused on data cleaning, exhibited relatively low computational requirements compared to the other pipeline stages, with execution times ranging from 0.096 s (VM 2) to 0.162 s (VM 5) and energy consumption spanning 7.28 J (VM 2) to 57.01 J (VM 9). Single-core configurations (VMs 1–3) demonstrated the highest energy efficiency, with VM 2 (1 CPU, 8 GB RAM) achieving the best overall performance by reducing execution time by 25.6% compared to VM 1 while consuming only 7.28 J. Increasing memory beyond 8 GB, as in VM 3, yielded negligible benefits, indicating that moderate memory capacity is sufficient to cache intermediate data without incurring unnecessary energy overhead.

In contrast, quad-core configurations (VMs 4–6) displayed counterintuitive behavior: their execution times were comparable to or slower than those of single-core VMs while consuming 2.5–5.4 times more energy. VM 5 (4 CPUs, 8 GB RAM) performed worst, with a 68.8% slowdown relative to VM 2 and a total energy cost of 39.00 J, likely due to thread-management overhead and poor parallelization efficiency.

Eight-core configurations (VMs 7–9) further underscored the inefficiency of over-provisioning, as they consistently underperformed their single-core counterparts while consuming 6.7–7.8 times more energy. For instance, VM 9 (8 CPUs, 16 GB RAM) consumed 57.01 J, nearly eight times the energy of VM 2, despite running 33.3% slower. These results reveal that data-cleaning workloads are most efficient on lightweight single-core nodes with moderate memory, as their sequential and I/O-bound nature prevents performance gains from parallelism while increasing energy waste.

Stage 2, which includes data preprocessing, also exhibited limited parallelization potential but a moderate computational load, with execution times ranging from 4.62 s (VM 3) to 8.13 s (VM 5) and energy consumption spanning from 359.03 J (VM 2) to 3,540.95 J (VM 9). Single-core configurations (VMs 1–3) proved most efficient, with VM 3 (1 CPU, 16 GB RAM) and VM 2 (1 CPU, 8 GB RAM) achieving the best performance, while VM 2 recorded the lowest energy consumption. In contrast, the 28.4% slowdown observed in VM 1 (1 GB RAM) highlights the penalty of memory insufficiency, which forces frequent disk I/O operations.

However, quad-core configurations (VMs 4–6) yielded inconsistent results, showing no clear performance advantage over single-core setups and consuming 3–5× more energy. VM 5 (4 CPUs, 8 GB RAM) recorded the worst outcome, with an 8.13-second execution time and 1971.98 J energy use, indicating thread-management overhead and memory bandwidth contention. Even VM 4 (4 CPUs, 1 GB RAM), which was the fastest among the quad-core nodes, achieved an execution time of 5.07 s while consuming 1222.97 J, representing 3.4 times more energy than VM 2 for 8.3% slower execution.

The octa-core group (VMs 7–9) further exposed the inefficiency of excessive parallelism: their runtimes were comparable to or slower than single-core VMs, yet their energy costs increased up to 9.9×, with VM 7 consuming 2140.59 J for nearly identical performance to VM 2. These findings reflect the dominance of sequential and memory-bound operations that prevent effective parallel scaling, as additional cores remain active but underutilized, dissipating energy through synchronization and context-switching overheads.

Stage 3, focused on model tuning, represented the most computationally demanding component of the pipeline, with execution times ranging from 184.36 s (VM 8) to 734.25 s (VM 1) and energy consumption spanning from 45,141.80 J (VM 3) to 260,924.83 J (VM 7). Single-core configurations exhibited severe performance limitations, with VM 1 requiring 734.25 s (over 12 minutes) and consuming 55,498.95 J, while VM 3 achieved the lowest energy consumption among these configurations (45,141.80 J) but still required 578.43 s to complete. The 21.2% improvement from VM 1 to VM 3 underscores the importance of adequate memory capacity for caching intermediate model states, although the absolute runtime remains prohibitive for rapid experimental cycles.

Quad-core configurations demonstrated the transformative benefits of parallelization in this stage, with VM 6 (4 CPUs, 16 GB RAM) emerging as the optimal balance between performance and energy efficiency. It achieved an execution time of 237.33 s, representing a 67.7% speedup over VM 1, while consuming 66,756.87 J. This corresponds to a 2.4× acceleration for only 1.5× the energy cost of VM 3. This efficiency gain arises from the concurrent execution of multiple cross-validation folds, with sufficient memory bandwidth to avoid contention. In contrast, VM 5 (4 CPUs, 8 GB RAM) required 327.25 s and 92,050.97 J, revealing that limited memory can bottleneck multi-core systems due to paging and cache contention. VM 4 (4 CPUs, 1 GB RAM) performed similarly to single-core configurations (602.80 s) due to insufficient memory preventing effective parallelization.

Among the octa-core setups, VM 8 (8 CPUs, 8 GB RAM) achieved the shortest runtime (184.36 s) and demonstrated that tuning workloads can effectively leverage high levels of parallelism when adequate memory is available to support concurrent model training. However, VM 9 (8 CPUs, 16 GB RAM) did not deliver further improvement, showing slower execution (218.75 s) and higher energy consumption, indicating that additional memory beyond 8 GB does not offer tangible performance gain and may introduce memory management overhead. Conversely, VM 7 (8 CPUs, 1 GB RAM) exhibited catastrophic inefficiency, taking 585.94 s and consuming 260,924.83 J due to extreme memory thrashing, negating all parallelization gains while maintaining peak power draw. Overall, these results demonstrate that model-tuning workloads benefit from balanced CPU and memory provisioning. However, resource imbalance, particularly low memory-to-core ratios, drastically reduces both performance and energy efficiency.

Finally, Stage 4, which involved model evaluation, showed execution times ranging from 0.231 s (VM 7) to 0.580 s (VM 5) and energy consumption spanning 18.61 J (VM 3) to 244.50 J (VM 9). Single-core configurations maintained a clear advantage in both runtime and energy efficiency, with VM 3 (1 CPU, 16 GB RAM) achieving the lowest energy consumption (18.61 J) and a near-optimal execution time of 0.238 s. The consistent results across VMs 1–3 (0.255–0.306 s, 18.61–23.17 J) confirm that evaluation tasks are not compute-intensive.

Quad-core configurations showed counterintuitive degradation, with execution times increasing substantially relative to single-core nodes; VM 5 (4 CPUs, 8 GB RAM) recorded the longest runtime (0.580 s) and consumed 140.79 J, indicating that the evaluation workload includes sequential or fine-grained operations that incur synchronization overhead when parallelized.

Eight-core configurations further revealed the limited efficiency of parallel scaling in this stage: although VM 7 (8 CPUs, 1 GB RAM) achieved the fastest runtime (0.231 s), it consumed 114.16 J, about six times more energy than VM 3 for nearly identical performance, while VMs 8 and 9 (8 CPUs, 8–16 GB RAM) exhibited both longer runtimes (0.509–0.546 s) and extremely high energy costs (227.76–244.50 J). The high energy usage in these configurations indicates that many cores remain active but underutilized, stalled at synchronization points or waiting for sequential computations to complete.

Moving beyond individual stages, this analysis provides a global perspective on how computational resources influence the pipeline's performance and energy behavior. Table 2 presents the Pearson and Spearman correlation coefficients between computational resources (CPU and RAM) and the analyzed pipeline metrics (execution time and energy consumption).

Table 2. Correlation coefficients between computational resources and pipeline metrics across stages.

Stage	Metric	**Pearson**		**Spearman**	
		CPU	RAM	CPU	RAM
Stage 1	Execution Time	0.011	-0.011	0.018	-0.021
	Energy Consumption	0.329	0.014	0.371	-0.014
Stage 2	Execution Time	0.085	0.067	0.173	0.144
	Energy Consumption	0.445	0.099	**0.632**	0.121
Stage 3	Execution Time	-0.170	-0.165	-0.158	-0.156
	Energy Consumption	0.241	-0.175	0.211	-0.123
Stage 4	Execution Time	0.124	0.125	0.183	0.175
	Energy Consumption	0.413	0.136	**0.516**	0.149

Based on these correlation coefficients, a clear pattern emerges: the most consistent and influential relationship across the pipeline is between CPU allocation and energy consumption. For Stages 1, 2, and 4, the number of CPU shows a strong positive correlation with energy consumption (Spearman coefficients of 0.371, 0.632, and 0.516, respectively). This indicates a robust monotonic trend where increasing the number of cores consistently raises power consumption, regardless of whether the task benefits from parallelization. In contrast, the correlation between CPU count and execution time for these same stages is weak or slightly positive (for example, Stage 4 execution time vs. CPU: 0.124 Pearson), confirming that additional cores do not accelerate performance and may even slightly hinder it due to synchronization overhead.

Stage 3 stands as the only exception, where CPU count shows a weak negative correlation with execution time ($r = -0.170$ Pearson). This is the expected and desired relationship for a compute-bound task, though the weakness of the coefficient suggests that the linear benefit is attenuated by resource-imbalance outliers (e.g., VM 7). Even in this case, the CPU correlation with energy consumption remains positive ($r = 0.241$ Pearson), confirming that parallel speedup consistently entails a direct energy cost.

Regarding RAM capacity, it plays a distinct and critical role as a stabilizer of efficiency rather than a primary driver of speed. Across the lightweight stages (Stages 1, 2, and 4), the correlation between RAM and all metrics is negligible ($|r| < 0.15$), confirming that once a threshold of adequate memory is met, further increases offer marginal returns. However, in Stage 3, the RAM correlations reveal a crucial dynamic related to preventing performance collapse. RAM shows a weak negative correlation with execution time ($r = -0.165$), supporting the observation that sufficient memory is necessary for effective parallel execution. More importantly, RAM exhibits a negative correlation with energy consumption ($r = -0.175$ Pearson). This finding is significant: sufficient memory actively reduces the total energy required to complete the workload. This occurs because adequate RAM prevents the performance-and-energy catastrophe of disk thrashing (as seen in VM 7), thereby stabilizing the energy footprint even as CPU allocation increases.

6 Conclusions and Future Directions

This work extended previous analyses by jointly evaluating the execution time and energy consumption of a MLOps pipeline across heterogeneous VM configurations, providing energy-aware insights that are critical to sustainable resource scheduling. Analysis in distinct pipeline stages confirmed that the optimal allocation of resources strongly depends on the computational characteristics of each stage.

The results show that lightweight stages, such as data cleaning and evaluation, have minimal computational demands and limited potential for parallelization. For these stages, increasing CPU or RAM resources provides negligible performance improvement but substantially increases energy consumption. In contrast, model tuning emerged as the most resource-intensive stage, benefiting effectively from parallelization when sufficient memory bandwidth is available. However, beyond a balanced CPU-to-RAM ratio, additional resources yielded diminishing returns, highlighting the inefficiency of over-provisioning. Finally, the correlation analysis confirmed that CPU allocation is the primary factor driving energy consumption across all stages, while adequate RAM acts as a stabilizing element that prevents energy surges caused by resource contention.

In general, these findings emphasize that achieving energy-efficient MLOps execution requires adaptive resource allocation policies that consider the heterogeneous nature of pipeline stages rather than uniform scaling. Incorporating energy awareness into orchestration mechanisms can significantly reduce unnecessary energy consumption while maintaining acceptable runtime performance, thereby contributing to greener and more sustainable AI practices.

Future work will focus on three main directions. First, the analysis will be extended to include specialized accelerators such as GPUs, TPUs, and FPGAs, enabling a broader evaluation of heterogeneous computing environments. Second, dynamic scheduling strategies will be incorporated into MLOps orchestration frameworks to enhance energy efficiency while maintaining acceptable runtime performance. Finally, predictive models will be developed to estimate execution time and energy consumption prior to deployment, enabling proactive resource allocation and sustainable workload placement across cloud and edge infrastructures.

Acknowledgements.. This work is supported by the European Regional Development Fund (FEDER), through the Regional Operational Programme of Centre (CENTRO 2030) of the Portugal 2030 framework [Project inMotion with Nr. 21359 (CENTRO2030-FEDER-02225900)].

References

1. Bolón-Canedo, V., Morán-Fernández, L., Cancela, B., Alonso-Betanzos, A.: A review of green artificial intelligence: towards a more sustainable future. Neurocomputing **599**, 128096 (2024)
2. Buyya, R., Ranjan, R., Calheiros, R.N.: Modeling and simulation of scalable cloud computing environments and the cloudsim toolkit: challenges and opportunities. In: 2009 International Conference on High Performance Computing & Simulation, pp. 1–11. IEEE (2009)
3. Chadli, K., Botterweck, G., Saber, T.: The environmental cost of engineering machine learning-enabled systems: a mapping study. In: Proceedings of the 4th Workshop on Machine Learning and Systems, pp. 200–207 (2024)
4. Chen, H.M., Chen, S.Y., Hsueh, S.H., Wang, S.K.: Designing an improved ml task scheduling mechanism on kubernetes. In: 2023 Sixth International Symposium on Computer, Consumer and Control (IS3C), pp. 60–63 (2023). https://doi.org/10.1109/IS3C57901.2023.00024
5. Chiang, M.C., Zhang, L.W., Chou, Y.M., Chou, J.: Dynamic resource management for machine learning pipeline workloads. SN Comput. Sci. **4**(5), 665 (2023)
6. Chicco, D., Jurman, G.: The advantages of the matthews correlation coefficient (mcc) over f1 score and accuracy in binary classification evaluation. BMC Genomics **21**(1), 1–13 (2020)
7. Corona, J., Rodrigues, P., Antunes, M., Aguiar, R.: Impact of resource heterogeneity on MLOps stages: a computational efficiency study. In: Proceedings of the 20th International Conference on Software Technologies - Volume 1: ICSOFT, pp. 246–253. INSTICC, SciTePress (2025). https://doi.org/10.5220/0013520600003964
8. Corona, J., Teixeira, R., Antunes, M., Aguiar, R.L.: Towards cost estimation of DRL for task scheduling and placement. In: IEEE EUROCON 2025-21st International Conference on Smart Technologies, pp. 1–6. IEEE (2025)

9. Derakhshan, B., Rezaei Mahdiraji, A., Abedjan, Z., Rabl, T., Markl, V.: Optimizing machine learning workloads in collaborative environments. In: Proceedings of the 2020 ACM SIGMOD International Conference on Management of Data, pp. 1701–1716 (2020)
10. Domingues, P., Araujo, F., Silva, L.: Evaluating the performance and intrusiveness of virtual machines for desktop grid computing. In: 2009 IEEE International Symposium on Parallel & Distributed Processing, pp. 1–8. IEEE (2009)
11. Dutta, G.: Network slicing recognition (2025). https://www.kaggle.com/datasets/gauravduttakiit/network-slicing-recognition
12. Eken, B., Pallewatta, S., Tran, N.K., Tosun, A., Babar, M.A.: A multivocal review of mlops practices, challenges and open issues (2024). https://arxiv.org/abs/2406.09737
13. Faubel, L., Schmid, K.: MLOps: a multiple case study in industry 4.0. In: 2024 IEEE 29th International Conference on Emerging Technologies and Factory Automation (ETFA), pp. 01–08. IEEE (2024)
14. Faubel, L., Schmid, K., Eichelberger, H.: MLOps challenges in industry 4. 0. SN Comput. Sci.**4**(6), 828 (2023)
15. Francisco, M., Linnér, B.O.: AI and the governance of sustainable development. an idea analysis of the european union, the united nations, and the world economic forum. Environ. Sci. Policy **150**, 103590 (2023)
16. Google: MLOps: continuous delivery and automation pipelines in machine learning (2024). https://cloud.google.com/architecture/mlops-continuous-delivery-and-automation-pipelines-in-machine-learning
17. Gupta, H., Vahid Dastjerdi, A., Ghosh, S.K., Buyya, R.: iFogSim: a toolkit for modeling and simulation of resource management techniques in the internet of things, edge and fog computing environments. Softw.: Pract. Experience **47**(9), 1275–1296 (2017)
18. Henderson, P., Hu, J., Romoff, J., Brunskill, E., Jurafsky, D., Pineau, J.: Towards the systematic reporting of the energy and carbon footprints of machine learning. J. Mach. Learn. Res. **21**(248), 1–43 (2020)
19. Jayaram Subramanya, S., Arfeen, D., Lin, S., Qiao, A., Jia, Z., Ganger, G.R.: Sia: heterogeneity-aware, goodput-optimized ml-cluster scheduling. In: Proceedings of the 29th Symposium on Operating Systems Principles, pp. 642–657. SOSP '23, Association for Computing Machinery, New York, NY, USA (2023). https://doi.org/10.1145/3600006.3613175
20. Kreuzberger, D., Kühl, N., Hirschl, S.: Machine learning operations (MLOps): overview, definition, and architecture. IEEE Access **11**, 31866–31879 (2023)
21. Le, T.N., Sun, X., Chowdhury, M., Liu, Z.: AlloX: compute allocation in hybrid clusters. In: Proceedings of the Fifteenth European Conference on Computer Systems. EuroSys '20, Association for Computing Machinery, New York, NY, USA (2020). https://doi.org/10.1145/3342195.3387547
22. Mitu, N.E., Mitu, G.T.: The hidden cost of AI: carbon footprint and mitigation strategies. SSRN Electron. J. (2025). https://doi.org/10.2139/ssrn.5036344
23. MKhubaiib: IoT attack prediction dataset (2025). https://www.kaggle.com/datasets/mkhubaiib/iot-attack-prediction-dataset
24. Moreno, C., Fischmeister, S.: Accurate measurement of small execution times–getting around measurement errors. IEEE Embed. Syst. Lett. **9**(1), 17–20 (2017)

25. Narayanan, D., Santhanam, K., Kazhamiaka, F., Phanishayee, A., Zaharia, M.: Heterogeneity-Aware cluster scheduling policies for deep learning workloads. In: 14th USENIX Symposium on Operating Systems Design and Implementation (OSDI 20), pp. 481–498. USENIX Association (2020). https://www.usenix.org/conference/osdi20/presentation/narayanan-deepak
26. Preciado-Velasco, J.E., Gonzalez-Franco, J.D., Anias-Calderon, C.E., Nieto-Hipolito, J.I., Rivera-Rodriguez, R.: 5g/b5g service classification using supervised learning. Appl. Sci. **11**(11), 4942 (2021)
27. Rodrigues, P., Almeida, L., Corona, J., Antunes, M., Aguiar, R.L.: Optimised task placement for MLOps. In: 2025 IEEE International Conference on Consumer Technology-Europe, pp. 1–4. IEEE (2025)
28. Sandeepa, C., et al.: From opacity to clarity: leveraging XAI for robust network traffic classification. In: Herath, D., Date, S., Jayasinghe, U., Narayanan, V., Ragel, R., Wang, J. (eds.) International Conference on Asia Pacific Advanced Network. LNCS, vol. 1995, pp. 125–138. Springer, Cham (2023). https://doi.org/10.1007/978-3-031-51135-6_11
29. Speedwall10: IoT device network logs (2025). https://www.kaggle.com/datasets/speedwall10/iot-device-network-logs
30. Strubell, E., Ganesh, A., McCallum, A.: Energy and policy considerations for modern deep learning research. In: Proceedings of the AAAI Conference on Artificial Intelligence, vol. 34 (09), pp. 13693–13696. Association for the Advancement of Artificial Intelligence (AAAI) (2020). https://doi.org/10.1609/aaai.v34i09.7123
31. Tamburrini, G.: The ai carbon footprint and responsibilities of AI scientists. Philosophies **7**(1), 4 (2022)
32. Tavallaee, M., Bagheri, E., Lu, W., Ghorbani, A.A.: A detailed analysis of the KDD cup 99 data set. In: IEEE Symposium on Computational Intelligence for Security and Defense Applications, pp. 1–6. IEEE (2009)
33. Teixeira, R., Almeida, L., Rodrigues, P., Antunes, M., Gomes, D., Aguiar, R.L.: Beyond performance comparing the costs of applying deep and shallow learning. Comput. Commun., 108312 (2025)
34. Thantharate, A., Paropkari, R., Walunj, V., Beard, C.: DeepSlice: a deep learning approach towards an efficient and reliable network slicing in 5G networks. In: 2019 IEEE 10th Annual Ubiquitous Computing, Electronics & Mobile Communication Conference (UEMCON), pp. 0762–0767. IEEE (2019)
35. Xin, D., Miao, H., Parameswaran, A., Polyzotis, N.: Production machine learning pipelines: empirical analysis and optimization opportunities. In: Proceedings of the 2021 International Conference on Management of Data, pp. 2639–2652. SIGMOD '21, Association for Computing Machinery, New York, NY, USA (2021). https://doi.org/10.1145/3448016.3457566
36. Zhang, K., Wu, B.: Task scheduling for GPU heterogeneous cluster. In: 2012 IEEE International Conference on Cluster Computing Workshops, pp. 161–169 (2012). https://doi.org/10.1109/ClusterW.2012.20
37. Zhang, X.: Mixtran: an efficient and fair scheduler for mixed deep learning workloads in heterogeneous GPU environments. Clust. Comput. **27**(3), 2775–2784 (2024). https://doi.org/10.1007/s10586-023-04104-9

Low-Resource Python Source Code Authorship Attribution Using Contrastive-Learning Embeddings

David Álvarez-Fidalgo[1] and Francisco Ortin[1,2(✉)]

[1] Computer Science Department, University of Oviedo, Calvo Sotelo 18, Oviedo, Spain
ortin@uniovi.es

[2] Munster Technological University, Rossa Avenue, Bishopstown, Cork, Ireland

Abstract. Authorship attribution of source code seeks to identify the programmer of a given fragment and is commonly applied in cybersecurity, intellectual property protection, and forensic analysis. We present an efficient and accurate Python authorship-attribution system built on CLAVE, a contrastive-learning framework originally designed for authorship verification. CLAVE produces compact stylometric embeddings that capture programmer-specific coding traits, which we use as input to a Support Vector Machine (SVM) classifier. With only six short code samples per programmer and modest computational resources, our system surpasses state-of-the-art methods, including deep-learning approaches trained on far larger datasets. Using a dataset of 595 Python programs from 85 programmers, we compare CLAVE embeddings with alternative verification models and large language model (LLM) encoders. The SVM trained on CLAVE embeddings consistently achieves the highest performance (0.923), reducing classification error by 45% relative to standalone CLAVE verification and outperforming all evaluated LLM encoders. Training completes in under 200 ms and requires less than 160 MB of memory on standard CPU hardware, enabling rapid retraining as new authors or samples are introduced. These results show that combining contrastive-learning embeddings with a classical classifier provides a practical, accurate, and resource-efficient solution for source-code authorship attribution.

Keywords: Source Code Authorship Attribution · Contrastive Learning · Source Code Stylometry · CLAVE · Machine Learning

1 Introduction

Authorship attribution is the task of determining the author of an anonymous work from a predefined set of candidates [1]. Such works may include books (e.g., to resolve cases of disputed or anonymous literary authorship), handwritten documents (for use in criminal investigations), paintings (to verify the authenticity of artworks), digital content (to identify the authors of anonymous online posts), or musical compositions (to settle disputes regarding the true composer). Authorship attribution typically relies on linguistic, stylistic, and structural features as distinguishing markers, collectively referred to as stylometry [1].

M. Mecella et al. (Eds.): ICSOFT 2025, CCIS 3144, pp. 183–204, 2027.
https://doi.org/10.1007/978-3-032-37353-3_8

```
def is_prime_number(number: int) -> bool:
    """Check if a given number is prime."""
    if number <= 1:
        return False  # 0 and 1 are not prime numbers
    for divisor in range(2, int(number ** 0.5) + 1):
        if number % divisor == 0:
            return False  # Found a divisor, not prime
    return True  # No divisors found, number is prime
```

```
def prime(n): return n>1 and all(n%d for d in range(2, int(n**0.5)+1))
```

Fig. 1. Different code stylometry for a Python function returning if the parameter is a prime number.

When applied to source code, authorship attribution refers to the task of determining which programmer wrote a particular piece of code [2]. This process often leverages techniques from natural language processing (NLP), machine learning, and software forensics to capture coding traits that distinguish one programmer from another. Source code authorship attribution has important applications in cybersecurity, intellectual property protection, and forensic analysis [3]. In cybersecurity, it is employed to trace malware developers, identify the origins of security vulnerabilities, and detect unauthorized code reuse. Within legal and intellectual property domains, it supports the verification of ownership claims and the detection of plagiarism in software projects. In forensic investigations, it enables law enforcement to identify cybercriminals by analyzing malicious scripts, ransomware, or other illicit software.

Figure 1 shows how the same program in Python can be expressed in different styles, a phenomenon known as code stylometry. In the upper example, the programmer includes type annotations for function parameters and return values [4], while in the lower example these are omitted. The former also provides explicit documentation through comments and docstrings and prefers longer, more descriptive identifier names, whereas the latter favors brevity. Differences in programming style are further reflected in the choice of control structures: one implementation adopts a more traditional approach using `if-else` statements, while the other leverages generator comprehensions. These stylistic decisions affect not only readability and maintainability but also the length and overall structure of the code.

Code authorship *verification* seeks to determine whether two code excerpts were written by the same programmer, even when the author was not observed during training [5]. The key distinction between authorship verification and authorship attribution lies in their objectives: *attribution* identifies the specific author of a code sample from a predefined set of candidates, whereas *verification* determines whether two samples originate from the same author without prior knowledge of possible candidates. Thus, attribution is framed as a multi-class classification problem in which the authors are known during training, while verification is treated as a binary classification task that evaluates whether two code samples share the same authorship, regardless of whether the author appeared in the training data.

In earlier work, we implemented CLAVE, a deep learning (DL) model for source code authorship verification that leverages contrastive learning and transformer encoders

[6]. CLAVE was pre-trained on 270,602 Python source code files and fine-tuned with code from 61,956 programmers for authorship verification. The model achieves an AUC of 0.9782, surpassing the state-of-the-art verification systems.

In this paper, leveraging the CLAVE's strong performance in source code authorship verification, we explore its effectiveness for authorship attribution when only a limited number of source code files per programmer are available. To this end, we develop several attribution systems based on CLAVE, alternative verification models, and Large Language Model (LLM) encoders trained on source code, to compare CLAVE's performance for authorship attribution against existing DL approaches.

The primary contribution of this paper is the development of a Python source code authorship attribution system that, using CLAVE, achieves accuracy comparable to current DL methods but only trained with six source files per programmer. Furthermore, the system requires substantially fewer CPU and memory resources than deep learning alternatives, allowing rapid retraining when new programmers or additional code samples are introduced. Notably, the accuracy of the authorship attribution system considerably enhances CLAVE's ability to operate as a one-shot classifier.

This paper builds upon our earlier work presented at the 20th International Conference on Software Technologies (ICSOFT) [7]. The extensions introduced here include an error analysis of the best-performing classifiers, a more detailed explanation of contrastive learning, expanded discussions on implications for cybersecurity, forensic investigations, ethical considerations, and limitations, as well as an overview of recently published related work. We also present a visualization of how CLAVE clusters code stylometry (Fig. 7), provide a more comprehensive description of the dataset (Figs. 5 and 6), evaluate two additional dimensionality reduction methods, analyze how performance varies with growing number of training files per programmer, and describe a probabilistic model currently under development.

The remainder of the paper is organized as follows: Sect. 2 reviews related work and Sect. 3 provides an overview of CLAVE. Section 4 details the methodology while Sect. 5 presents the results. Section 6 discusses the findings, and Sect. 7 concludes the paper.

2 Related Work

2.1 Source Code Authorship Attribution

Kurtukova et al. propose a hybrid neural network (HNN) combining Convolutional Neural Networks (CNNs) with Bidirectional Gated Recurrent Units (BiGRUs) for Python code authorship attribution [8]. They evaluate their approach with groups of 5, 10, and 20 programmers (10–30 files per programmer), obtaining 0.85 accuracy for 20 programmers. In their design, CNN layers capture local structural code patterns, while BiGRU layers model long-range dependencies.

Alsulami et al. leverage Abstract Syntax Tree (AST) information extracted from source code to design a deep learning model for authorship attribution [9]. They implement both Long Short-Term Memory (LSTM) and Bidirectional Long Short-Term Memory (BiLSTM) models to automatically learn discriminative features from AST representations of programmers' code. Their dataset consists of 700 Python files written by

70 programmers across 10 problems from the Google Code Jam competition. The BiLSTM model achieves the best performance, with 0.96 accuracy when classifying 25 programmers and 0.88 accuracy when extended to 70 programmers.

Abuhamad et al. introduce DL-CAIS, a Deep Learning-based Code Authorship Identification System [10]. The system integrates a TF-IDF-driven deep representation with multiple Recurrent Neural Network (RNN) layers and fully connected layers. This representation is then combined with a random forest classifier, improving scalability for de-anonymizing authors. DL-CAIS is trained on the complete Google Code Jam dataset from 2008–2016 and on real-world code samples from 1,987 GitHub repositories. It achieves 94.38% accuracy in identifying 745 C programmers.

RoPGen is a deep learning model for authorship attribution that combines data augmentation with gradient augmentation during adversarial training to improve robustness against adversarial attacks [11]. This strategy increases training diversity, introduces meaningful perturbations to neural network gradients, and encourages the model to learn varied representations of coding styles. They train RoPGen on four datasets of Java, C, and C + + programs.

2.2 Source Code Authorship Verification

White and Sprague present a neural network architecture based on a bidirectional LSTM that learns stylometric representations of source code [12]. The model is trained with the NT-Xent loss function from the SimCLR framework [13]. For evaluation, the trained network is applied to authorship verification by comparing cosine similarity between representations, and to authorship attribution using a support vector machine classifier. On a dataset of C/C + + programs from Google Code Jam (2008–2017), the network achieves a verification accuracy of 92.94%.

FDR (Feedforward Duplicated Resolver) is a method for authorship verification built on a neural network initially trained for authorship attribution [14]. The network uses Variable-Independent Nested Bigrams, novel features extracted from the AST of each program. After being trained to classify source code files by known authors, part of the network is repurposed to generate representations of source code, which are then compared for verification. Their approach achieves an AUC of 0.96 in predicting whether pairs of samples from 43 unknown authors were written by the same individual.

Ou et al. introduce a neural network architecture for source code authorship verification that combines a bidirectional LSTM with a Generative Adversarial Network (GAN) [3]. Trained as a Siamese network, it learns stylometric representations of source code, while the GAN enforces the removal of functionality-related information from these representations. Authorship verification is performed by comparing the representations using cosine similarity.

Wang et al. develop a neural network that takes as input a set of manually engineered features extracted from pairs of programs and outputs the probability that both were written by the same author [15]. The features include static properties (extracted without execution) and dynamic metrics (collected during execution), such as runtime and memory usage.

2.3 Large Language Models for Source Code

Deep learning techniques in Natural Language Processing (NLP) have advanced rapidly since the introduction of the Transformer architecture and large language models (LLMs) [16]. Many of these innovations have also proven effective when adapted to source code.

CodeBERT is a bimodal pre-trained model for source code and natural language built on the architectures of BERT and RoBERTa [17]. The model is pre-trained jointly on source code and natural language, then fine-tuned for downstream tasks such as natural language code search and code documentation generation.

CuBERT is a pre-trained model for generating contextual embeddings of source code, also based on the BERT architecture [18]. CuBERT is pre-trained on a large dataset of Python files from GitHub and fine-tuned on multiple code understanding tasks, including variable-misuse classification and function-docstring mismatch detection.

A wide range of LLMs for source code has since been developed, typically categorized into general models trained on both natural and programming languages, and specialized models trained exclusively on code [19]. These models adopt encoder-only, decoder-only, or encoder–decoder architectures.

2.4 Contrastive Learning

Contrastive learning is a self-supervised deep learning paradigm designed to learn data representations by ensuring that similar instances are closer in the representation space, while dissimilar instances are farther apart [20]. The central idea is to obtain meaningful representations by contrasting positive (similar) pairs of data points against negative (dissimilar) ones.

This technique has been applied to improve the robustness of LLMs for source code. Jain et al. observe that while existing LLMs capture program functionality effectively, they remain highly sensitive to even semantically neutral code edits, leading to significant performance degradation and susceptibility to adversarial attacks [21]. To address this issue, they propose ContraCode, a contrastive pre-training model that leverages compiler transformations for data augmentation. ContraCode outperforms RoBERTa by 39% AUC on adversarial code clone detection tasks. A related approach, ContraBERT, applies nine source code transformations for contrastive pre-training of CodeBERT and GraphCodeBERT using the InfoNCE loss function [22]. ContraBERT yields substantial improvements in clone detection performance for both models.

Contrastive learning has also achieved notable success in natural language processing. Reimers and Gurevych introduce a BERT variant that employs Siamese and triplet networks to learn semantic sentence embeddings, which can be compared via cosine similarity [23].

Given the nature of authorship verification, contrastive learning has become a widely used approach in this domain as well. In the context of natural language documents, Tyo et al. adapt BERT with alternative objective functions to produce document representations that are closer for texts written by the same author and farther apart otherwise [24].

SimCLR is a widely adopted self-supervised contrastive learning framework originally developed for computer vision [13]. In SimCLR, positive instances are generated through data augmentation: for each input in a mini-batch, two augmented versions are created. The model is trained using the NT-Xent loss, which encourages representations of augmented views of the same input to be pulled closer together, while pushing apart those derived from different inputs.

3 Clave

The code attribution system presented in this paper builds upon our previous research, CLAVE: Contrastive Learning for Authorship Verification with Encoder Representations [6]. Figure 2 depicts the architecture of CLAVE, which takes source code as input and produces a single vector (embedding) that captures its stylometric representation. Embeddings of code authored by the same individual are positioned close together in the vector space, whereas embeddings from different authors are placed farther apart.

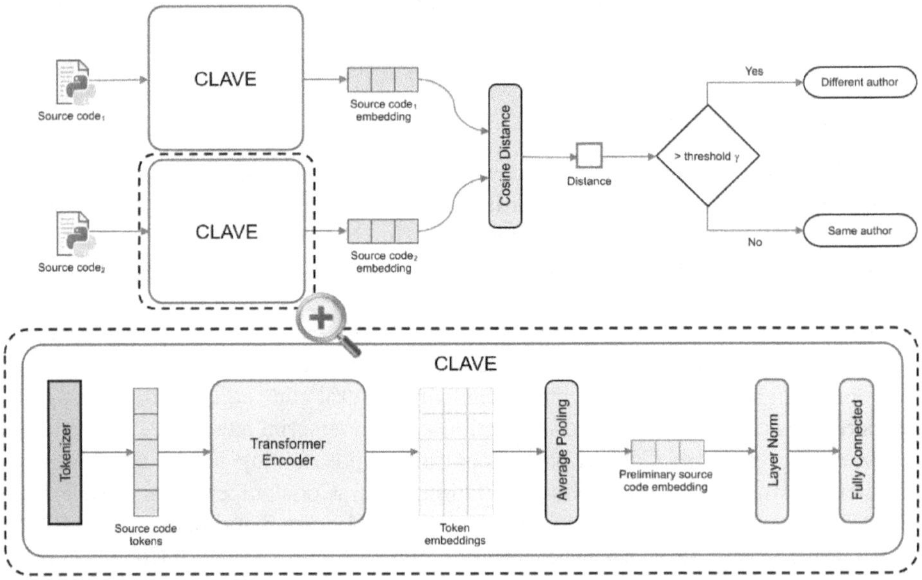

Fig. 2. Architecture of CLAVE. The lower panel provides a detailed view of the CLAVE component appearing in the upper part of the figure.

Because CLAVE generates a single embedding that encapsulates the stylometry of the input code, it is particularly well-suited for authorship verification. Two code excerpts are passed through CLAVE, producing two stylometric embeddings (upper part of Fig. 2). If the cosine distance (1 − cosine similarity) between these embeddings exceeds a threshold γ, the excerpts are classified as belonging to different authors; otherwise, they are attributed to the same author.

The first component of CLAVE (lower part of Fig. 2) is a SentencePiece tokenizer for Python, which transforms input code into a vector representation [6]. We explore three tokenization strategies: (i) SentencePiece customized for Python code, (ii) a newly designed tokenizer tailored for Python that we call the Stylometric Tokenizer, and (iii) a hybrid approach combining both. Among these, the customized SentencePiece tokenizer yielded the best results [6].

The resulting token vectors are then passed through a six-layer Transformer Encoder, which outputs a matrix of embeddings, one for each token. The encoder follows the architecture of Vaswani et al. [16] and, like BERT [25], employs learned positional embeddings instead of sinusoidal encoding. It also adopts the GELU activation function in place of ReLU [26]. The encoder is configured with model dimension $d_{model} = 512$, feed-forward dimension $d_{ff} = 2048$, and $h = 8$ attention heads.

To derive a single embedding that represents the entire code excerpt, the token embedding matrix produced by the encoder undergoes pooling, yielding a fixed-length vector regardless of input size. This embedding is then normalized to reduce internal covariate shift, improving training stability and performance. Finally, a fully connected layer with a ReLU activation function refines the representation. The final vector constitutes the model's output, encapsulating the stylometric features of the source code.

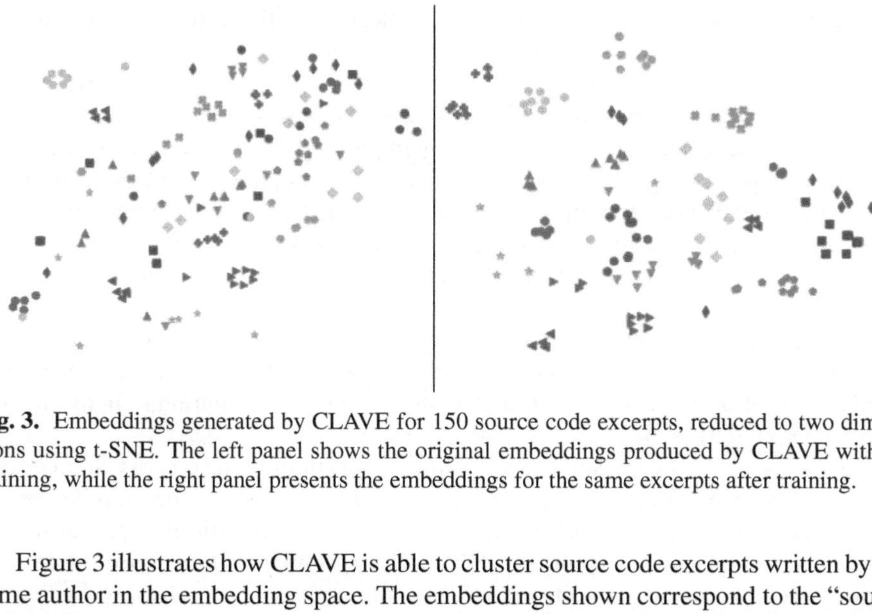

Fig. 3. Embeddings generated by CLAVE for 150 source code excerpts, reduced to two dimensions using t-SNE. The left panel shows the original embeddings produced by CLAVE without training, while the right panel presents the embeddings for the same excerpts after training.

Figure 3 illustrates how CLAVE is able to cluster source code excerpts written by the same author in the embedding space. The embeddings shown correspond to the "source code embeddings" from Fig. 2, reduced to two dimensions using t-SNE. The examples are randomly sampled from the test set, comprising 15 authors with 10 code files selected per author.

3.1 Training of CLAVE

CLAVE is first pre-trained using Masked Language Modeling (MLM) [25, 27], where tokens are randomly masked or replaced. The Transformer Encoder is trained to recover the original tokens at these positions, with the pre-training loss computed as the cross-entropy between the predicted token probabilities and the ground-truth tokens. For pre-training, we used 6,132 GitHub Python repositories comprising 270,602 Python files, with 90% of the files allocated for training and 10% for validation.

After pre-training, CLAVE is fine-tuned through a contrastive learning process based on the SimCLR framework (Sect. 2.4) [13], adapted for authorship verification as proposed by White and Sprague [13]. In this stage, we employ the NT-Xent (Normalized Temperature-Scaled Cross-Entropy) loss function introduced in SimCLR [6, 13].

For fine-tuning, we used code from the Google Code Jam programming contest (2003–2023), comprising 819,405 Python files authored by 77,703 programmers. The dataset was split into 80% for training, 10% for validation, and 10% for testing.

4 Methodology

The proposed source code attribution system is depicted in Fig. 4. The system takes as input $n \times p$ source code files, where p denotes the number of programmers and n the number of source files per programmer (Sect. 4.1). Each file is processed by a code authorship verification system—CLAVE and alternative methods are evaluated, as described in Sect. 4.2—to produce an embedding that captures the stylometric characteristics of the code. These embeddings are standardized using a z-score transformation to ensure zero mean and unit variance, thereby improving the stability and effectiveness of subsequent processing. Given that the dimensionality of the embeddings ranges from 512 to 1024, and that our system is designed for a limited number of samples, we investigate several dimensionality reduction techniques (Sect. 4.4). The reduced embeddings are compiled into a dataset, with each instance labeled according to its corresponding programmer.

We then train multiple classifiers (Sect. 4.3) across varying numbers of programmers to construct authorship attribution models. These models are evaluated and compared against prior work, while CPU and memory consumption during training are also analyzed (Sect. 4.5).

During inference, the classification pipeline mirrors the training process. Source code from an unknown programmer is processed through the authorship verification system to generate an embedding, which is then standardized and reduced using the optimal dimensionality reduction method identified during hyperparameter tuning (Sect. 4.4). The resulting vector is passed to the classifier, which outputs the most probable programmer label.

4.1 Dataset

To train the classifiers, we gathered Python source code files from multiple programmers. Because our objective is to capture the programmers' stylistic features rather than the functionality of their code, we selected solutions to the same set of problems written by different individuals. For this purpose, we used data from the Google Kick Start programming competitions held between 2019 and 2022.

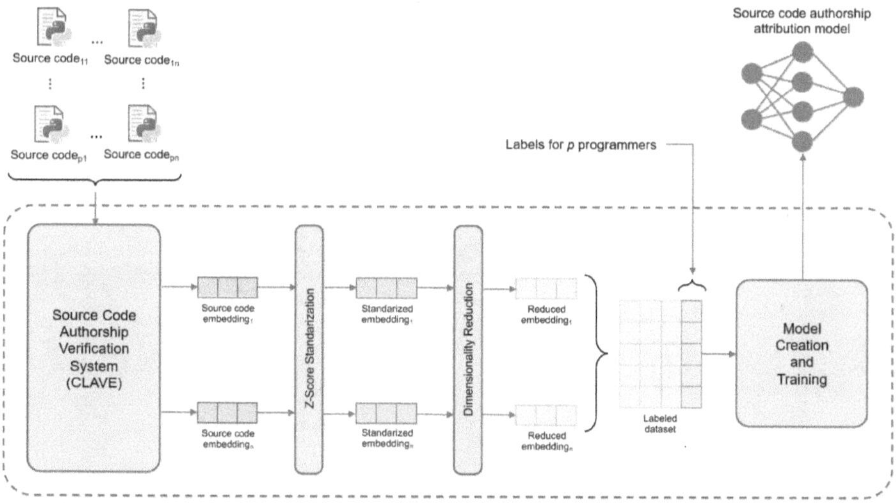

Fig. 4. Architecture of the source code authorship attribution system proposed.

In these contests, participants solve seven distinct programming problems in their language of choice and may submit multiple solutions, with only the final submission being evaluated. We considered only Python code from programmers who submitted a non-empty final solution for all seven tasks. To avoid any overlap with CLAVE's training data, we excluded files and programmers that were part of its training phase.

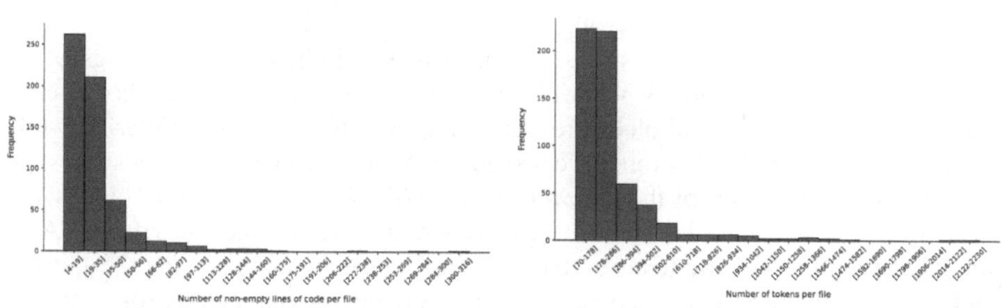

Fig. 5. Distribution of Python non-empty lines of code (left) and tokens (right) per program across the dataset.

The resulting dataset comprises 85 Python programmers, each contributing seven source files, for a total of 595 programs. Because all programs address the same set of problems, classification cannot rely on functional differences. The dataset is intentionally limited in size to evaluate whether classifiers can be trained efficiently in both time and memory while still achieving strong performance with a few samples.

Figure 5 shows the distribution of non-empty lines of code (LoC) and tokens per program across the dataset. The Python programs are relatively short: 80% of the files contain at most 36 LoC (331 tokens), with a median of 21 LoC (196 tokens) and a mean of 29.13 LoC (269.9 tokens). This brevity of source code programs adds an extra challenge for the classifier.

Figure 6 presents the distribution of LoC per problem using a boxplot. As mentioned, each programmer in the dataset provides solutions to seven programming problems. There is no significant difference in LoC across problems (Kruskal–Wallis test, $p < 0.01$), consistent with the visual observation that the interquartile ranges (IQRs) [Q1, Q3] overlap substantially for all problems.

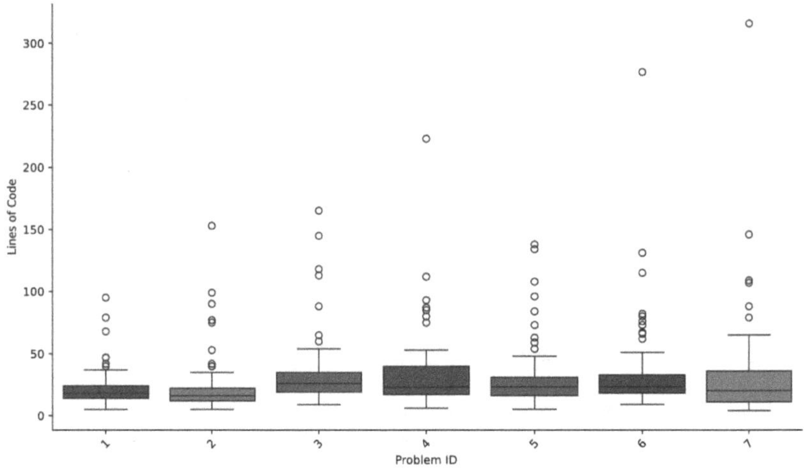

Fig. 6. Lines of code distribution per problem.

Figure 7 depicts pairwise cosine similarities between CLAVE embeddings of 10 randomly selected programmers, with rows and columns grouped by the author of each program. The 7 × 7 diagonal blocks reveal strong intra-programmer similarity, while inter-programmer similarities remain consistently lower. Cosine similarities between embeddings of code written by the same programmer (the 7-program diagonal blocks) are markedly higher than those between different programmers. This indicates that CLAVE embeddings capture stylistic features that distinguish programmers beyond the specific problem solved. However, the separation is not perfect: Programmer 2, for example, exhibits lower intra-programmer similarities, and their final program (ID 14) shows cosine values comparable to inter-programmer cases.

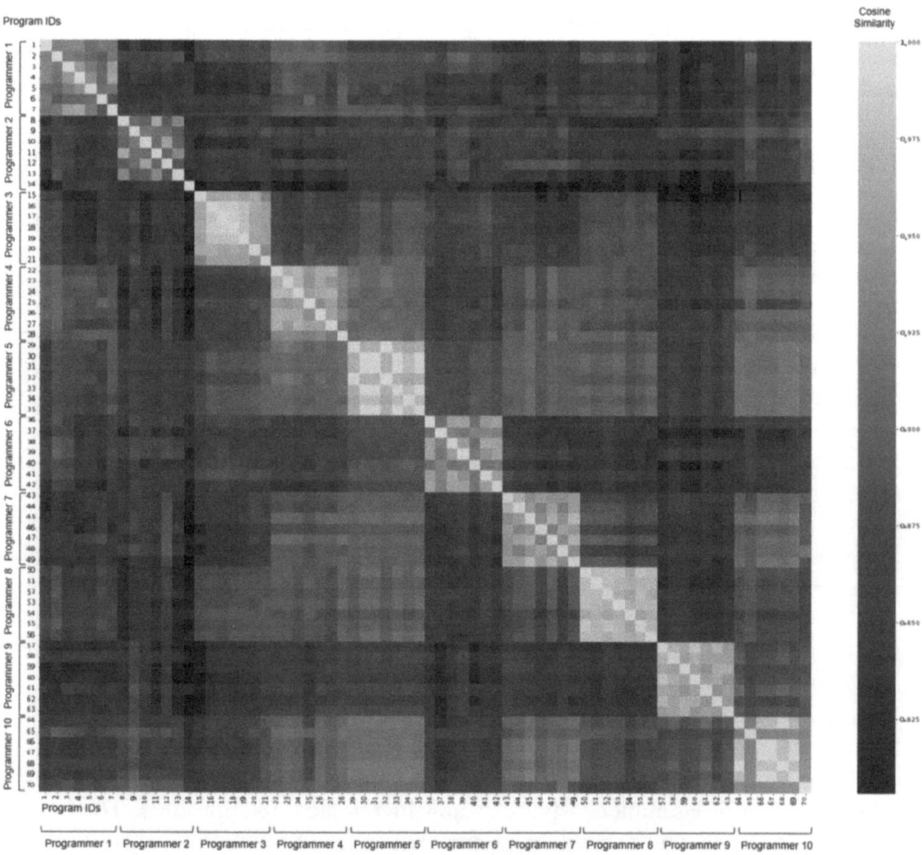

Fig. 7. Heatmap of pairwise cosine similarities between CLAVE embeddings of 10 random programmers. Rows and columns are grouped by programmer.

4.2 Source Code Authorship Verification Systems

The first component of the code authorship attribution framework shown in Fig. 4 is the authorship verification module. We evaluate the state-of-the-art systems discussed in Sect. 2, including CLAVE [6], FDR [14], SCS-GAN [3], and the model introduced by White and Sprague [12]. All models were trained on the same fine-tuning dataset described by Álvarez-Fidalgo and Ortin [6].

We also incorporated cutting-edge Large Language Models (LLMs) designed specifically for source code. Drawing on the survey of code-focused LLMs by Zhang et al. [19], we selected specialized encoder models pre-trained on source code: CodeBERT, GraphCodeBERT, SynCoBERT, Code-MVP, SCodeR, and CodeSage, excluding those not publicly available (SynCoBERT, Code-MVP, and SCodeR). In addition, we included StarEncoder, a high-performing encoder-based LLM for source code that was not covered in Zhang et al.'s survey.

Because these LLMs produce a matrix of token embeddings, we applied average pooling to derive a single vector representation for each source file, following the same procedure used for CLAVE.

4.3 Classification Algorithms

Another essential component of the code authorship attribution system shown in Fig. 4 is the classification model. We evaluated the following classifiers:

1. *k*-Nearest Neighbors (*k*-NN). A non-parametric, instance-based learning algorithm that assigns a label to a new data point based on the most frequent class among its *k* nearest neighbors in the training set. This method is well suited to our task because the authorship verification system produces embeddings that cluster files from the same programmer in close proximity.
2. Multiclass Logistic Regression (LR). A linear model that estimates class probabilities using the softmax function, offering a simple yet reliable baseline for multiclass classification.
3. Support Vector Machines (SVM). A classifier that identifies the hyperplane maximizing the margin between classes in a high-dimensional space, using kernel functions to address non-linear boundaries. SVM handles high-dimensional embeddings effectively, provides strong generalization, and remains robust even with relatively small datasets such as ours.
4. Multi-Layer Perceptron (MLP). A fully connected feedforward neural network that learns non-linear mappings between inputs and outputs through multiple hidden layers. It can capture complex stylometric patterns in the embeddings and is particularly effective when programmers' styles exhibit hierarchical relationships. This model requires careful tuning of several hyperparameters (see Sect. 4.4).
5. Random Forest (RF). An ensemble of decision trees, each trained on a random subset of features and data. By aggregating predictions across trees, Random Forest reduces variance, improves generalization, and captures non-linear relationships in the embeddings.
6. Extreme Gradient Boosting (XGBoost). A gradient-boosting framework that builds decision trees sequentially, with each tree correcting errors from its predecessors. XGBoost is well suited for high-dimensional embeddings, performs strongly on structured data such as stylometric features, and includes built-in regularization and pruning mechanisms to prevent overfitting.

4.4 Hyperparameter Optimization

We selected six files per programmer for training and validation (510 files) and one file per programmer for testing (85 files). To determine the best hyperparameters for each configuration of the architecture shown in Fig. 4, we performed six-fold stratified cross-validation. In each fold, five programs from every programmer were used for training, and the remaining program was reserved for validation. This procedure evaluates the classifier on unseen data while preserving a balanced representation of each programmer across folds.

The architecture in Fig. 4 includes several hyperparameters that strongly affect learning and generalization. To find the best combinations, we carried out an exhaustive grid search. For every candidate set of hyperparameters, the model was trained and its performance measured by validation accuracy, defined as the ratio of correctly classified instances to the total number of instances in the balanced dataset.

Dimensionality reduction, also highlighted in Fig. 4, was treated as an additional hyperparameter. We explored several options.

- Principal Component Analysis (PCA) was used to retain either 99% or 95% of the explained variance, providing an efficient method when the stylometric features of code embeddings are linearly dependent.
- Linear Discriminant Analysis (LDA). Since the dataset is labeled, we also tried LDA to project the data into a space that maximizes class separability, reducing the dimensionality to "number of programmers − 1."
- Uniform Manifold Approximation and Projection (UMAP). For non-linear reduction, we applied UMAP with target dimensions of 10, 30, and 50.
- T-distributed Stochastic Neighbor Embedding) (t-SNE). We evaluated t-SNE to capture complex non-linear structures in the embeddings by preserving local neighborhood relationships in a lower-dimensional space. Although typically used for visualization, t-SNE was tested here as a potential preprocessing step to enhance class separability before classification, exploring perplexity values between 5 and 30 [28] and output 2 and 3 dimensions.
- Autoencoders. We investigated deep autoencoders as a data-driven approach to learn compact representations of the source code embeddings [29]. The encoder compresses the input into a lower-dimensional latent space, and the decoder reconstructs the original embeddings. We tuned the size of the latent space across 10, 20, 30, and 50 dimensions and varied the depth of the encoder–decoder architecture from two to five hidden layers. These ranges were chosen to balance reconstruction fidelity with dimensionality reduction, aiming to preserve stylistic information relevant to authorship.
- No dimensionality reduction. As a baseline, we also considered using the original embeddings without any reduction.

Under this framework, we also conducted hyperparameter searches for each of the six classification models described in Sect. 4.3. The full list of parameters and the best-performing configurations are provided in [30].

To evaluate statistical significance, we applied bootstrapping with 10,000 repetitions to compute 95% confidence intervals for each metric [32]. This involved repeatedly sampling the test set with replacement to create multiple resampled datasets. Confidence intervals for the mean of each metric were then derived from these samples, enabling us to test for significant differences between the systems under comparison [32].

4.5 Error Analysis

A detailed error analysis was conducted to gain a deeper understanding of the misclassifications produced by the best-performing model. Examining the distribution of these errors provides insights into stylistic similarities among programmers and reveals potential limitations of the embedding space.

We computed the full confusion matrix on the 85-programmer test set, where each row corresponds to the true author and each column to the predicted author; off-diagonal entries indicate misattributions. The source code of misclassified authors was then reviewed to identify possible reasons for the model's decisions, focusing on representative code snippets that exhibit shared stylistic traits.

4.6 Training Resources

Beyond its classification accuracy, a key advantage of the proposed system is its modest CPU and memory footprint when training a code authorship attribution model across multiple programmers. As noted in Sect. 2, the highest-performing approaches are typically deep learning models that demand substantial training time [33].

To assess computational cost, we measured the training time of each model on the full dataset using the optimal hyperparameters. Each experiment was repeated 30 times to obtain the mean execution time and its 95% confidence interval, following the procedure described by Georges et al. [32].

Memory usage was monitored with the `psutil` library [34]. We recorded the maximum resident set size during training, representing the non-swapped physical memory consumed by the process [35]. This metric enabled us to quantify RAM requirements and evaluate the system's efficiency in terms of memory resources.

All hyperparameter searches and model training were carried out on an Intel Core i9-10900X CPU (3.7 GHz) with 48 GB of RAM, running a 64-bit version of Windows 11 without GPU acceleration. Python 3.13.2 was used for training and hyperparameter tuning, together with scikit-learn 1.6.1 and XGBoost 2.1.4 for model implementation.

5 Results

Figure 8 shows the accuracies of the source-code authorship attribution systems trained with the method described in Sect. 4. For each system, only the best-performing classifier is reported; the complete results are available in [30]. As the number of programmers grows, the accuracy of all models declines. Among them, the SVM classifier with CLAVE embeddings achieves the highest accuracy, outperforming every other system by a wide margin—when distinguishing 85 programmers, its accuracy is 22 percentage points higher than that of the second-best system. Across the various systems, the top classifiers were SVM and LR.

Figure 9 provides a learning-curve analysis, showing test accuracy as the number of training programs per programmer grows. The ranking of methods mirrors that in Fig. 8, with CLAVE + SVM achieving the highest accuracy across all training sizes. All models improve as the number of training programs per programmer increases, although some begin to converge (e.g., CLAVE) at six training programs, while others, such as FDR, continue to gain accuracy.

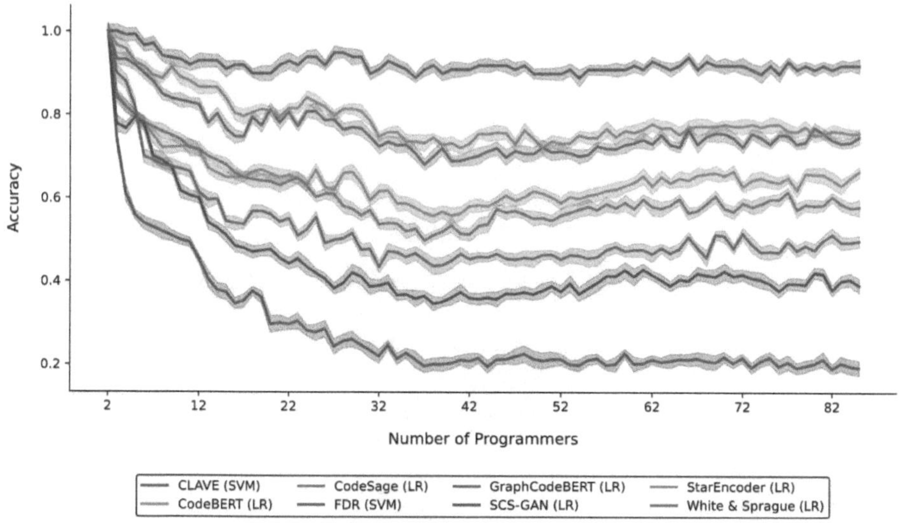

Fig. 8. Accuracy of the source code authorship attribution systems as the number of programmers increases, using the best classifier for each verification system and LLM [7]. Shaded areas represent 95% confidence intervals. SVM denotes Support Vector Machine, and LR stands for Logistic Regression.

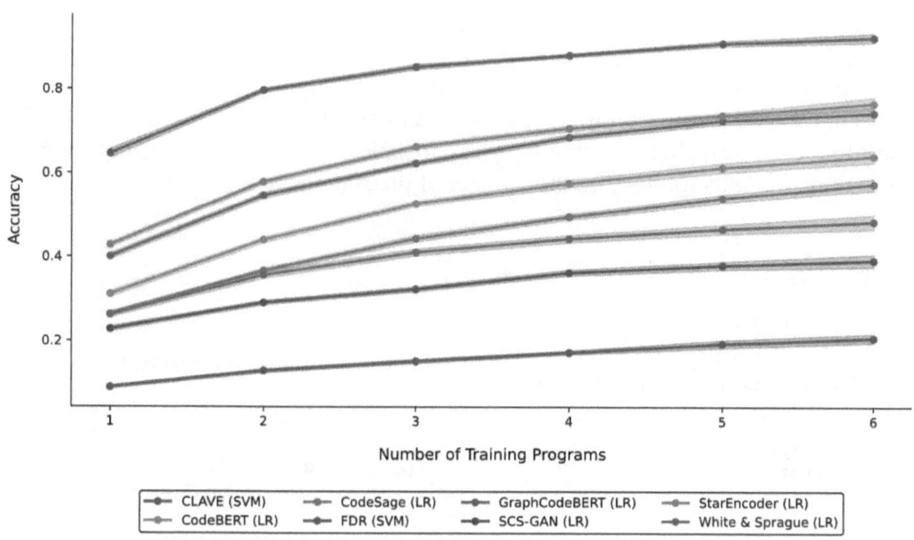

Fig. 9. Accuracy of the source-code authorship attribution systems as the number of training programs per programmer increases, using the best classifier for each verification system and LLM. Shaded regions indicate 95% confidence intervals. SVM denotes Support Vector Machine, and LR denotes Logistic Regression.

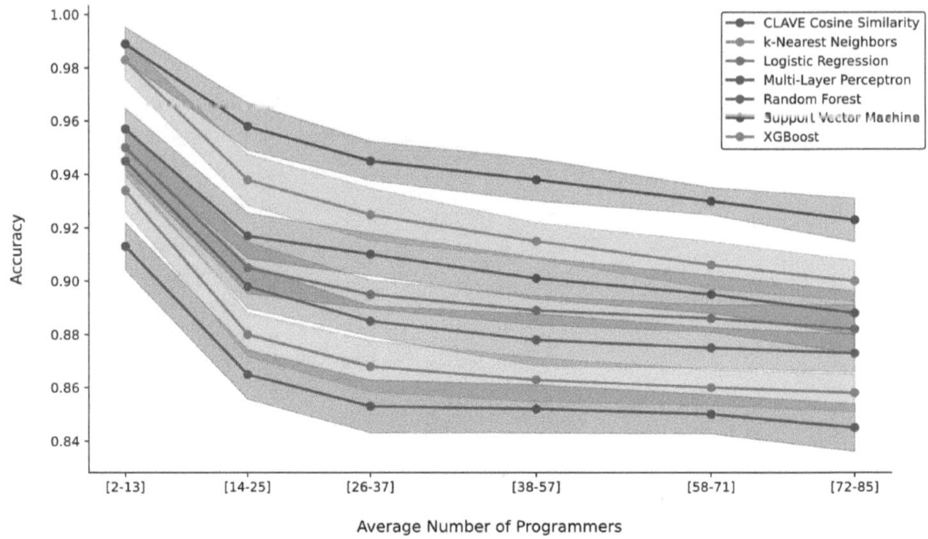

Fig. 10. Accuracy of the classifiers trained with the CLAVE source code authorship verification systems as the number of programmers increases [7]. Shaded areas represent 95% confidence intervals. The CLAVE cosine similarity classifier assigns authorship based on the closest embedding to the sample to be predicted, using cosine similarity distance.

Figure 10 reports the accuracies of classifiers trained with CLAVE embeddings, averaged over groups of 12 programmers to reduce fluctuations and highlight overall trends. SVM again attains the highest accuracy, with statistically significant gains over the next-best classifier (k-NN); the 95% confidence intervals do not overlap [32]. The third-best approach, CLAVE Cosine Similarity, assigns authorship by selecting the embedding closest to the test sample according to cosine distance. All classifiers display a similar pattern of decreasing accuracy as the number of programmers increases.

```
t=int(input())
for jj in range(t):
   n=int(input())
   a=list(map(int,input().split()))
   count=0
   for i in range(1,n-1):
      if(a[i]>a[i-1] and a[i]>a[i+1]):
         count+=1
   print("Case #",end="")
   print(jj+1,end=": ")
   print(count)
```

```
c = int(input())
b = 0
while(c>0):
   b += 1
   n = int(input())
   arr = list(map(int,input().split()))
   peak = 0
   for i in range(1,len(arr)-1):
      if arr[i-1] < arr[i] and arr[i] > arr[i+1]:
         peak += 1
         initial = arr[i]
   print("Case #{}: {}".format(b,peak))
   c-=1
```

Fig. 11. Programs written by two different programmers to solve the same problem. The program on the left was attributed by CLAVE + SVM to the same author as the program on the right.

In the error analysis, we examined the stylometric differences between each pair of programmers whose code excerpts were misclassified by CLAVE + SVM. Figure 11 displays two programs written by different authors to solve the same problem. The program on the left was mistakenly attributed to the author of the program on the right. Both programmers employ very short, lowercased identifiers, omit functions and comments, avoid spaces around operators and comma-separated expressions, and occasionally use unnecessary parentheses in the conditions of `while` and `if` statements.

Table 1 lists the training times for models with 85 programmers and six files per programmer, without hyperparameter tuning, using the hardware described in Sect. 4.6. Among the classifiers, *k*-NN and SVM require the least CPU resources, whereas XGBoost is the most computationally demanding. No single verification system consistently yields the fastest training: CLAVE and White & Sprague record the shortest times for two classifiers each, while FDR and SCS-GAN achieve the minimum for one classifier each.

Table 1. Execution times (in seconds) for training each classifier with 85 programmers and 6 program files per programmer (510 files in total), without hyperparameter search [7]. 95% confidence intervals were below 3.5%.

	CLAVE	Code BERT	Code Sage	FDR	GraphCodeBERT	SCS-GAN	Star Encoder	White & Sprague
k-NN	0.136	0.119	0.074	0.062	0.158	0.021	0.123	0.043
LR	3.765	5.559	4.863	4.707	5.193	5.134	4.487	4.819
MLP	0.550	1.002	1.226	18.160	4.965	13.076	6.652	18.813
Random Forest	1.160	0.632	0.963	0.459	0.870	0.807	1.301	0.495
SVM	0.156	0.185	0.240	0.133	0.192	0.123	0.200	0.119
XGBoost	37.402	25.827	75.195	11.384	56.108	9.946	54.237	8.512

Table 2 reports memory usage during model training. The final row shows the memory footprint of the base code-authorship verification model (or base LLM) without any classifier, ranging from 153.86 MB to 155.33 MB. Differences in memory consumption across verification systems remain under 1%, though all classifiers increase the baseline requirement. On average, *k*-NN, SVM, and LR add roughly 1%, 2.7%, and 2.9% more memory, respectively. RF raises memory usage by 14.6%, while XGBoost increases it by 55.9%.

6 Discussion

The SVM classifier trained with CLAVE embeddings achieved the highest performance among all evaluated code-authorship attribution systems, outperforming the best non-CLAVE classifier by 22% (Fig. 8). Its accuracy exceeds that of all other classifiers across varying numbers of programmers and programs per programmer. The learning curve for CLAVE + SVM demonstrates rapid convergence with just six programs per programmer (Fig. 9), indicating that SVM can achieve high accuracy without requiring large numbers of training programs. These results highlight that the stylometric vectors generated by CLAVE are well suited for source-code attribution tasks.

Table 2. Memory consumption (in MBs) for training each classifier with 85 programmers and 6 program files per programmer (510 files in total), without hyperparameter search [7]. 95% confidence intervals were below 1%.

	CLAVE	Code BERT	Code Sage	FDR	GraphCodeBERT	SCS-GAN	Star Encoder	White & Sprague
k-NN	155.20	155.31	159.47	154.65	155.71	155.07	155.66	157.60
LR	158.31	160.74	163.12	155.36	160.98	155.49	160.92	156.32
MLP	162.01	162.18	167.71	158.07	163.07	157.03	162.86	160.21
Random Forest	187.10	167.57	167.68	161.38	167.52	178.56	212.83	173.37
SVM	157.58	163.56	160.89	156.41	159.38	155.74	159.26	156.79
XGBoost	343.79	212.25	232.49	179.46	294.43	212.15	216.77	234.80
Verification	154.01	154.66	155.24	153.86	155.33	153.99	154.59	154.09

Figure 8 also highlights the strength of LLM encoders when trained on large source-code datasets. With only six Python files per programmer, the LLM-based models outperform the three state-of-the-art code-authorship verification systems described in Sect. 2. The sole exception is CLAVE, which exceeds the accuracy of all four evaluated LLM models.

When comparing classification error (1 – accuracy), the SVM trained on CLAVE embeddings reduces the error rate by 45.4% relative to using CLAVE authorship verification alone (which selects the closest embedding to the test sample using cosine similarity) (Fig. 10). This indicates that training a classifier on CLAVE embeddings is preferable to relying solely on the verification system, even with only six Python files per programmer. However, this improvement is evident primarily with the SVM and *k*-NN algorithms for such a limited training set; other algorithms achieve accuracy similar to or worse than that of the standalone CLAVE verification method.

We further compare our SVM + CLAVE system with state-of-the-art deep-learning models for Python authorship attribution (Sect. 2). Alsulami et al. trained a BiLSTM on 700 Python files from 70 programmers [9]; despite having more samples and fewer authors than our study, their classification error (0.12) is 55.8% higher than ours (0.077). Kurtukova et al. proposed a hybrid CNN–BiGRU network that achieved 0.85 accuracy for 20 programmers [8]. Other systems discussed in Sect. 2 focus on C, C++, or Java. These comparisons show that the SVM + CLAVE approach offers competitive performance for Python authorship attribution, outperforming existing verification systems and even deep-learning methods that are far more computationally expensive to train.

Our model design promotes stronger generalization than typical deep-learning authorship-attribution approaches. By leveraging source-code embeddings derived from a one-shot verification system, it captures deeper stylistic and structural patterns while avoiding overfitting to dataset-specific artifacts. In contrast, end-to-end deep-learning classifiers require large labeled datasets for each author and often struggle with unseen authors [1]. Projecting code into a structured embedding space allows authorial styles to cluster naturally, enabling effective classification without extensive retraining and improving robustness to adversarial modifications [36].

We also measured the computational resources needed to train the CLAVE authorship-attribution system. Training on the full dataset required only 156 ms and 157.6 MB of memory on the computer described in Sect. 4.6, without a GPU. These requirements are far lower than those of deep-learning-based authorship-attribution models, which typically consume several gigabytes of memory and require much longer training times. This efficiency highlights CLAVE's suitability for resource-constrained environments and deployment on standard hardware, and it enables rapid model retraining when new code fragments or programmers are added to the training set.

CLAVE + SVM struggled to correctly attribute authorship except in cases involving particularly short files. Although 80% of the programs in the dataset contain 36 lines of code or fewer, CLAVE + SVM still achieves 0.923 accuracy with only six training files per programmer. Together with the inherent challenges of attributing authorship for short programs, our error analysis revealed that CLAVE has difficulty classifying code in which the programmer uses short identifiers, omits functions, and excludes comments. These stylistic patterns reduce the distinctiveness of small code excerpts, making it harder for the embeddings to capture unique authorial traits.

The proposed CLAVE + SVM framework can accurately attribute source-code authorship from only a few code samples while requiring minimal computational resources. These characteristics make it particularly suitable for time-critical contexts such as malware attribution, intellectual-property enforcement, and detection of unauthorized code reuse across distributed development teams.

Despite these advantages, code authorship attribution poses significant ethical and privacy concerns. The same techniques that aid legitimate investigations could also be misused for developer surveillance or the deanonymization of open-source contributors. Because attribution is inherently probabilistic, misclassifications may result in false accusations if findings are treated as conclusive evidence. To reduce these risks, any operational deployment should enforce strict access controls, maintain transparency about data retention, undergo independent validation, and comply with applicable privacy regulations. This method should be regarded as an investigative aid rather than definitive proof of authorship and must be used in conjunction with due process and corroborating evidence.

7 Conclusions

The stylometric embeddings generated by the contrastive-learning CLAVE authorship verification model enable efficient and accurate source-code authorship attribution. The proposed system achieves state-of-the-art accuracy, including deep-learning approaches, while requiring only six short source files per programmer and modest computational resources, demonstrating that high-quality attribution does not depend on large training corpora or GPU acceleration.

The use of a classifier such as SVM to process the CLAVE embeddings includes additional performance to using the CLAVE embeddings with a distance metric for authorship attribution. Its low resource requirements allow rapid retraining as new programmers or programs are added to the training set, increasing its classification accuracy.

Our experiments further demonstrate the method's robustness as the number of authors grows, its rapid accuracy convergence with increasing programs per programmer, and its ability to generalize to challenging short-program scenarios. Collectively, these results establish CLAVE + SVM as a practical, resource-efficient, and reliable solution for source-code authorship attribution.

We are developing a probabilistic model that takes n programs written by programmer A and m programs written by programmer B and returns the probability that A and B are the same individual, using CLAVE stylometry embeddings. We also plan to extend CLAVE to additional programming languages and evaluate its performance on more diverse datasets to assess generalizability across different coding styles. In addition, we intend to examine the model's robustness against adversarial attacks, such as code obfuscation or style imitation, and to explore strategies for enhancing its reliability in security and forensic applications.

All the source code used in this study—including the training dataset, CLAVE source code and binary models, performance results from model evaluation, optimal hyperparameters for each model, and CPU and memory measurement data—is available for download at https://www.reflection.uniovi.es/bigcode/download/2025/ccis.

8 Disclosure of Interests.

The authors have no competing interests to declare that are relevant to the content of this article.

Acknowledgments. This work was funded by the Government of the Principality of Asturias, with support from the European Regional Development Fund (ERDF), under project GRU-GIC-24–070. Additional funding was provided by the Ministry of Science, Innovation and Universities (grant PID2024-155586OB-I00).

References

1. He, X., Lashkari, A. H., Vombatkere, N., Sharma, D. P.: Authorship attribution methods, challenges, and future research directions: a comprehensive survey. Information, **15**(3), 131, 1–42 (2024)
2. Kalgutkar, V., Kaur, R., Gonzalez, H., Stakhanova, N., Matyukhina, A.: Code authorship attribution: methods and challenges. ACM Comput. Surv. **52**(1), 1–26 (2019)
3. Ou, W., Ding, S.H.H., Tian, Y., Song, L.: SCS-GAN: Learning functionality-agnostic stylometric representations for source code authorship verification. IEEE Trans. Software Eng. **49**, 1426–1442 (2023)
4. Ortin, F., Garcia, M., Perez-Schofield, B.G., Quiroga, J.: The StaDyn programming language. SoftwareX **20**, 101211–101222 (2022)
5. Stamatatos, E., et al.: Overview of the authorship verification task at PAN 2023. In: Working Notes of the Conference and Labs of the Evaluation Forum (CLEF 2023), pp. 2476–2491, Thessaloniki, Greece (2023)
6. Álvarez-Fidalgo, D., Ortin, F.: CLAVE: a deep learning model for source code authorship verification with contrastive learning and transformer encoders. Inf. Process. Manage. **62**(3), 104005–104020 (2025)

7. Álvarez-Fidalgo, D., Ortin, F.: Efficient source code authorship attribution using code stylometry embeddings. In: 20th International Conference on Software Technologies (ICSOFT), Bilbao (Spain), pp. 167–177 (2025)
8. Kurtukova, A., Romanov, A., Shelupanov, A.: Source code authorship identification using deep neural networks. Symmetry **12**(12), 1–17 (2020)
9. Alsulami, B., Dauber, E., Harang, R., Mancoridis, S., Greenstadt, R.: Source code authorship attribution using long short-term memory-based networks. In: Computer Security (ESORICS 2017). LNCS, **10492** (2017)
10. Abuhamad, M., AbuHmed, T., Mohaisen, A., Nyang, D.: Large-scale and language-oblivious code authorship identification. In: Proceedings of the ACM SIGSAC Conference on Computer and Communications Security (CCS '18), pp. 101–114 (2018)
11. Li, Z., Chen, G. Q., Chen, C., Zou, Y., Xu, S.: RoPGen: towards robust code authorship attribution via automatic coding style transformation. In: Proceedings of the 44th International Conference on Software Engineering (ICSE '22), pp. 1906–1918 (2022)
12. White, R., Sprague, N.: Deep metric learning for code authorship attribution and verification. In: 20th IEEE International Conference on Machine Learning and Applications (ICMLA), pp. 1089–1093 (2021)
13. Chen, T., Kornblith, S., Norouzi, M., Hinton, G.E.: A simple framework for contrastive learning of visual representations. arXiv:2002.05709, pp. 1–20 (2020)
14. Hozhabrierdi, P., Hitos, D. F., Mohan, C. K: Zero-shot source code author identification: A lexicon- and layout-independent approach. In: International Joint Conference on Neural Networks (IJCNN), pp. 1–8 (2020)
15. Wang, N., Ji, S., Wang, T.: Integration of static and dynamic code stylometry analysis for programmer de-anonymization. In: Proceedings of the 11th ACM Workshop on Artificial Intelligence and Security (AISec '18), pp. 74–84 (2018)
16. Vaswani, A., et al.: Attention is all you need. In: Advances in Neural Information Processing Systems, (vol. 30), Curran Associates, Inc (2017)
17. Feng, Z., et al.: CodeBERT: a pre-trained model for programming and natural languages. arXiv:2002.08155, pp. 1–12 (2020)
18. Kanade, A., Maniatis, P., Balakrishnan, G., Shi, K.: Learning and evaluating contextual embedding of source code. In: Proceedings of the 37th International Conference on Machine Learning (PMLR), pp. 5110–5121 (2020)
19. Zhang, Z., et al.: Unifying the perspectives of NLP and software engineering: a survey on language models for code. Trans. Mach. Learn. Res. **9** (2024)
20. Hadsell, R., Chopra, S., LeCun, Y.: Dimensionality reduction by learning an invariant mapping. In: IEEE Computer Society Conference on Computer Vision and Pattern Recognition (CVPR'06), vol. 2, pp. 1735–1742 (2006)
21. Jain, P., Jain, A., Zhang, T., Abbeel, P., Gonzalez, J. E., Stoica, I.: Contrastive code representation learning. arXiv:2007.04973v4, 1–19 (2022)
22. Liu, S., Wu, B., Xie, X., Meng, G., Liu, Y.: ContraBERT: enhancing code pre-trained models via contrastive learning. arXiv:2301.09072, 1–12 (2023)
23. Reimers, N., Gurevych, I.: Sentence-BERT: sentence Embeddings using Siamese BERT-Networks. In: Proceedings of the Conference on Empirical Methods in Natural Language Processing (EMNLP), Hong Kong, China, pp. 3980–3990 (2019)
24. Tyo, J., Dhingra, B., Lipton, Z. C.: Siamese BERT for Authorship Verification. In: Proceedings of the Working Notes of CLEF, Conference and Labs of the Evaluation Forum volume 2936, Bucharest, Romania, pp. 2169– 2177 (2021)
25. Devlin, J., Chang, M.-W., Lee, K., Toutanova, K.: BERT: Pre-training of deep bidirectional transformers for language understanding. In: Proceedings of the 2019 Conference of the North American Chapter of the Association for Computational Linguistics: Human Language Technologies, pp. 4171–4186 (2019)

26. Hendrycks, D., Gimpel, K.: Gaussian error linear units (GELUs). ArXiv: 1606.08415v5, 1–10 (2023)
27. Liu, Y., et al.: RoBERTa: a robustly optimized BERT pretraining approach. arXiv:1907.11692, 1–13 (2019)
28. van der Maaten, L., Hinton, G.E.: Visualizing data using t-SNE. J. Mach. Learn. Res. **9**(86), 2579–2605 (2008)
29. Hinton, G.E., Salakhutdinov, R.R.: Reducing the dimensionality of data with neural networks. Science **313**(5786), 504–507 (2006)
30. Ortin, F., Álvarez-Fidalgo, D.: Support webpage of the article Low-Resource Python Source Code Authorship Attribution using Contrastive-Learning Embeddings, https://www.reflection.uniovi.es/bigcode/download/2025/iics, last accessed 2025/9/17
31. Noma, H., Matsushima, Y., Ishii, R.: Confidence interval for the AUC of SROC curve and some related methods using bootstrap for meta-analysis of diagnostic accuracy studies. Communications in Statistics: Case Studies. Data Analysis and Applications **7**, 344–358 (2021)
32. Georges, A., Buytaert, D., Eeckhout, L.: Statistically rigorous Java performance evaluation. ACM SIGPLAN Notices **42**(10), 57–76 (2007)
33. Rodriguez-Prieto, O., Pato, A., Ortin, F.: PLangRec: Deep-learning model to predict the programming language from a single line of code. Futur. Gener. Comput. Syst. **166**, 107640–107655 (2023)
34. Rodola, G.: Psutil: A cross-platform library for process and system monitoring in Python, https://psutil.readthedocs.io, last accessed 2023/10/25
35. Ortin, F., Facundo, G., Garcia, M.: Analyzing syntactic constructs of Java programs with machine learning. Expert Syst. Appl. **215**, 119398–119414 (2023)
36. Abuhamad, M., Jung, C., Mohaisen, D., Nyang, D.: SHIELD: thwarting code authorship attribution. ArXiv: 2304.13255, pp. 1–13 (2023)

Beyond Preconditions and Postconditions: Frame Specifications for Modern Design by Contract

Yoonsik Cheon(✉) and Benjamin Good

The University of Texas at El Paso, El Paso, TX 79968, USA
ycheon@utep.edu, bgood@miners.utep.edu

Abstract. Design by Contract (DbC) traditionally emphasizes preconditions, postconditions, and invariants, but provides no explicit means to constrain state modifications. This limitation complicates reasoning about side effects and weakens behavioral guarantees. We address this gap by integrating frame specifications—declarations of which parts of program state may change—into DbC. Our approach models program objects as abstract state tuples and introduces lightweight annotations to specify, include, or exclude state elements. A proof-of-concept implementation in Dart combines compile-time instrumentation with selective runtime reflection, supporting both statically and dynamically typed entities. Compared with manual assertion-based techniques, our method reduces annotation overhead, improves maintainability, and enforces frame properties without entangling them with core logic. A case study of a strategy game demonstrates reduced specification effort while retaining expressive power. This work advances DbC toward a more complete framework for specifying and verifying intended software behavior.

Keywords: Design by Contract · Frame Specifications · Annotations · Runtime Verification · Dart

1 Introduction

Design by Contract (DbC) has long been recognized as a cornerstone of rigorous software development. It provides a disciplined way to specify the expected behavior of programs through preconditions, postconditions, and invariants [38,39]. These constructs serve as precise agreements between clients and providers of methods, enabling robust reasoning about correctness and fostering reliability in both industrial and academic settings [1,26,29,40,43,44,47,48]. By ensuring obligations are met before execution and guarantees are established afterward, DbC reduces ambiguity in software behavior and encourages modular development.

Despite its strengths, classical DbC lacks an explicit mechanism for controlling what must remain unchanged during execution. Preconditions describe

M. Mecella et al. (Eds.): ICSOFT 2025, CCIS 3144, pp. 205–228, 2027.
https://doi.org/10.1007/978-3-032-37353-3_9

admissible initial states, and postconditions define expected final states, but neither prevents methods from inadvertently altering unrelated variables. This missing dimension—known as *frame conditions* [9]—is critical for modular reasoning and avoiding unintended side effects, which are a well documented source of subtle faults. Such faults can degrade maintainability or, in safety-critical domains, lead to severe failures [3,22]. As systems grow more complex, with state distributed across nested objects, collections, and dynamically typed structures, explicit and enforceable frame specifications become increasingly important.

In this work, we present a lightweight, annotation-based framework that integrates frame specifications directly into DbC and enforces them at runtime. Developers can declare precisely which parts of an object or program state may be modified, using object states abstracted as tuples of named components. Runtime checks ensure that only the declared modifications occur, supporting modular reasoning without intrusive changes to program logic. Our approach combines compile-time instrumentation with selective runtime reflection, which is particularly effective in optionally typed or dynamically typed languages.

We chose Dart [10] as the implementation platform, motivated by its adoption in cross-platform development and its hybrid typing system. Prior work has extensively explored static approaches to frame conditions [21,23,24,27,34, 35,37], but runtime enforcement in optionally typed settings has received little attention. To our knowledge, our work is the first to provide integrated, annotation-based runtime support for frame conditions in DbC for such languages.

This article extends our earlier work presented at ICSOFT 2025 [16]. Its main contributions are:

1. A lightweight annotation model for frame specifications, including `@Modifies` for permissible modifications and `@State` for abstracting state components. The model supports inclusions, exclusions, and custom abstractions, drawing inspiration from model variables [13,14] and data groups [32].
2. A runtime verification mechanism based on snapshot comparison and wildcard substitution, which ensures that only declared state changes occur while remaining non-intrusive to program logic.
3. A prototype implementation in Dart that demonstrates feasibility, highlights challenges in optional typing, and evaluates expressiveness and maintainability in applications.
4. A preliminary evaluation through a case studiy, illustrating the approach's generality and practical benefits.
5. Comparison with existing DbC and verification tools, highlighting advantages in flexibility, expressiveness, and runtime safety.

The remainder of this article is organized as follows. Section 2 revisits DbC and motivates the need for frame conditions, outlining the key challenges. Section 3 develops the underlying conceptual model by formalizing the state-as-tuple abstraction. Section 4 presents our annotation model and verification strategy, while Sect. 5 describes the prototype implementation and design choices. Section 6 reports on a preliminary evaluation through a Dart/Flutter case study. Section 7 reviews related work, including advances in runtime verification and modular reasoning. Finally, Sect. 8 summarizes the contributions, discusses implications, and outlines directions for future research.

2 Background and Motivation

Design by Contract (DbC) is a well-established methodology for improving software correctness and reliability by making the assumptions and guarantees of software components explicit [38–40,43]. Contracts capture the rules of engagement between clients and providers of functionality, reducing ambiguities that often lead to defects.

DbC relies on three central constructs:

- *Preconditions*, which constrain the state that must hold when a method is invoked;
- *Postconditions*, which describe how the state must look after execution; and
- *Invariants*, which must hold across all stable states of an object or module.

These assertions serve as executable documentation that is both human-readable and machine-checkable. For example, consider a simple bank account with a withdrawal operation:

```
@Requires('amount > 0 && amount <= balance')
@Ensures('balance == balance@pre - amount')
void withdraw(long amount) {
  balance -= amount;
}
```

Here, the contract specifies that only valid amounts may be withdrawn and that the balance must be updated consistently. The special notation `balance@pre` references the initial state before execution. Invariants complement pre- and postconditions by ensuring persistent properties, such as "the account balance must never be negative."

2.1 Limitations of Traditional DbC

Despite their utility, preconditions, postconditions, and invariants do not answer a crucial question: *what must remain unchanged during method execution?* Without explicit frame specifications, methods may silently modify unrelated parts of the program state. Such unintended side effects are often difficult to detect and can lead to subtle bugs, compromised modular reasoning, or even critical failures in safety-sensitive systems.

Frame conditions (or frame properties) explicitly declare which variables, fields, or abstract state components a method is permitted to modify [9,46]. They enforce the principle of "*and nothing else changes*" [8]. For instance, in the `withdraw()` method, the intended modification scope is the account balance only. Without a frame condition, unrelated fields such as account owner or transaction history could be altered without violating pre- or postconditions. Frame specifications eliminate this ambiguity, clarifying intent and preventing hidden bugs.

Frame conditions extend DbC in several ways:

- Modular reasoning: Developers can understand a method's impact without inspecting its implementation.
- Clarity and maintainability: Explicit modification scopes reduce the risk of side effects.
- Automation: Runtime or static tools can verify that only declared modifications occur.

2.2 Challenges in Enforcing Frame Conditions

Although conceptually simple, enforcing frame conditions at runtime in practice is nontrivial:

1. Capturing object states: Comparing pre- and post-states requires deep snapshots. Reference semantics can track aliases but not true object content.
2. Nested and composite structures: Methods often modify nested objects or collections (e.g., `game.players[i].score`). Deciding between shallow and deep state capture affects correctness and performance.
3. Optional and dynamic typing: In languages like Dart, runtime reflection is needed to traverse objects whose structure is unknown or only partially known at compile time.
4. Equality semantics: Preservation by value versus identity can lead to different interpretations of frame constraints.
5. Performance trade-offs: Snapshotting and comparing complex graphs incur runtime overhead. Efficient yet precise enforcement is essential, particularly in resource-constrained environments.

These challenges explain why frame conditions have seen limited adoption in practical runtime verification. Our work addresses them via a lightweight annotation mechanism supported by hybrid compile-time instrumentation and selective runtime reflection, making frame specifications practical even in dynamically and optionally typed languages.

3 Conceptual Model of Frame Conditions

Frame conditions capture *state-preservation guarantees*: they declare which parts of a program's state may change during method execution, while implicitly asserting that all other components remain unchanged. This section develops a formal yet lightweight conceptual model that underpins our annotation-based approach.

3.1 Program State as Tuples

We model a program's state as a collection of named components, or *state tuples*, which record the values of relevant objects and variables at a given execution point. The *pre-state* represents the program state before a method executes, while the *post-state* represents the state afterward. A frame specification marks which components of the pre-state may change; all remaining components are implicitly required to be preserved.

Formally, a program state σ is a mapping from variable names to object states:

$$\sigma : \text{Var} \rightarrow \text{ObjState}$$

where `ObjState` is itself a mapping from field names to values or nested object states. For example, consider a board game method defined in a `Board` class that places a game piece for a player at a specified position on the board:

```
placeStone(Player player, int x, int y)
```

A corresponding pre-state could be represented as:

$$\{\texttt{this} : \texttt{this}, \texttt{player} : \texttt{player}, \texttt{x} : 11, \texttt{y} : 10\}$$

Here, `this` denotes the receiver board object, and the other entries record the argument values. If an object consists of nested objects, it is modeled hierarchically within its object state, producing a tree-like structure of fields and values. This representation enables reasoning about modifications at varying levels of granularity, from top-level objects down to nested subcomponents. For example, Fig. 1 illustrates the state of a `Game` object containing a `Board` and two `Player` objects, one of whom has the turn.

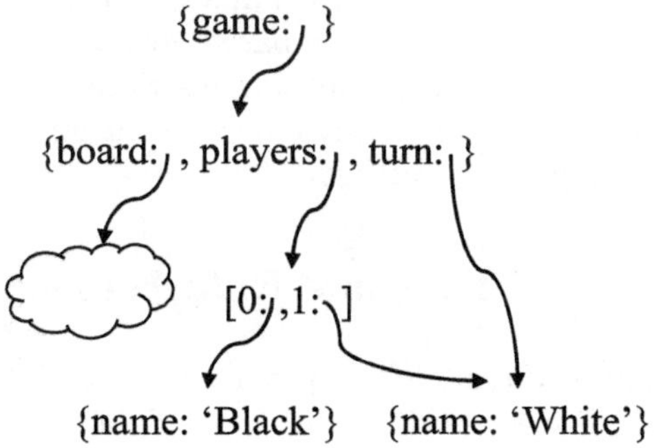

Fig. 1. A game object illustrating nested state: the board, two players, and the active player.

3.2 Frame Conditions as State Patterns

Frame conditions define a *pattern* over the pre-state that the post-state must match. Mutable fields are explicitly marked with a wildcard (`*`) to indicate permissible changes. For instance, consider a simplified state pattern for a game:

$$\{\texttt{board} : \text{board}, \texttt{players} : \text{players}, \texttt{turn} : *\}$$

This frame condition allows updates to `turn`, while requiring that `board` and `players` remain unchanged. Such pattern-based specifications reduce runtime comparison complexity and provide developers with an intuitive way of declaring modification scopes.

Conceptually, this aligns with *frame axioms* in logic and formal specification languages, which stipulate that "everything not explicitly mentioned remains the same" [8,9]. In our tuple-based model, wildcards serve as a conceptual device for representing the explicitly mentioned components of state, providing a concise model for reasoning about and verifying state preservation at runtime.

3.3 Relation to Effect Systems and Ownership Types

Frame conditions are related to—but distinct from—effect systems and ownership type systems. Effect systems track which variables or references a method may modify, supporting static reasoning about side effects [36,42]. However, their scope is typically coarse-grained and not designed for dynamic or runtime enforcement. Ownership type systems restrict aliasing and enforce encapsulation boundaries, thereby controlling modifications indirectly [17,18]. While powerful for ensuring safety properties, they are intentionally restrictive and often require non-trivial restructuring of data representations.

In contrast, our frame conditions directly express modification scopes. They combine tuple-based state abstraction, wildcards for mutable components, and annotation-driven runtime enforcement. Compared to effect systems, they offer finer precision and runtime support; compared to ownership types, they provide flexibility without imposing rigid aliasing restrictions. This positions frame conditions as a lightweight yet expressive mechanism for state control in both statically and dynamically typed settings.

4 Annotation-Based Runtime Enforcement

Building on the tuple-based model of program states introduced in Sect. 3, we translate abstract frame specifications into lightweight annotations that drive runtime checks. Each annotation declares the set of fields or objects a method may modify, while implicitly requiring that all other state components remain unchanged.

The process is straightforward at least conceptually: (a) capture the pre-state of the method, (b) mark the fields declared as mutable, (c) execute the method body, and (d) validate that the post-state differs from the pre-state only in the allowed places. The following example illustrates this workflow. Instrumented lines generated from the annotation are shown with a gray prefix:

```
@Modifies('balance')
void withdraw(long amount) {
| State preState = state;|
| preState.frame('this.balance');
   ... // original method body
  assert(preState == state);
}

 get state => State({'this': {'balance': balance, /* ... */ }});
```

The `@Modifies` annotation specifies that only the `balance` field of the receiver may change. The current state is first captured as `preState`, represented as a mapping from object and field names to values. The `frame()` method declares which fields are allowed to be modified. After method execution, the equality check compares the pre- and post-states, ignoring fields explicitly marked as modifiable. If any other component differs, a contract violation is raised at runtime. The `state` getter is a helper method that constructs a `State` object representing the current state (see Sect. 5 for the `State` framework class).

This mechanism allows developers to write simple, declarative annotations while delegating the enforcement logic to the underlying framework. More complex examples, including additional annotations and nested object structures, are discussed below.

4.1 Custom Annotations and State Modeling

Our framework introduces a small but expressive set of annotations that allow developers to declare frame conditions in a direct and lightweight manner. The core annotation, `@Modifies`, enumerates those parts of the program state a method is permitted to change. Its dual, `@Preserves`, specifies fields that must remain invariant throughout execution, offering a declarative way to state negative frame conditions. Finally, the `@State` annotation provides a mechanism for shaping and abstracting the notion of state itself, including or excluding fields, defining composite properties, or selecting equality semantics for comparison (see below).

At runtime, a frame condition asserts that all elements of the pre-state not listed as modifiable must remain unchanged. Formally:

$$\forall x \bullet x \in \text{State}_{\text{pre}} \wedge x \notin \text{Modifies} \Rightarrow x_{\text{post}} \equiv x_{\text{pre}}$$

In practice, this means that standard program elements—such as the receiver `this` and method parameters—are automatically included in the default state. More complex or external components can be declared explicitly with `@State` (see below). Frame conditions can then be expressed using annotations such as `@Modifies` and `@Preserves`. For example, in a banking application, one might write:

```
@Modifies(''balance")
@Preserves(''owner")
void withdraw(long amount) { ... }
```

This specifies that the account balance may change, while the owner reference must remain invariant, even if future refactorings might otherwise introduce unintended modifications. Although the `@Preserves(''owner")` annotation is technically redundant in this case, it emphasizes the intended immutability of the `owner` field and documents the contract more clearly.

Nested objects and composite structures are addressed through path expressions such as `x.y.z`, with limited wildcards (`x.p*`) for sets of fields. Collections are supported with fine-grained references, ranges, or wildcards, for instance:

```
@Modifies('a[3], a[1..10], a[*]')
```

This level of precision allows developers to specify exactly which elements may be mutated. State can also be expressed in terms of getters or query methods, aligning with Dart's idioms:

```
@Modifies('this.getPlace(x,y)')
void placeStone(Player player, int x, int y) { ... }
```

State Annotations. Beyond concrete fields, `@State` supports abstract or user-defined state properties. In principle, it is possible to determine all objects that exist and are accessible in the pre-state—either statically, dynamically, or through a combination of both. Typically, these include the receiver (`this`) and the method parameters. However, identifying objects referenced indirectly through nested method calls may require whole-program analysis, which is often impractical. Moreover, not all objects are relevant to frame properties.

To address this, we provide custom annotations to include or exclude objects from frame-condition checks. These annotations effectively define the universe of objects used for specifying and verifying a method's frame properties. Both explicit and implicit state information are considered: public fields supply explicit state data and are included by default, whereas implicit states such as getters or observer methods are excluded unless explicitly annotated. To support flexible state modeling, we introduce specialized annotations for the following purposes:

- Including or excluding fields and getters: Annotations such as `@State.includes` and `@State.excludes` allow developers to specify which fields and getters should be treated as part of a class's program state.
- Defining additional state elements: The annotation `@State('name', 'expression')` enables programmers to declare custom state components at either the method or class level.

For example, player statistics fetched through external services can be incorporated into the state model:

```
@State('stat', 'getStat(player)')
@Modifies('getPlace(x,y), stat.moves')
void placeStone(Player player, int x, int y) { ... }
```

The @State annotation above introduces a new abstract state component named stat, whose value is computed by evaluating getStat(player). The corresponding @Modifies annotation specifies that both the board cell at getPlace(x,y) and the moves field of stat may be changed by this operation.

Multiple fields can also be aggregated into a single logical property, simplifying frame declarations. Consider a player's full name composed of three separate fields

```
@State('name', '''$_first $_middle $_last"',
   parts: '_first,_middle,_last')
@Modifies('name')
void changeName(...) { ... }
```

In this example, the annotation defines an abstract state element, name, which groups three fields into a single conceptual unit. This grouping makes specifications more concise and better aligned with the program's intended semantics. When an abstract state is referenced in an @Modifies annotation, all constituent fields listed in the parts parameter are considered modifiable.

Together, these annotation mechanisms enable precise, flexible, and developer-friendly frame specifications. Rather than forcing an all-or-nothing treatment of object fields, they allow the state model to be tailored to the needs of each method, striking a balance between expressiveness and runtime enforceability.

Object Comparison and Equality. Frame checking requires comparing pre- and post-state values to determine whether unauthorized modifications occurred (see Sect. 4.2). Since objects may be equal either by reference or by value, our system provides a configurable equality mechanism. Dart distinguishes between identical() (reference equality) and == (value equality), and our annotations allow developers to select the desired method for each field or object:

```
@State('currentPlayer', '_currentPlayer', equality=identity)
final Player _currentPlayer;
```

The equality parameter accepts built-in comparisons (==, identical()) as well as custom functions. Developers may also specify defaults at the class or application level, which apply unless overridden. Equality choice determines how object states are captured: reference equality records only identities, value equality requires shallow or deep copies, and custom equality may necessitate tailored cloning strategies, also declared via annotations.

Snapshots can be captured eagerly (at pre-state initialization) or lazily (when constraints are checked), trading storage for runtime overhead. Although many developers expect value equality, capturing entire object graphs in Dart can be prohibitively expensive, since all values are objects. We therefore default to reference equality, while still allowing value or custom semantics where correctness demands it.

4.2 Translation to Runtime Checks

To operationalize annotation-based frame specifications, our approach translates contracts into executable runtime checks through compile-time instrumentation augmented with runtime reflection, accommodating Dart's optional typing system. During compilation, methods annotated with `@Modifies`, `@Preserves`, or `@State` are instrumented with code that (a) captures a snapshot of the relevant pre-state, (b) marks elements declared as mutable, and (c) verifies after execution that all other elements remain unchanged. When static type information is available, state access is efficient; otherwise, reflection ensures correctness (see Sect. 5). This hybrid strategy balances safety and performance across Dart's statically and dynamically typed modes.

The following example illustrates the instrumentation process for a board game method:

```
@Modifies(''board.getPlace(x,y), currentPlayer")
void placeStone(int x, int y) {
| State pre = State({'this': {'board': board, 'players': players,|
| /* ... */}});|
| pre.capture({'x':x, 'y':y});|
| pre.frame('this.board.getPlace(x,y), this.currentPlayer');|
  // original method body
| assert(pre == State({'this': {'board': board, 'players': players,|
| /* ... */}})..capture({'x': x, 'y': y}));|
}
```

In this instrumented code, the pre-state is captured, the frame condition specifies permissible modifications, and the post-state comparison ensures that only those modifications occur. Here, the receiver (`this`) is captured statically at compile time, while its components such as `board` and `players` are resolved dynamically at runtime (see Sect. 5.2). Equality semantics are configurable via `@State` annotations: developers may choose identity, structural equality, or custom comparators. Reference equality is used by default to minimize overhead, while deep copies or lazy snapshots can be requested where value semantics are needed. This flexibility allows fine-grained control without burdening developers with low-level instrumentation details.

Practically, the translation process is integrated into Dart's build system, ensuring consistent code generation (see Sect. 5). Runtime checks are compiled away in production when assertions are disabled, eliminating overhead in deployed applications. While the current implementation targets sequential execution, the framework could be extended to concurrent or reactive systems through transactional wrappers or temporal frame conditions. Tooling support—such as IDE overlays that visualize frame annotations or testing frameworks that exploit them for mutation testing—represents a further step toward making frame conditions a practical part of everyday software development.

5 Implementation

To demonstrate our approach, we developed a prototype for frame annotations in Dart [10], targeting cross-platform mobile applications. We chose Dart because of its growing role in cross-platform frameworks like Flutter and its hybrid type system, which introduces unique challenges for runtime verification of design-by-contract (DbC) properties. The prototype currently supports two categories of annotations: framing, such as `@Modifies`, which declares the parts of the program state a method is allowed to change, and state abstraction, such as `@State`, which enables abstract and user-defined state components.

5.1 Code Instrumentation Pipeline

The prototype builds on the standard Dart build infrastructure, leveraging three key components: `source_gen` for automatic generation of instrumented code from annotations, `build` to coordinate the execution of these generators during compilation, and `analyzer` to provide static inspection of Dart sources. These components form the backbone of code generation workflows in Dart and Flutter, and are distributed through the official package repository [45].

During compilation, annotated code is scanned and transformed into an instrumented version. Builders inject additional logic to capture the relevant program state before and after annotated operations. When type information is explicit, the generated code produces optimized state models with minimal overhead; when types are implicit or omitted, the framework falls back on reflection to reconstruct object structures dynamically. For example, given an annotated method, the generator introduces state-capturing logic that models the receiver (`this`) and its fields as key–value mappings. This allows the runtime to maintain a snapshot of the relevant state before execution. Reflection is used only when strictly necessary, ensuring that performance costs are proportional to the absence of static typing.

By embedding these transformations into the build pipeline, frame conditions become first-class specifications rather than comments, with their enforcement seamlessly woven into the runtime behavior of the application.

5.2 Managing Optional Typing

A central challenge in Dart is its optional typing system. To balance flexibility and efficiency, the prototype adopts a hybrid strategy. When type information is present, object structures are determined at compile time and the generator emits specialized state constructors. For example:

```
State preState = State({'this': {'board': board, /* ... */ }});
```

In this case, the structure of the receiver (`this`) is statically known, allowing a tailored state model to be created and passed to the `State` constructor. Elements such as `board` are captured directly, but need not be abstracted into separate state models unless necessary. If finer-grained modeling is required, the system can construct these dynamically at runtime (see below). By contrast, when type declarations are absent, the system generates generic instrumentation that relies on reflection to inspect object structures on the fly. This hybrid approach ensures that well-typed code benefits from optimized, efficient checks, while dynamically typed code remains fully supported. As a result, frame enforcement remains feasible in a language that mixes static and dynamic features.

To support this dual strategy, the program state model of Sect. 3 is extended to: $\Sigma : \mathit{Var} \rightarrow \mathit{ObjState} \cup \mathit{Obj}$. When the internal structure of an object can be determined and is relevant to frame reasoning, it is stored as an `ObjState` capturing its fields and subcomponents. Otherwise—either because the structure is unknown or such detail is unnecessary—the object itself is stored directly. At runtime, if a frame annotation requires finer granularity (e.g., marking fields of an object), the system converts the stored object into its state representation via reflection (see the next subsection). This lazy conversion avoids unnecessary overhead while ensuring that frame checks remain precise whenever deeper inspection is required.

5.3 State Modeling and Frame Semantics

Another key aspect of our implementation is the modeling of program states for frame validation, where the initial state serves as a template against which the final state is checked. The core runtime library centers on the `State` class, which represents program states as nested collections of name-value pairs. It provides operations for (a) capturing pre- and post-states, (b) comparing them against declared frame conditions, and (c) marking fields permitted to change using *wildcards*. For instance, the annotation `@Modifies('this.board.getPlace(x,y)')` generates:

```
assert(preState.frame('this.board.getPlace(x,y)'));
```

The `frame()` method traverses the `preState`, locates the specified element, and replaces it with a wildcard to indicate that it may change. States are represented as nested name-value maps, and each value is checked to determine whether it is already modeled as a state object. If not, reflection is used to dynamically construct a new state model, ensuring that even previously unseen or dynamically typed objects are incorporated into validation. For example, if `board` is not initially represented as a state object, the method inspects it at runtime to build a model that includes `getPlace(x,y)` and any other accessible fields. In this way, when a composite object contains a mutable field, the field is replaced with a wildcard that accepts any value during comparison, while the remainder of the structure must remain unchanged. This combination of tree traversal and dynamic reflection ensures that both declared and previously unseen objects participate in frame validation. As a result, developers can specify precisely which parts of the program state may evolve, while the runtime automatically guards against unintended side effects—even in the presence of dynamically typed or partially known structures.

5.4 Performance Considerations

Capturing program states can be costly for deep object graphs. To mitigate this, the prototype exploits Dart's compilation model: instrumented code is embedded in `assert` statements, which are stripped from production binaries when compiled with the `--release` flag. In addition, Dart's tree-shaking removes unused helper code, ensuring that no residual overhead remains in deployed applications.

In debug mode, runtime checks do introduce measurable costs. Our benchmarks showed that contracts relying only on static typing added negligible overhead, while reflection-heavy checks incurred a slowdown of approximately 3–8%. Since these checks disappear entirely in release builds, developers benefit from strong runtime guarantees during testing without sacrificing production performance.

5.5 Prototype Limitations and Future Directions

The prototype validates the feasibility of lightweight frame annotations in Dart, but several limitations remain:

- Deep structures: Capturing and comparing nested object graphs can be expensive. Optimizations such as selective hashing or shallow cloning may be investigated to improve efficiency.
- Granularity: The current system enforces contracts at the field level, but support for quantified frame conditions (e.g., "all elements of a list except specified objects remain unchanged") is limited.
- Expressiveness: Compared to JML [11,19,30,31] and Spec# [5], the prototype provides a lightweight, annotation-based approach that integrates directly into Dart's build system, but lacks the richer specification mechanisms available in behavioral interface specification languages (BISLs) [25].

Future work focuses on enhancing both usability and expressiveness. On the tooling side, an analyzer plugin could provide immediate feedback by highlighting inconsistencies between annotations and code mutations, surfacing them as editor diagnostics with quick-fix suggestions. On the specification side, the framework was designed to be extensible: custom annotations may introduce fine-grained collection-level constraints or alias-aware permissions, while the `State` class can be extended with richer comparison strategies (e.g., semantic equality for domain-specific objects). These directions position frame annotations not only as a runtime enforcement mechanism but also as a practical aid for everyday software development.

6 Preliminary Evaluation and Discussion

In our earlier work [15], we demonstrated how frame specifications can be encoded as executable assertions for runtime verification. Building on that foundation, we now evaluate the annotation-based approach through a small case study implemented as a cross-platform mobile application in Dart/Flutter. The application implements the Omok game (also known as Gomoku or Gobang), a two-player strategy game played on a 15×15 grid (see Fig. 2). Players alternate turns placing stones on the board with the goal of forming an unbroken line of five stones vertically, horizontally, or diagonally.

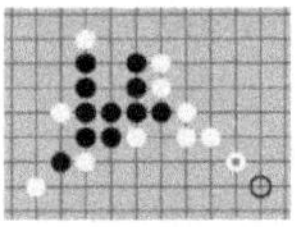

Fig. 2. Screenshot of the Omok game.

6.1 Case Study and Code Impact

The game model was implemented with three primary classes: `Board`, `Player`, and `Game`, totaling 256 source lines of code (SLOC) across 21 methods. To create a controlled basis for evaluation, frame conditions were specified for every method.

When assertions were written manually, the code size grew to 408 SLOC (a 59% increase). By contrast, using annotations reduced the total to 284 SLOC (only an 11% increase). Table 1 summarizes these results, highlighting the primary benefit of annotations: a significant reduction in specification overhead compared to manual assertions.

Table 1. Source code size comparisons for the Omok model classes.

	SLOC	Increase (%)
Base code	256	N/A
Manual assertions	408	59
Annotations	284	11

To illustrate how the annotation-based approach is applied, consider the `Game` class, a key component of the Omok game (see below). Using annotations, we can clearly specify which parts of the game state are allowed to be modified within each method. Declarative shorthand such as `this.* except players` makes specifications both concise and readable, while `@ModifiesNothing` identifies pure observer methods, which represented 57% of methods in our prior study [15].

```
class Game {
  @State('board')
  final Board _board;
  // and other fields ...

  @Modifies('this.* except players')
  void newGame() { ... }

  @ModifiesNothing
  Player get currentPlayer => _currentPlayer;

  @Modifies('currentPlayer')
  Player changePlayerTurn() { ... }

  @Modifies('players[1]')
  set opponentPlayer(Player opponent) { ... }

  @Modifies('board.places[x][y], board.winRow, currentPlayer')
  Outcome makeMove(int x, int y) { ... }

  // and other methods ...
}
```

In the example, the `newGame()` method is annotated with `@Modifies('this.* except players')`, allowing modifications to all fields of the `Game` state except for `players`. This concise pattern notation simplifies specifying the mutable parts of complex objects. The `currentPlayer` getter is marked as read-only with the `@ModifiesNothing` annotation, which is effectively shorthand for `@Modifies('')`. Since a large portion of methods in most applications—57%, according to our previous work [15]—are observer methods that do not modify object state, this annotation is crucial for reducing boilerplate code and improving clarity. The `changePlayerTurn()` method allows modifications to the `currentPlayer` field, while `opponentPlayer()` enables changes to the second player (`players[1]`). The use of familiar array indexing notation in frame conditions clarifies that only the second player in the list can be altered. The `makeMove()` method, which represents a player making a move on the board, illustrates the specificity of the approach: it allows changes only to the `places[x][y]` and `winRow` fields of the `board`, as well as the `currentPlayer`. Importantly, when a composite object such as `board` appears in a frame condition, it denotes an abstraction—specifically, the tuple of its relevant state elements (`places` and `winRow` in this case)—rather than the concrete object itself.

From a quantitative perspective, annotation density averaged one per method (1 annotation/method) and 0.67 per field (0.67 annotation/field), with each annotation line contributing approximately 9.86% of the total code volume. Compared to the manual assertion version, the annotation-based implementation achieved a 3.8× reduction in specification volume per line of code (densities of 0.0986 vs. 0.3725), while requiring less developer effort. Qualitatively, we believe that annotation-based specifications are easier to maintain and reason about, as they localize behavioral intent without cluttering method bodies with explicit state-checking logic.

6.2 Findings, Performance, and Open Issues

The case study yielded several insights. First, annotations reduce visual and cognitive clutter by decoupling frame specifications from method logic, promoting a declarative style that scales well in large classes. Second, they enable fine-grained mutability control—e.g., specifying `board.places[x][y]` rather than an entire `board` object—thereby improving precision in describing permissible state changes. Overall, the results suggest that annotation-based specifications enhance maintainability by reducing SLOC, clarifying mutability constraints, and managing state modifications more effectively, particularly in optionally typed languages such as Dart.

Performance Considerations. Runtime checking involves capturing pre- and post-states, which may incur overhead for deeply nested objects. In practice, all checks are encapsulated in `assert` statements and removed in release builds, leaving production performance unaffected. Benchmark measurements showed negligible slowdown for type-informed checks and a modest 3–8% overhead for reflection-heavy cases during testing—an acceptable trade-off for runtime assurance.

Semantic Precision. A key consideration is whether to include call-by-value parameters, such as `x` and `y` in `playStone(int x, int y)`, in the program state. For primitive types, changes are local and invisible to the caller, but for reference types, the objects pointed to can be mutated even though the references themselves are passed by value. Frame specifications must account for such mutations to accurately capture permissible state changes.

Related to this is the distinction between *reference assignment* and *state mutation*. For fields, specifications must clearly state whether a reference (e.g., `board`) may be reassigned or whether only the internal structure of the referenced object may change. This distinction affects both reasoning precision and verification cost.

Open Issues. Building on the preceding discussion of semantic precision, several open issues remain regarding the soundness and scalability of annotation-based specifications. One concerns the treatment of getters when modeling an object's abstract state. Internal state may be encapsulated and inaccessible directly, especially in third-party or external objects whose values are exposed only through getters. These values may correspond to data stored remotely, such as in databases or cloud storage, making direct field access infeasible. However, incorporating getters raises questions about redundancy and semantic overlap, since multiple getters may reflect the same underlying state. A practical approach is to group related getters into unified abstract components, ensuring that annotations capture consistent and non-redundant views of an object's state.

Inheritance presents another challenge for maintaining precise and sound annotations. Subclasses may extend or refine the abstract state of their superclass, but it must be clear whether existing state components may also be modified. Similarly, method overriding must preserve the frame conditions declared in the superclasses. Ideally, the overriding method should specify a frame that is at least as restrictive as the inherited one, maintaining behavioral substitutability while allowing controlled extension. Addressing these issues is essential for scaling annotation-based specifications to larger object hierarchies and ensuring that inherited contracts remain consistent, precise, and enforceable. Future work will explore automated inference and consistency checking of inherited frame conditions to further reduce developer burden and improve annotation reliability.

6.3 Summary

Compared to established contract systems such as Eiffel and JML (see Sect. 7 for detailed comparison), the proposed approach offers a lightweight, annotation-based mechanism that integrates seamlessly with a language supporting optional typing. Whereas Eiffel emphasizes preconditions and postconditions, and JML provides a rich yet type-intensive specification language, our work addresses an intermediate point in this design space by focusing on frame conditions as a practical and expressive means of capturing allowable state changes.

Overall, the evaluation indicates that annotation-based frame conditions can provide a scalable and expressive mechanism for reasoning about side effects in Dart applications. The resulting annotations reduce specification overhead, enhance code clarity, and improve maintainability without sacrificing precision. Future work will investigate richer abstractions of program state, refined treatment of inheritance, and optimized runtime instrumentation for validation and enforcement.

7 Comparison with Related Work

Frame specifications have long been recognized as an essential element of program specification, but existing approaches differ considerably in how they are expressed, verified, and enforced. In this section, we contrast our annotation-based, runtime-oriented approach with well-established frameworks ranging from traditional Design by Contract (DbC) to heavyweight formal verification systems. The comparison highlights the originality of our contribution: lightweight runtime enforcement of frame specifications in a practical programming language.

7.1 Eiffel and Traditional DbC

Eiffel pioneered DbC with built-in support for preconditions, postconditions, and invariants [38,39]. While these constructs can be checked at runtime, Eiffel provides no explicit syntax for frame conditions. Developers must infer permissible state changes from method behavior, leaving room for ambiguity and potential side effects. Runtime violations can be detected for contracts, but not for unintended state modifications.

In contrast, our approach extends the DbC philosophy with explicit frame clauses expressed as annotations. By specifying exactly which parts of an object may change, and by checking these constraints at runtime, we make state-change reasoning both explicit and enforceable.

7.2 JML and Spec#

Behavioral interface specification languages (BISL) [25] such as the Java Modeling Language (JML) [11,19,30,31] and Microsoft's Spec# [5] extend DbC with explicit frame constructs: `assignable` in JML and `modifies` in Spec#. These clauses precisely define the set of modifiable locations (see an example JML specification below).

```
/*@ requires amount > 0 && amount <= balance;
  @ assignable balance;
  @ ensures balance == \old(balance) - amount; @*/
public void withdraw(int amount) {
  balance -= amount;
}
```

Such specifications are powerful but often verbose and heavily coupled to verification toolchains. JML's runtime checker enforces pre/postconditions and invariants, but not frame clauses. Spec# requires theorem prover integration (via Boogie [4] and Z3 [41]) and also restricts frame checking to static verification.

By comparison, our Dart annotations retain the spirit of `assignable/modifies` but present them in a lightweight, developer-friendly style. Frame specifications are embedded directly in code and enforced dynamically without reliance on external provers.

7.3 DbC in Dart

The only existing work on DbC in Dart is Chalin's Dart Contracts proposal [12], which introduces mechanisms for specifying function and class behavior but does not provide provisions for defining or enforcing frame properties. Our annotation-based approach addresses this gap by allowing developers to explicitly specify frame conditions in Dart and verify them at runtime.

In particular, beyond the `@Modifies` annotation for declaring frame conditions, our approach introduces the `@State` annotation, which provides an abstract representation of an object's state to facilitate frame checks (see Sect. 4.1). This concept is analogous to specification-only variables, such as model variables found in BISLs like JML and Spec# [13,14,34], which define abstract variables based on concrete program variables for use only in specifications.

Furthermore, the `parts` parameter within the `@State` annotation functions similarly to data groups [32], allowing developers to group mutable fields under an abstract state element for more structured and modular specification of frame conditions.

7.4 Formal Verification Frameworks

Frameworks such as Dafny [33], Frama-C [6,20,28], and KeY [2,7] provide rigorous specification and verification environments. Frame specifications are first-class citizens in these systems, expressed as part of the formal semantics and discharged through SMT solvers or proof assistants (see an example in Dafny below):

```
method withdraw(amount: int)
  requires amount > 0 && amount <= balance
  modifies this
  ensures balance == old(balance) - amount
{
  balance := balance - amount;
}
```

These approaches deliver strong guarantees but at a significant cost: they require comprehensive formal models, heavy annotation overhead, and specialized verification expertise. Importantly, they lack runtime checking—any violations during program execution remain undetected if the static proof is incomplete or omitted.

Moreover, frame axioms can also be automatically inferred through static analysis [46], demonstrating that frame reasoning can be mechanized, though at the cost of scalability and runtime applicability. In contrast, our approach emphasizes lightweight, annotation-driven enforcement that complements, rather than replaces, formal verification.

7.5 Lightweight Runtime-Oriented Contribution

Across these traditions, runtime enforcement of frame specifications has been underexplored. Eiffel checks contracts at runtime but omits frame axioms. JML and Spec# include frame clauses but enforce them only statically. Dafny, Frama-C, and KeY provide the strongest verification support, yet again through static reasoning only. None of these frameworks offer direct runtime verification of frame axioms.

Our approach fills this gap by combining:

- *Lightweight syntax:* annotations embedded directly in source code, minimizing verbosity and integration effort.
- *Dynamic enforcement:* runtime reflection and instrumentation ensure that violations are detected during execution rather than at compile time.
- *Practical applicability:* seamless integration with optionally typed languages like Dart, where static analysis alone is insufficient.

This positions our work between two extremes: it is more expressive than traditional DbC systems without frame conditions and far more accessible than heavyweight formal verification frameworks. To our knowledge, it is the first practical framework to provide runtime verification of frame axioms within an annotation-based DBC system.

7.6 Effect Systems and Ownership Types

Beyond explicit frame specifications, two other major families of techniques address reasoning about side effects and state changes: *effect systems* and *ownership types*.

Effect systems extend type systems with annotations that describe the effects a program construct may have on state or control flow [36,42]. For example, an effect system can classify functions as pure (no state changes) or impure (state-changing), or track which regions of memory a function can read or write. While powerful for modular reasoning, effect systems typically operate at the type level, limiting their granularity and requiring explicit type/effect annotations throughout the program. They emphasize static enforcement and compositional reasoning rather than runtime verification.

Ownership types [17,18] restrict aliasing by structuring object references into ownership hierarchies. By ensuring that each object is owned by a unique context, these systems enable developers and tools to reason about which objects a method can mutate, thereby bounding the scope of side effects. Ownership types have been successfully applied to encapsulation, modular verification, and safe concurrency, but they typically require pervasive annotations and impose structural constraints on object graphs.

In contrast, our annotation-based frame specifications do not rely on global type or aliasing disciplines. They are local, lightweight, and expressed directly within method contracts, making them accessible to everyday developers. Most importantly, frame conditions are enforced at runtime, complementing static analyses such as effect systems and ownership types with dynamic guarantees. This duality makes our approach particularly well-suited for dynamically evolving codebases and optionally typed languages like Dart, where purely static methods are less effective.

8 Conclusion

This paper presented an annotation-based extension to Design by Contract (DbC) that incorporates frame specifications, moving beyond the traditional emphasis on preconditions and postconditions. Our approach enables developers to declaratively specify which parts of an object's state may change during method execution, making side-effect constraints both explicit and enforceable. By modeling objects as abstract tuples of state components, the method supports fine-grained frame checking without cluttering program logic or introducing unintended dependencies.

A key contribution is the integration of frame specifications into a runtime verification framework for Dart. The hybrid design combines compile-time code generation with runtime reflection, supporting both statically and dynamically typed code in optionally typed languages. Compared to manual assertion-based implementations, the annotation-based approach significantly reduces code complexity and improves maintainability while preserving strong runtime guarantees. A small case study demonstrated the feasibility and practicality of the approach in realistic application contexts.

Several directions for future research remain. First, we plan to evaluate the approach on larger and more complex codebases to assess scalability and performance trade-offs. Second, we intend to extend the model to capture key object-oriented features—such as inheritance, method overriding, and polymorphism—to ensure that frame specifications integrate naturally with advanced design structures. Finally, we aim to evolve the prototype into a full-fledged developer toolchain, making frame-aware DbC more accessible and practical for everyday software development.

In summary, incorporating frame conditions into DbC strengthens the methodology by clarifying not only what a method must achieve but also what it is permitted to modify. This balance of expressiveness and enforceability enhances the reliability, maintainability, and clarity of modern software systems—particularly in languages like Dart, where optional typing and dynamic behaviors introduce additional challenges. Frame conditions thus complete the DbC paradigm, extending contracts beyond obligations and guarantees to the disciplined management of state change.

References

1. Ahmed, S., Imtiaz, S.M., Khairunnesa, S.S., Cruz, B.D., Rajan, H.: Design by contract for deep learning APIs. In: Proceedings of the 31st ACM Joint European Software Engineering Conference and Symposium on the Foundations of Software Engineering (ESEC/FSE), pp. 94–106 (2023). https://doi.org/10.1145/3611643.3616247
2. Ahrendt, W., Beckert, M., Hähnle, R., Schwichtenberg, P.H.H., Wolff, B.: The KeY platform for verification and analysis of Java programs. In: Giannakopoulou, D., Kroening, D. (eds.) Verified Software: Theories, Tools and Experiments. VSTTE 2014, Lecture Notes in Computer Science, vol. 8471, pp. 65–81. Springer (2014). https://doi.org/10.1007/978-3-319-12154-3_4
3. Amusuo, P.C., Sharma, A., Rao, S.R., Vincent, A., Davis, J.C.: Reflections on software failure analysis. In: ACM Joint European Software Engineering Conference and Symposium on the Foundations of Software Engineering (ESEC/FSE), pp. 1615–1620. Singapore (2022). https://doi.org/10.1145/3540250.3560879
4. Barnett, M., Chang, B.Y.E., DeLine, R., Jacobs, B., Leino, K.R.M.: Boogie: a modular reusable verifier for object-oriented programs. In: Formal Methods for Components and Objects (FMCO 2005), LNCS, vol. 4111, pp. 364–387. Springer (2006). https://doi.org/10.1007/11804192_17

5. Barnett, M., Leino, K.R.M., Schulte, W.: The Spec# programming system: an overview. In: Construction and Analysis of Safe, Secure, and Interoperable Smart Devices (CASSIS 2004), LNCS, vol. 3362, pp. 49–69. Springer (2005). https://doi.org/10.1007/978-3-540-30569-9_3
6. Baudin, P., et al.: The dogged pursuit of bug-free C programs: the Frama-C software analysis platform. Commun. ACM **64**(8), 56–68 (2021). https://doi.org/10.1145/3470569
7. Beckert, B., Hähnle, R., Schmitt, P. (eds.): Verification of Object-Oriented Software: the KeY Approach. Springer, Berlin, Heidelberg (2007)
8. Borgida, A., Mylopoulos, J., Reiter, R.: and nothing else changes': the frame problem in procedure specifications. In: Proceedings of 1993 15th International Conference on Software Engineering, pp. 303–314 (1993). https://doi.org/10.1109/ICSE.1993.346034
9. Borgida, A., Mylopoulos, J., Reiter, R.: On the frame problem in procedure specifications. IEEE Trans. Software Eng. **21**(10), 785–798 (1995). https://doi.org/10.1109/32.469035
10. Bracha, G.: The Dart Programming Language. Addison-Wesley Professional, Boston, MA (2016)
11. An overview of JML tools and applications. Int. J. Softw. Tools Technol. Transf. (STTT) **7**, 212–232 (2005). https://doi.org/10.1007/s10009-004-0167-4
12. Chalin, P.: Ensuring that your Dart will hit the mark: an introduction to Dart contracts. In: International Conference on Information Reuse and Integration, pp. 369–377. San Francisco, CA (2014). https://doi.org/10.1109/IRI.2014.7051913
13. Chalin, P., Kiniry, J.R., Leavens, G.T., Poll, E.: Beyond assertions: advanced specification and verification with JML and ESC/Java2. In: Formal Methods for Components and Objects (FMCO 2005), Lecture Notes in Computer Science, vol. 4111, pp. 342–363. Springer (2005). https://doi.org/10.1007/11804192_16
14. Cheon, Y., Leavens, G.T., Sitaraman, M., Edwards, S.: Model variables: cleanly supporting abstraction in design by contract. Softw. Pract. Exp. **35**(6), 583–599 (2005). https://doi.org/10.1002/spe.649
15. Cheon, Y., Liu, B., Rubio-Medrano, C.: Asserting frame properties. In: International Conference on Software Technologies (ICSOFT 2024), pp. 145–152. Dijon, France (2024). https://doi.org/10.5220/0012786600003753
16. Cheon, Y., Good, B.: Enhancing design-by-contract with frame specifications. In: Proceedings of the 20th International Conference on Software Technologies (ICSOFT 2025), pp. 378–385. Bilbao, Spain (2025). https://doi.org/10.5220/0013578400003964
17. Clarke, D.G., Potter, J.M., Noble, J.: Ownership types for flexible alias protection. In: Proceedings of the 13th ACM SIGPLAN Conference on Object-Oriented Programming, Systems, Languages, and Applications (OOPSLA), pp. 48–64. ACM (1998). https://doi.org/10.1145/286936.286947
18. Clarke, D.G., Wrigstad, T., Noble, J., Potter, J.M.: Ownership types: a survey. Lect. Notes Comput. Sci. **2277**, 15–48 (2002). https://doi.org/10.1007/978-3-642-36946-9_3
19. Cok, D.R.: OpenJML: software verification for Java 7 using JML, OpenJDK, and Eclipse. In: NASA Formal Methods Symposium (NFM 2011), LNCS, vol. 6617, pp. 472–479. Springer (2011). https://doi.org/10.1007/978-3-642-20398-5_35
20. Cuoq, P., Kirchner, F., Kosmatov, N., Prevosto, V., Signoles, J., Yakobowski, B.: Frama-C: A software analysis perspective. In: International Conference on Software Engineering and Formal Methods (SEFM 2012), LNCS, vol. 7504, pp. 233–247. Springer (2012). https://doi.org/10.1007/978-3-642-33826-7_16

21. Darvas, A., Leino, K.R.M.: Practical reasoning about invocations and implementations of pure methods. In: International Conference on Fundamental Approaches to Software Engineering (FASE 2007), ETAPS, pp. 336–351 (2007).https://doi.org/10.1007/978-3-540-71289-3_26
22. Gazzola, L., Mariani, L., Pastore, F., Pezze, M.: An exploratory study of field failures. In: IEEE International Symposium on Software Reliability Engineering (ISSRE), pp. 67–77. (2017). https://doi.org/10.1109/ISSRE.2017.10
23. Hähnle, R., Schmitt, P.H., Beckert, B.: Verification of Object-Oriented Software: The KeY Approach, Springer (2007)
24. Hatcliff, J., Dwyer, M.: Using the Bandera tool set to model-check properties of concurrent Java software. In: CONCUR 2001: Concurrency Theory, International Conference, pp. 39–58. Aalborg, Denmark (2001). https://doi.org/10.1007/3-540-44685-0_5
25. Hatcliff, J., Leavens, G.T., Leino, K.R.M., Müller, P., Parkinson, M.: Behavioral interface specification languages. ACM Comput. Surv. **44**(3), 1–58 (2012). https://doi.org/10.1145/2187671.2187678
26. Jazequel, J.M., Meyer, B.: Design by contract: the lessons of Ariane. Computer **30**(1), 129–130 (1997). https://doi.org/10.1109/2.562936
27. Kassios, I.T.: Dynamic frames: support for framing, dependencies and sharing without restrictions. In: FM 2006: Formal Methods, 14th International Symposium, pp. 268–283. Hamilton, Canada (2006). https://doi.org/10.1007/11813040_19
28. Kosmatov, N., Prevosto, V., Signoles, J.: Guide to Software Verification with Frama-C, Springer (2024)
29. Le Traon, Y., Baudry, B., Jezequel, J.M.: Design by contract to improve software vigilance. IEEE Trans. Software Eng. **32**(8), 571–586 (2006). https://doi.org/10.1109/TSE.2006.79
30. Leavens, G.T., Baker, A.L., Ruby, C.: Preliminary design of JML: a behavioral interface specification language for Java. ACM SIGSOFT Softw. Eng. Notes **31**(3), 1–38 (2006). https://doi.org/10.1145/1127878.1127884
31. Leavens, G.T., Cheon, Y., Clifton, C., Ruby, C., Cok, D.R.: How the design of JML accommodates both runtime assertion checking and formal verification. Sci. Comput. Program. **55**(1), 185–208 (2005). https://doi.org/10.1016/j.scico.2004.05.015
32. Leino, K.R.M.: Data groups: specifying the modification of extended state. In: Proceedings of OOPSLA '98, ACM SIGPLAN Conference on Object-Oriented Programming, Systems, Languages, and Applications, pp. 144–153 (1998). https://doi.org/10.1145/286936.286953
33. Leino, K.R.M.: Dafny: an automatic program verifier for functional correctness. In: Logic for Programming, Artificial Intelligence, and Reasoning (LPAR 2010), LNCS, vol. 6355, pp. 348–370. Springer (2010). https://doi.org/10.1007/978-3-642-17511-4_20
34. Leino, K.R.M., Müller, P.: A verification methodology for model fields. In: Programming Languages and Systems, 15th European Symposium on Programming (ESOP 2006), pp. 115–130. Vienna, Austria (2006). https://doi.org/10.1007/11693024_9
35. Leino, K.R.M., Nelson, G.: Data abstraction and information hiding. ACM Trans. Program. Lang. Syst. (TOPLAS) **24**(5), 491–553 (2002). https://doi.org/10.1145/582153.582154
36. Lucassen, J.M., Gifford, D.K.: Polymorphic effect systems. In: Proceedings of the 15th ACM SIGPLAN-SIGACT Symposium on Principles of Programming Languages (POPL), pp. 47–57. ACM (1988). https://doi.org/10.1145/73560.73564

37. Marché, C., Paulin-Mohring, C., Urbain, X.: The Krakatoa tool for certification of Java/JavaCard programs annotated in JML. J. Logic Algebraic Program. **58**(1–2), 89–106 (2004). https://doi.org/10.1016/j.jlap.2003.07.006
38. Meyer, B.: Applying 'design by contract'. IEEE Comput. **25**(10), 40–51 (1992) https://doi.org/10.1109/2.161279
39. Meyer, B.: Object-Oriented Software Construction, 2nd edn. Prentice Hall, Upper Saddle River, NJ (1997)
40. Mitchell, R., McKim, J.: Design by Contract, by Example. Addison-Wesley, Boston, MA (2001)
41. de Moura, L., Bjørner, N.: Z3: an efficient SMT solver. In: Tools and Algorithms for the Construction and Analysis of Systems (TACAS 2008), LNCS, vol. 4963, pp. 337–340. Springer (2008). https://doi.org/10.1007/978-3-540-78800-3_24
42. Nielson, F., Nielson, H.R.: Type and Effect Systems. In: Texts in Theoretical Computer Science, Springer (1999).https://doi.org/10.1007/978-3-662-03822-9
43. Ozkaya, M.: Teaching design-by-contract for the modeling and implementation of software systems. In: International Conference on Software Technologies (ICSOFT), pp. 499–507 (2019). https://doi.org/10.5220/0007950904990507
44. Ozkaya, M., Kloukinas, C.: Design-by-contract for reusable components and realizable architectures. In: Proceedings of the 16th ACM SIGSOFT Symposium on Component-Based Software Engineering (CBSE '14), pp. 129–138. ACM (2014). https://doi.org/10.1145/2602458.2602462
45. pub.dev: dart and Flutter package repository. https://pub.dev. Accessed 30 Sept 2025
46. Rakamaric, Z., Hu, A.J.: Automatic inference of frame axioms using static analysis. In: 23rd IEEE/ACM International Conference on Automated Software Engineering (ASE 2008), pp. 89–98. IEEE (2008). https://doi.org/10.1109/ASE.2008.19
47. Schiller, T.W., Donohue, K., Coward, F., Ernst, M.D.: Case studies and tools for contract specifications. In: Proceedings of the 36th International Conference on Software Engineering (ICSE 2014), pp. 596–607 (2014). https://doi.org/10.1145/2568225.2568285
48. Zhang, J., Ristin, M., Schanely, P., Van De Venn, H.W., Gligoric, M.: Python-by-contract dataset. In: Proceedings of the 30th ACM Joint European Software Engineering Conference and Symposium on the Foundations of Software Engineering (ESEC/FSE), pp. 1652–1656 (2022). https://doi.org/10.1145/3540250.3558917

Author Index

M. Mecella et al. (Eds.): ICSOFT 2025, CCIS 3144, p. 229, 2027.
https://doi.org/10.1007/978-3-032-37353-3

FSC
www.fsc.org
MIX
Papier | Fördert gute Waldnutzung
FSC® C083411

Kolibri 360 GmbH
Ferdinand-Jühlke-Straße 7
99095 Erfurt, Deutschland
produktsicherheit@kolibri360.de